TO THE
END
OF THE
WORLD

TO THE
END
OF THE
WORLD

TRAVELS WITH OSCAR WILDE

RUPERT
EVERETT

Little, Brown

LITTLE, BROWN

First published in Great Britain in 2020 by Little, Brown

1 3 5 7 9 10 8 6 4 2

A CIP catalogue record for this book
is available from the British Library.

ISBN 978-1-4087-0511-7
C Format ISBN 978-1-4087-0512-4

Typeset in Caslon by M Rules
Printed and bound in Great Britain by Clays Ltd, Elcograf S.p.A.

Papers used by Little, Brown are from well-managed forests
and other responsible sources.

MIX
Paper from
responsible sources
FSC® C104740

Little, Brown
An imprint of
Little, Brown Book Group
Carmelite House
50 Victoria Embankment
London EC4Y 0DZ

An Hachette UK Company
www.hachette.co.uk

www.littlebrown.co.uk

For Jörg, Katja, Philipp, Thorsten,
Sébastien and Stefaan. Without all of you,
none of this would have been possible.

Contents

Twelve years ago I had a dream. Fatal in middle age.

I decided to write, direct, star in and produce a film.

I would be Oscar Wilde in exile. A gigantic leading role, pages of flighty dialogue, a Visconti-meets-CCTV aesthetic, all those friends and relations from a thirty-year career press-ganged into supporting roles, the dream seemed as clear as yesterday and went all the way to the Oscars where, receiving my second award of the night, I would hold one glittering statuette up to each ear and scream, 'Are these earrings too garish?'

The dream soon turned into a nightmare. This is the story of that bad trip.

Prologue

This year for the first time I have invested in an appointments diary. It's big and blue and looks important, with a ribbon for a bookmark like a bible. Up until now I have committed everything to memory – my mantra being that if I don't remember something it can't be that important anyway. This modus operandi may have worked in the seventies when I still had a short-term memory and little to recall but now – in the cold May of 2010 – the fringes of my brain have frayed while the interior looks like a tie-dye T-shirt during a recent scan searching for drug-induced black holes. Still desperate to please like a toothless old circus dog, I yap yes to everything and then forget all about it until it's too late and I am doing something else. In such a way I have lost the friendship of Joan Collins, among other things, having double-booked myself one evening after a performance of *Pygmalion* when I was supposed to be dining with her.

I am sitting with two young men and a skeletal lady in J Sheekey's restaurant in the West End of London. They are from Paramount Pictures or 20th Century Fox, I can't remember which. What I can remember is that this is the last meeting I have at such an exalted level – actually feasting with the high priests of Hollywood – to discuss possible involvement in a picture, rather than what is to come crashing in next, and is, by the way, the harsh reality faced by most actors competing for jobs today, which involves recording a scene on your iPhone and texting it with fingers crossed to the casting director. The rest, as Hamlet said, is normally silence.

But all this is for the future. For the time being I am at a comfortable corner table holding forth. The men, Andy and Loeg, lean in black suits, white shirts, thin ties and neon teeth, are producers – and the thin lady is called Hope. Thunderbirds are go. She is there for the ride, an executive from another studio. Her face is fixed in a surgical grin. Over her shoulders a frayed fur coat at which she distractedly picks. The men are as unfathomable as Martians, downloading my every gesture, while Hope chatters away like a self-harming parrot about the project, a family-viewing fairy story in which the villain is a giant.

The men play that trick of not talking or moving a muscle so that the room spins around them and I babble on, revealing too much too soon while they fix me with their Paul Newman eyes, pupils like pins, unwavering in their scrutiny, ready to play back later against the wall of their hotel suite in a satellite link-up with their superiors back at the studio.

I am used to this by now, although perhaps I have been too long back in England to know exactly how to measure myself or them, added to which I am definitely drinking more these days and have already hoovered up a couple of dry martinis to conjure up a bit of sloshed sparkle – the dregs of my star quality.

But I am strutting my stuff, acting butch and generally giving the impression of being a no-nonsense, take charge kind of giant and things seem to be going pretty well. A couple of well-wishers have enjoyed me in the play tonight. I have been gracious and natural, waving them on with bonhomie and will settle up with them later, but now I must finish my pitch for the role, which considering I have only read three pages of the script has been quite long and detailed. (The first, the last and a couple in between are largely sufficient for the seasoned hack to be able to spout preludes and fugues of shit.)

I grind to a halt and they stare back – no helpful chirrup of encouragement – and there is a moment of silence.

'What you say is true,' proclaims Loeg finally. 'This picture will die without soul.' (Translation: It's so bad we're going to need some good actors.)

'It's a smart script,' trills Hope pecking at her coat. Smart is a Hollywood word.

'There's got to be a three-dimensional quality to all these characters. We need actors who know how to do that,' continues Loeg. (Take the money and don't ask too many questions.) 'Otherwise they're just . . . ' A long, important pause.

'Giants?' I have a terrible habit of finishing everyone's sentence, but I can't stand silence. This is the fifth time I have done it in the last ten minutes, and a shadow of impatience scuds across Loeg's face.

'What we need is . . . ' I surge on regardless, 'a bit of rehearsal. Will there be any time for rehearsal, Loeg?' I am intense, a humble craftsman, Daniel Day-Lewis in fact. Simple. Direct. And deep. (The polar opposite to interior me right now, which is devious, superficial and bored.)

It works.

'Oh yeah. Sure. We're gonna rehearse out there at Pinewood.' He beams at me, reassured. 'You Brits,' his eyes are saying, twinkling with shock and awe. I am an actor brandishing his tools. He is about to say 'You got the part' when Johnno, the plotting queen d' (new word incorporating maître d' and queen bee) of the restaurant, a man camper even than me, sashays over with his little finger up at his mouth and baby eyes twinkling, wide as saucers.

'Houston, we got a problem,' she hisses in that flat South Coast drawl of hers, bending towards me in a vaudevillian aside. Everyone looks up.

'What?' I snap. I cannot be put off my stride at this delicate stage and be forced by her to slip into giggly-girl banter. It would be fatal. Needless to say she's clocking that I am acting butch and her eyes narrow slightly.

'Ooh. Very Victor Immature, dear.' She sneers, at the same time gathering the table with her hands. 'Well. Get this. Joan Collins is waiting for you at The Ivy. You stood her up. She's FURIOUS!'

It takes us all a moment to move from one fairyland to another.

'Oh no! I completely forgot,' I moan, cancer cells replicating.

'Joan Collins?' Andy lights up. 'Is she still around? Maybe we could get her in the movie.'

'*Maybe*??' barks Loeg. 'She's been circling the studio in a helicopter, ready to drop in – fully made-up – since the last episode of *Dynasty*.'

The three Americans explode with mirth. Queen Dee watches with a delighted smile.

'She's dizzy!' she declares when the laughter dies down.

'Dizzy in the helicopter,' screams Hope. 'You English get me. That dry frickin' humour.'

'Not Joan. I'm talking about HER,' giggles QD, prodding me in the ribs. I scream. 'I don't know how she remembers her lines.' He has got the party going, and the Martians are coming out of their shell. They may even end up being queens, which will mean curtains for my role in the film. (Queens never employ other queens and if they do, watch out. One will probably eat the other. It's an unspoken rule.)

'That could be a problem. SHE has a lot of dialogue,' trumpets Loeg, throwing his arm over my shoulder. We all laugh heartily, topped by Johnno, who trills like an alarm clock.

'They're on the phone now. What do you want me to say?'

'Can't you just say I'm not here?'

Johnno looks at me solemnly. 'No. Not really. They already know.'

'How?'

'I told them. I'll tell them you'll come after dinner.'

'That won't work. Who is she with?'

'Biggins.'

'Biggins?' screams Andy. He's tipsy now. Definitely gay. 'Bilbo Biggins?'

'No. Chris. As in more – bricks – please – Biggins.'

Andy is befuddled.

Johnno has got his hand on his hip now and is really getting into the swing. My new job is out the window. 'You know,' she hisses in a theatrical aside. 'The one that was done for shoplifting.'

'We'll get them to come here,' says Loeg, clutching at Johnno. 'Lemme talk to them. We could ask her to sing at the wedding.'

'Whose wedding?' I ask weakly. This is getting out of hand.

'Ours.' The two producers wave ringed hands over the table.

'Ker-ching!' they scream in unison.

'She can't sing.' I want to pull the evening back on track, but it's too late.

'Let's get them over here right now.'

'I doubt they will,' whines Queen D.

'I'll send my car.'

'Oooh, the limo! That could work. I'll go back and tell them.' Johnno minces off, threading his way through the tables, hands waving.

I try to get the business side of things going again, but there is little point. We are in the world of Joan Collins, Biggins and Johnno. I salute bravely as my ship sinks.

'Yeah. As Loeg was saying. I agree. It's important to get a dimensional feel to these characters. Otherwise they're just . . . '

'Listen,' beeps Andy. 'We love you. We want you in the picture, but you know what? None of the giants are right for you.' I am about to protest but he ploughs right on. 'What could be BRIlliant – don't you agree, Loeg – is the role of the hairdresser!'

I feign puzzled.

'He has this cute little salon right high up in the branches. It's really neat, all made out of leaves.'

'Oh sure! That's a great role. It's pivotal. You could steal the picture.'

I'd rather steal the negative, I think but do not say. Instead, I fix an excited glow onto my face as an image materialises with alarming clarity. On the edge of a vast sound stage there is a little set all made of leaves – leaf sink, leaf hairdryer, leaves through the windows with leaf curtains – and me in the middle – hipsters and a green quiff – backcombing an ogre. It is too vivid to be anything but a premonition and I nearly puke.

Out of the corner of my eye I can see Johnno skimming back over the horizon.

'You're in deep shit,' he says, swivelling to a halt. 'They don't want a car. They just want to know why you don't come. I told them you're in a meeting. I've got an idea. Why don't I nip over with your credit card and pay their bill? That would be a nice touch.'

'Good idea.' Anything to get him away. I hand over my card.

'See ya!' he giggles, and dashes out.

I am quite drunk now and longing to be at the other restaurant with Joan and Biggins and having a good chinwag about Leslie Bricusse and Tony Newley and the old days instead of arse-licking my way up the beanstalk, when Johnno reappears.

'They refused!' she proclaims to the whole restaurant, waving my credit card over her head.

'Oh my God. She must be really angry. What did they say?'

'They said they could pay for their own dinner, thank you very much.'

'Unheard of!'

'I'll say. A first.'

At which point there seems to be very little else to do than scream and high-five, followed by a little chorus of 'There's no business like show business'. The table next to us joins in.

'Oh my God,' says Loeg. 'This is so *My Best Friend's Wedding*.'

Needless to say, I do not get the role of the giant, or any other role for that matter. Not for a while. Joan and I don't speak for years, and darling Johnno is going to die. The evening has all these threads running through it. I walk home in a blur. I'm drunk, of course. The West End on a Saturday night is a funfair. Screaming heads spin across my path on invisible whirligigs. The gridlocked traffic grinds and billows. Somewhere nearby Percy is handing a spangled Joan Collins into a purring limo. Or maybe a minicab. Escaping the crowds on Long Acre, I find myself in front of Bow Street police station – boarded up for years – and as usual I think of Oscar Wilde.

He arrived at this place on an April evening in 1895. The libel suit he had brought against the Marquess of Queensbury dramatically collapsed that morning. At the Cadogan Hotel, pissed as a newt, he was arrested on a charge of gross indecency and brought here in a cab by two policemen.

All for a visiting card left at a club by a lunatic.

I stand there, swaying slightly, wondering what it must have been like in the cell that night. The noise of the crowd outside. The large group of journalists inside, allowed by the police to taunt him in the cell – the most famous man in London, reduced to a fairground oddity.

Shooting star. Shot.

Every time I pass that police station I am freshly amazed. There but for the grace of God. Oscar Wilde is the patron saint of anyone who ever made a mess of their life. More than that, I think to myself, weaving my way towards Holborn, he is also the Christ figure of the gay movement. Crucified so that our sins may be forgiven. After all, Wilde in exile is the first snapshot in modern times of an openly gay man. Still recognisable, still famous. You could see him drifting down the Boulevard Saint-Germain and say, 'That man is a homosexual.'

Ecce homo(sexual).

Oscar put a face to it. It was only a matter of time. The road to liberation had begun.

And THAT's when I have the dream. Drifting off towards Great Ormond Street, through Drury Lane and Bloomsbury Square, Oscar Wilde is following me. From the shadows into the lamplight, through the black brick squares, all the way to my house. Big mistake. Now he knows where I live. He's been stalking me ever since.

PART ONE

CHAPTER ONE

The Little Spare Room

The little spare room is tucked under the gables of our little
pink farmhouse, cut off from the endless banging about
and hoovering of my mother and Twiddles, our daily. Its sloping
walls are covered with faded yellow paper seething with tiny
white garlands, and the room smells musty and unused. Pipes
gurgle in the walls and two tiny windows are square eyes on the
face of our house, peeking foolishly from under the fringe of the
roof at the flat cornfields of Essex, waving at us in the breeze
as far as the eye can see, scribbled over with hedgerows and
fences, and in the distance Braintree, our local town, which plays
Grandmother's Footsteps with our house, always coming closer,
year after year, field by field, claiming the surrounding countryside, in brick closes of ghastly (my mother's word) bungalows,
eating a view that has hardly changed since Constable's time.

I am five years old and have moved into the little spare room
because a weird thing has happened. I have begun to hear a
deafening silence in bed at night. It comes in waves as I am falling asleep. Today I would be bundled off to a child psychiatrist

for a prescription of giggle pills, but my family are resolutely pre-Freudian, even though this is the sixties, and despite the fact that I become seriously anguished most nights, we all keep buggering on, and anyway it is impossible to explain what is going on to any of the grown-ups. I hardly understand myself.

'But darling, you said it wasn't a noise,' reasons Mummy, holding my tear-stained face to her bosom.

'It isn't.' Renewed screams. Mummy will never understand.

'You were having a dream,' she says, tucking me back in and smoothing my hair.

'No,' I moan, realising right there, five years old, the big gaping truth, as big as the silence, and just as deafening – I'm on my own.

'Oh dear,' I sob, trying to put on a brave face.

'Stop now, or you won't have any tears left.'

That's what you think, Mummy. There's plenty more where these came from. She is a silhouette in the doorway now and she's going back downstairs. I turn away from her and snuffle hopelessly into my pillow.

Here are the facts. After my light has been turned off (six thirty), I lie in my bed and wiggle my toes against the Aertex sheets. The dusk is pale through the curtains, and I wait until the room emerges from the sudden dark in all the familiar shapes and shadows of my teddies and puppets, while outside pigeons flap about in the trees and Mummy loads the dishwasher downstairs. A door opens. A snatch of conversation. It closes. I begin to drift off, and THEN it starts. I hear – or become aware of – what can only be described as a huge static silence. It's inside me. I try to ignore it, but the more I do, the deeper it becomes. It is neither a noise nor a thing, though it has the qualities of both. It burns my eardrums with its hiss and presses against me with the weight of an entire ocean so that soon I am flailing against it, tangling myself in the sheets like a fish in a net. At first I make noises to stop it, sing one of my favourite hits – 'Little Children' or 'Julie' – and then I thump the bed with my hands but each time I stop it comes back bigger, buzzing, heavy and huge. A vast, gaping silence. Within a few minutes I am desperate, and so the curtain rises on my nightly performance.

'Mummy?'

The first call is calm. I pretend I have a sensible question to ask. (I know, even now, that I must appear rational.) Pause. Nothing. 'Mu-mee!' I sing this one – still calm – with just an edge of hysteria, louder. I listen out, head cocked – still more animal than human, relying on noises. Nothing.

'MUMMY!' This one is loud and staccato. I wait. No movement downstairs. And then I go for it, screaming and puce, flooding with molten tears. It's a battle of wills. They think I will get bored if they don't react, and before the silence I did. But now things have changed. Someone has got to do something unless I am to be swallowed by it. Sometimes Mummy plays a nasty trick and sends Daddy up. (There's no point explaining to a man. I realise this even now.) But mostly they just wait. They don't know me yet. It's only been five years. I have a will of steel and I WANT MY MUMMY NOW.

Eventually a door opens below, footsteps carefully climb the stairs and there she is, my mummy, a vision in curlers and a blue towelling minidress with white flowers.

'Darling, you are naughty. We're going out to dinner with the Barkers and I have to get ready. What are we going to do with you?'

Well, funny that you should ask, Mummy, because I have always had my eye on the little spare room – I just love the wallpaper there. So now I suggest that the noise is coming from my room and that maybe I should move, and – lo and behold – Mummy says yes. Within five seconds all my teddies (and dolls) are having tea on the little spare room bed and Mummy has come in to read to me before she goes out.

And it is in this bed that I hear the words Oscar Wilde for the first time.

Mummy looks like Jackie Onassis tonight. She has short hair, big white earrings and a long dress she made herself. She has Granny V's pearls round her neck and she sits on the edge of my bed. She opens a purple book and begins to read. I can still hear her now.

'High above the city, on a tall column, stood the statue of the Happy Prince.' She speaks softly, a whisper almost, and I can feel the silence subside. I nestle my head on her knee and watch her face with adoration. There is nothing unfamiliar in it, nothing I don't know. She reads with simplicity but with feeling, and little by little over the next few days the story of the derelict statue and the migrating swallow turns my world around as my brain cells are ignited and my imagination soars for the first time. By the end of the story, a week or so later, the swallow has stripped the Happy Prince of all his jewels and given them to the poor. Both Mummy and I are stunned.

'"Dear little swallow," said the Prince, "you tell me of marvellous things, but more marvellous than anything is the suffering of men and women."'

I don't have a clue what she is on about. I don't think Mummy does either, but we are both in floods of tears anyway as the swallow dies of cold and drops at the Prince's feet.

Introducing me to Oscar Wilde is Mummy's most audacious move, and her greatest contribution to my emotional development. That summer in the little spare room, tucked up in the pale dusk, in the safety of our little pink house folded into the sleeping fields, is the first time another's voice – words written under long-forgotten moons – builds that extraordinary bridge that art can make across time, and Wilde is here. The pigeons may not be pink and white, and our house is certainly not the temple at Baalbek, but they still coo softly in the eaves and we all listen as Mummy tells us about the fisherman who sells his soul, the nightingale who sacrifices herself for another's happiness, of the giant living in permafrost. It is here that I learn for the first time that there is a thing called love and that it usually has a price.

The terrible silence goes on for about a year, fading away as my character quickly develops. In fact it is the silence of innocence, the one I will spend the rest of my life trying to regain. It appears to be a deafening noise from the perspective of the developing brain as little by little one is coaxed by thought into 'being', becoming something. We start to be soldiers or stockbrokers at this little age, and soon we will have a favourite football team and religion. We will try to become our parents, and the silence of the universe becomes a threat. Thought submerges it like Braintree covers the cornfields.

CHAPTER TWO

Swiss Cottaging

Forty-nine years later I am a wheezy matinee idol in a halo of light bulbs, watching myself across a dirty mirror scribbled with phone numbers written in lipstick. It is seven o'clock at night in a run-down West End dressing room. I have caught an everlasting cold and for the last three months have felt death in the air, which is probably the perfect mindset because tonight I AM Oscar Wilde, performing in *The Judas Kiss* by David Hare at the Duke of York's Theatre in St Martin's Lane. For the last time. It is the end of a long, cold winter and I have performed this play eight times a week since last September. First at the Hampstead Theatre, then on tour – Dublin, Bath, Brighton, Richmond and Cambridge – and now we are here in one of London's filthiest playhouses, caked in dust, riddled with moth and mould, as cold as the tomb and smelling of cabbage. Luckily there are other odours in the air. The sweet smell of success is one of them. With the right nose, standing upwind of the drains, I can feel it blowing against my face.

*

FLASHBACK. I know on the first day of rehearsals that *The Judas Kiss* is going to be a life-changing embrace. The planets are aligned. Not the ones in outer space perhaps, but certainly at Swiss Cottage (far enough) where the production is born. My moon is in the Hampstead Theatre – built on the foundations of the old Studio One at the Central School of Speech and Drama – the very room from which I was unceremoniously expelled thirty-three years ago.

Walking up the steps from Swiss Cottage station on that first day of rehearsal is a journey across time. Over the horizon looms my alma mater, the Embassy Theatre, hardly recognisable. The original Victorian building, dirty white and double-fronted with its blue-framed windows and matching marquee, its bare brick flank that seemed to lean over the Finchley Road, has shrunk with age, dwarfed in the clutch of the new university faculty. The doors are open, so I step inside.

Everything has changed except the noise. Cataracts of traffic still gush past and the whole school shivers, gripped in that familiar low fever that only cools late at night. The hall is empty and unrecognisable except for the portrait of the founder, Elsie Fogerty. She eyes me warily from the wall by the old masters' common room, a picture worthy of *St Trinian's*, or the set of a long-dead drawing room comedy. IS she looking slightly desperate, or is it my imagination? Perhaps she is as confused as I at the changes the building – the world – has undergone. The organs and arteries of the old school, the changing rooms and staircases, have all been ripped out, and the place no longer smells of that delicious theatrical perfume, REP, with its 'top' of Leichner tinged with gin, its 'coeur' of face powder and Elnette and that overwhelming 'bottom' scent of dust and carbolic with a little scoop of shit.

The Embassy Theatre itself, an archetypal provincial fleapit in my day, with its bumpy purple walls and ratty velvet drapes – unchanged since 1910 – is now an amphitheatre. American students on a summer course wade through Shakespeare with upward inflections on the stage. I am early for rehearsals, so I sit in the auditorium and watch.

How I had wanted to go to RADA each day I walked up the steps from the Tube to this gloomy spot. With its corrugated iron roof it felt like a mental home or a mission, its teachers a vengeful group of singing nuns and monks in jazz pants in a neighbourhood of bedsits and mediums and sad old Viennese ladies, but of course looking back it all seems quite enchanting.

After two unsatisfactory years at Central I was expelled, but that has not stopped my name being engraved on the front steps along with all the other dead heroes. I sit on mine now and survey the avenue sloping down towards Belsize Park, still and hazy in the summer morning – impossibly romantic – and there is the bench in the trees below on which my best friends Tim, Peter and I (the outcasts) pretended to hold auditions with all our favourite directors every day during the lunch break. Listening very carefully I can still hear the echo.

'That was super, Tim. I'd really like to see more of that bum of yours. It looks terrific,' one of us would say, pretending to be Peter Brook.

'Could you drop your trousers a little? Super.' We imagined everything ended up on the casting couch. If only it had.

It happened on the last day of the summer term of 1979. 'Baker Street' played on the radio in the school canteen. For once I was early. There was no one about. Just Jerry and Marianne peeling potatoes in the kitchen. I sat in the window, watching. The same white misty morning. The radio said it was going to be a 'scorcher' and the chestnut trees on Eton Avenue oozed sap and shimmered in the diesel breeze. The traffic on the Finchley Road roared along to the song, tinny and reduced by the radio in the kitchen while Jerry and Marianne bickered in Portuguese. They were a sitcom all of their own, school caterers from hell, her fat, him thin, framed inside the hatch between the canteen and the cooking area.

'... give up the booze and the one-night stands ...' Gerry sang.

'Ah believe dat when ah see it, Jeery,' screamed Marianne, suddenly appearing through the hatch. 'Ees true, Rupert. You know Jeery!' It was all a big joke. Jerry winked and slapped Marianne's gigantic bum.

With her scream – as if by magic – the school suddenly came to life. From all directions the alumni converged on the building and the windows shook as doors slammed, footsteps crashed across the ceiling, up and down the stairs. You could tell they were all actors as they screamed and laughed, bursting in and rushing out, colliding into theatrical clinches.

'See you in Aberdeen?'

'Actually I'm going to Stratford. Just heard.'

'Oh. Fabulous!' Shock and suspicion disguised as pleasure made for half-hearted squeals of joy.

Our class – stage 80 – assembled in Studio One, eagerly anticipating the end-of-year 'crits', those individual, in-depth illuminations about our progress towards the senior year and 'the profession' as manifested by the principal and the teaching staff. We huddled on the floor, jubilant and competitive, a pack of theatrical hounds baying for attention as our masters converged behind a trestle table and sat down neatly into a kind of theatrical Last Supper. In the middle George Hall – the principal – radiated Christlike concern as my turn came to be evaluated. Stigmata would suddenly spurt from his wrists if he had to catalogue one more of my shortcomings. I liked him tremendously and remember looking beseechingly into his eyes, but he continued anyway. What we all dreaded was happening to me and you could hear a pin drop. Finally George stopped, apparently struck dumb, but then another thought crossed his mind. He just couldn't understand – he said with a frown – what induced me to wear so much make-up as Posthumus. (We had clunked through *Cymbeline* for our end-of-term show.)

'I didn't know I was!' I replied, my throat tightening.

'What do you think, John?' asked George, turning to his boy-friend the head teacher – the most poisonous of them all on a bad day but otherwise quite a laugh. He was called John Jones, and he normally called me Cunty or Everard (I should have known). Actually I liked him, too. He looked like the Milky Bar Kid's stage mother. He ruled the roost at Central with a constitution of exclusion and favouritism that kept us all on our toes. His approval meant everything and you could tell who had it. They swaggered with talent in the common room. Some of the girls had crushes on him, and it was rumoured he was bisexual but I doubt it.

'Yes, George,' he said in his neat suburban clip, icy-calm, pushing his spectacles up his nose with a middle finger while he consulted his notes. 'I was completely disappointed with you this term.' He looked up. 'You seem to be going backwards fast.'

Tears were now balancing on the lids of my eyes. John Jones looked straight into them, daring them to fall. 'Actually, it's pretty much a disgrace, a waste of all our time.'

Leonie, the prettiest girl in our year, who was writing down my 'crits' for me – that's what we did – looked up and gasped, 'What?'

He repeated himself and continued killing me off while George watched with the same doleful face under exhausted-from-being-constantly-surprised eyes.

I was crushed. OK, I hadn't been easy. I had rebelled against the system of rib reserve and vocal technique. I had skipped every fencing class. I didn't want to learn tap. I never bothered to go to the zoo for animal studies. I wore pink tights and drop earrings at movement class, but so what?

Apropos. 'Your movement show was just second-rate Lindsay Kemp. What were you thinking? What was the point? Did you tell your scene partners you were going to be using blood capsules?'

'No.'

John sat thoughtfully with his legs crossed, leaning forward, elbows on his knees, looking at his hands. I could feel my heart thump. He took his time (*X Factor* technique before its time). 'I just don't know what the next step is,' he said finally.

'I do,' piped the voice teacher, Bardy Thomas.

My gaping face was dragged into the magnetic field of her cruel, sharp eyes – mine had dilated with terror.

'I think we've got to think very carefully whether it's worth you coming back next year,' she said evenly.

'Really?' was all I could muster, tears now pouring down my face.

Bardy observed them with a wry smile. 'Yes, really,' she sneered in vulgar imitation.

I disliked this woman as much as she disliked me. Remembering this helped – drew me back from the edge – and the tears stopped dead in their tracks. Bardy had Pebbles hair worn up in a tuft held together by a brightly coloured plastic clip. It gave her a poultry quality. As she clucked and pecked, scratched with her claws at the roots of all my defects, I fixed my attention on the tuft. It waggled comically above her head and the sound cut out. While the rest of the teachers hammered nails into my coffin – with uniform voracity – the reality of my situation dawned. I was about to be expelled, exiled by the business before I was even out of the stable. Was this the end of my dreams? I had been plotting to go to drama school from the moment I set foot on stage as Titania aged twelve. Suddenly I felt hopelessly out of my depth.

It was unfair. I was quite interesting. Without question I had something. It may not have been Posthumus or Cymbeline or even Thumbelina – but it was something that didn't deserve to be squashed. Yes, I was weirdly tall and thin – beyond size zero. Yes, I was already taking heroin and fucking everything in sight and I never wore shoes. But at least all that gave me a kind of creepy quality, an experience. An actor who's done something is normally more interesting than an actor who's done nothing. In an art school I would have been encouraged. But there was something pitiless about British entertainment, something grim and soot-stained from the war, and that day was just the beginning of a peculiar slow-motion wrestling match with the establishment. Behind all the trestle tables for all time, the same old chippy hippies and opera queens sat in judgement, at first in those strange prefab offices perched over bomb sites (not just of the war but of the class system as well) and then through the glass walls of boardrooms and at the central tables during awards seasons. Something between me and the world I longed for just never quite worked. I should have pushed 'freeze' and stepped out of the picture because nothing was going to change, but I didn't. Instead at the end of 'crits' I was asked to go to the principal's room.

Alone and stripped of all dreams, I watched as my assassin gathered his things, ready for the holidays. He had a bicycle pump in his hand. I was not even going to leave a trace on the atmosphere; no echo. George confirmed that I would not be coming back. He looked at me with those raisin eyes for some reaction. There was no point in saying anything so I turned and left the room. I walked down into the Tube for the last time, down that long escalator to the train. I briefly considered throwing myself in front of it as it screeched from the dusty tunnel but couldn't really be bothered, so I went home instead, straight to bed where I lay surrounded by empty bottles and overflowing ashtrays, plates of congealed food, glasses half-full of wine, all the debris from the end-of-term party I had thrown the night before, and coiled myself up in dirty sheets and drifted off in a mist of depression. These were the days of answering machines, and endless voices echoed across the deserted party with dreary messages of commiseration.

I slept for three days. Then I rose from my tomb, dramatic and romantic, barefoot in a kaftan and stared glumly into thin air at Picasso's coffee shop on the King's Road, day after day trying to have an idea in wraparound dark glasses from Seditionaries. The only flicker of life was the odd reflected leaf falling across their black lenses.

It was at Picasso's that I came up with my first live performance. I had been reliably informed that Ken Russell was going to be walking down the King's Road one Saturday and I decided to stage a one-man show so that he could discover me. For my libretto I chose Barbara Cartland's book of etiquette. I prepared my costume carefully. Polka-dot minidress, drop earrings, stilettos. My hair was blue-black, cut into a towering wedge by Antony Price. I painted my face a greenish-white with a red gash of lipstick. In a moment of madness just before leaving home I shaved off my eyebrows. (They have never grown back properly.)

I was told that Russell would be around after lunch, scouting for extras for his new film. I could hardly believe my luck as I imagined myself throwing that elusive double six and elbowing my way up the ladder straight to stardom. Obviously he would take one look at me and sign me up on the spot. 'Just you wait, Henry Higgins,' I hummed to myself as I set off from home with a little stool and a begging bowl.

For the first hour I was doing rather well. I gathered quite a crowd, and the plastic bucket was full of coins until a group of punks coming down the street from Sloane Square elbowed their way through the spectators, took the bowl and ran off with it towards the World's End. I did not validate them by giving chase. I simply went on with my reading – I'd just got to the bit about how to address royalty – but then the police arrived and I was moved on. Ken Russell never appeared.

It was the summer of '79.

Clearly I would have to resort to more conventional methods. I bought sixty envelopes and stamps and wrote letters to all the directors named in *Contacts* – a theatrical directory I had shop-lifted one day in Covent Garden. I even sent one to a theatre in Nairobi called the Donovan Maule. I enclosed the sickly child star headshot that had been taken by an extorting hag (also from *Contacts*) who kept telling me to look happy during the shoot. (We weren't on the same page. They ended up looking very Operation Yewtree before its time.) I licked endless stamps onto envelopes during all-night sessions listening to disco standards, smoking and dreaming in my basement flat. The game was on!

For thirty-five years I managed to avoid Swiss Cottage.

CHAPTER THREE

Back to the Future

Now I am back on the Finchley Road, looking for the Cosmo Restaurant where all the little old ladies used to have tea in the old days. It's gone, replaced by a down-at-heel coffee shop run by a couple of grumpy Eastern bloc Berthas who never seem to have enough of anything, either food or humour. The *Judas Kiss* company lunches there every day.

The Cosmo used to be an elegant – if dull – oasis for those poor old birds who flapped in from Budapest and Prague via West Hampstead and Golders Green during the years follow-ing the war. Bent double on sticks, in twos and threes, white hair in coils and buns, their tiny, intense eyes scrutinising the pudding trolley for apple strudel piled with cream, these ladies could remember the death camps. Thick lace curtains shielded them from the relative horrors of the Finchley Road, throwing a dreary light on the pale green walls. The whole thing looked like a worn-out photograph, a distant echo of Vienna between the wars, all the red and gold drained into the colours of autumn leaves falling. They came to all the school productions and sometimes paid for our tea. We told them about our plans for stardom and they listened enraptured even though they'd heard it all before. We beseeched them to share our dreams and were thrilled when they declared – their eyes shining and charmed, or marbleised by cataracts – that we would definitely be big stars. In those days we discussed the future. Now we discuss the past and their ghosts lean in.

In the new virtual world a troupe of actors preparing a play seems impossibly quaint, as romantic and old-fashioned as a village post office. Actors must communicate. Through the face, not Facebook. We must have spatial awareness. We cannot plough through the crowds like bumper cars. We need manners (not necessarily good ones but some code of behaviour), and must respond to discipline. We only have ourselves and each other with which to construct a performance and we generally go at it wholeheartedly, trusting one another with all the gory details of our lives over the lunch break. Our foibles and phobias, highs and lows, health scares and messy divorces are the building bricks, the individual currency with which we trade, and this August, in the shadow of the old acting school, the whole process seems miraculous and meaningful, very much at odds with the grab it world outside.

Rehearsals take place in a subterranean studio with no windows, only skylights. This is what it feels like being a fish. Life waves above us in the branches. Our director is called Neil Armfield (Neil Armstrong in one review) and has been imported – at great expense – from Sydney. He has a round furry face with hidden features – kind brown eyes obscured by thick glasses and a foxy smile peeking out from his untrimmed beard. He could be laughing with you or at you. He is calm at all times, dressed usually in plaid shirts and wide, flat shoes with thick brightly coloured laces in which he clomps around the set, arms outstretched – a dowser searching for water, or a medium gathering ectoplasm – plotting the moves and the action of the play.

He is immediately enthralled by Freddie Fox. We all are. They spend hours discussing whether Freddie should sit at this moment or maybe that one, in the middle of a certain line or after. The rest of us wait patiently wondering what we're going to cook for dinner while Freddie brilliantly drags the whole rehearsal process into his magnetic field. He is an extraordinary invention, twenty-two going on seventy-two, appearing in a room rather than entering, a Hollywood star from the thirties in Gatsby pants. He is the head boy of a theatrical family. His uncle Robert is one of my closest friends and is also the producer of our play, so I have known Freddie all his life. As I vividly recall him upstaging everyone at the age of five it is no surprise to discover that he fully intends to walk away with the show. His jihad is not aggressive – Queensberry Rules all the way – but as far as he is concerned the show has been written for him and the world is waiting for him to take over.

I fully approve of this modus operandi. He reminds me of myself except that he scribbles endless notes in his script, as if somehow the guise of a diligent student will throw us all off the scent. In rehearsals he is quite astonishing, but even if he sets himself on fire – and he could – he will never manage to steal the show, because he has overlooked one thing. One cannot swim against a writer's tide. David has created one of the best parts ever written for an actor, and it's MINE, and even if I am stumbling through it at the moment, looking a little indistinct, he does not know – and nor does anyone else – that I have ordered the most incredible fat suit from the master of disguise Rob Allsopp, replete with baboon moobs, a wobbling midriff and a marvellous knee-length arse. I shall wear it under a tightly laced corset, to squeeze me into the perfect Wildean waddle.

Oscar's cock will be the key to my performance, and Rob has

made a Christmas stocking of a thing, with low-hanging balls filled with dried beans. This appendage will be visible to the audience, squelched within my trousers. (I had to cut it down a size or two after a couple of previews. It was taking over. Big cocks always do.)

I have two incredible sets of dirty teeth with enlarged gums to give my cheeks the Oscar silhouette. (They are made by Fangs, who created my Miss Fritton overbite and are truly inspired.) I have two amazing wigs from the queen of hair, Alex Rouse. One is thick and bouncy for act one and the other is thin and balding for act two. I am going to look astonishing as Oscar before I even open my mouth. I have spent the whole year fine-tuning this look, if not my performance.

There are three other young actors in the play. We call them the kids – Ben, Kirsty and Tom. By the way, Freddie is NOT one of the kids, even though he is younger than two of them. They all have to perform naked. We have been putting off the moment of truth in rehearsals, but finally the day comes and we have decided to have a nude run. Luckily for them they are all very alluring. The rest of us sit behind the trestle tables trying not to look fascinated as Ben performs cunnilingus on Kirsty.

At least they have each other to hide behind, but poor Tom who plays Galileo the Neapolitan fisherman must prance around the stage for a whole act nude. His parents are both mounted police officers in Suffolk, and he is naturally worried what they may think. (In fact, they turn out to be charming, and love him in the show.) His part is quite shocking. He must begin the act entwined with Freddie Fox on a bed, and has had to show Neil his private parts in the audition since there is a particular reference in the play to them, their dimensions and hue. Also he must speak Italian with a Neapolitan accent.

On the day of the nude run he gets quite upset. Why has he taken the part? He feels like a piece of meat. Actually, he is an excellent actor, one of the best things in the play, but we don't know this yet. Freddie, our unelected head boy, swiftly takes control of the situation and marches him off to the disabled loo so that they can undress together and get used to one another's nudity. (If only Freddie had been there in the Garden of Eden humanity mightn't have ended up in this mess!)

The rest of us have a coffee break. In rehearsals I live for the coffee breaks. All I want to do is chat. The director has insisted on named cups. It's rather like school. Does he have some terrible disease? Or does he think one of us has? God knows what happens in the disabled loo, because Tom stumbles back into the room as if he has seen a ghost, while Freddie 'appears' a few seconds later. 'He's not ready,' is all Mr Fox will say.

He gets ready pretty quick and is one of the high points of the show. At one moment in the evening he must cross the stage wet to answer the front door, while I sit slumped in an armchair. From this bird's eye position I am able to observe the heads of the entire audience move with him – as one – and I resign myself to the fact, once and for all, that even I could set myself on fire at this point and nobody would notice.

One morning in the first week of rehearsals Neil, our director, arrives very upset. The actor who played Oscar in his Sydney production died last night. They had been great friends, and according to him had been a marvellous Oscar.

'What was his name again?'

'Bille Brown.'

The hairs on my arms stand up on end. I am walking on someone else's grave.

At some point at the end of the seventies, probably during my second year at drama school, there was a large Australian on the prowl at night in Earl's Court, good-looking but shaped like a pear drop. I first saw him one evening as I was sitting in the large bow window of my friend Tom's flat on Coleherne Road. It was where I perched most nights, ready at any given moment to tear from the room and pounce on the passing trade in the street.

And there was a lot. The Coleherne pub was next door on the corner of the Old Brompton Road and at closing time all the cowboys and leather queens spilt onto the street and stood in exotic shadows under the street lights. They looked like divine expressionless mutants – just lips and cheekbones with black sockets for eyes.

(Later, at their place, unpeeled from their kit, in the cosy light emanating from a fringed lampshade they might present a less thrilling picture. The harsh line of a firm jaw often turned to a sagging swag in its warm glow, ruched at the earlobe and under the chin. Remove a biker's cap at your peril. Almost everyone was bald. The Marlon Brando you had just cruised – a little too easily, perhaps – ended up looking like a baby bird recently dropped from the nest, flapping around with a whip, and all rather unconvincing. But that was part of the fun.)

The block around Tom's flat – right onto Wharfedale Road, right again on Finnborough and back onto the Old Brompton Road – was a legendary cruising spot and went on until dawn during the good years. A couple of revolutions and one normally got lucky. If not then some ghastly chemical reaction set in and you could cruise that block till dawn and you wouldn't even be able to entice Bird Woman – the name we gave to the vagrant queen who lurked under the arch into the mews.

In such a way I met and made it with Bille a few times. We were neither of us at the top of one another's list, but in those days just to be doing it was as important as who you were doing it with. He smelt of aftershave and soap and submerged sweat. In the minimum of conversation I discovered he was working as an actor and going back to Australia next year. He must have been in his late twenties and already had a slightly elephantine gait.

The encounter had nothing particular to write home about and we both rushed off in opposite directions as soon as the deed was done. The last time we made out – behind a car halfway down the mews, with Bird Woman watching from the shadows and making weird 'phwoaah' and 'yeeah' sounds, which I rather enjoyed but Bille did not – his temper cracked. I never wanted to talk. I NEVER gave my real name. Was I Kevin or Ryan or Brad? There was no point explaining so I just looked glum. Sex was a separate thing from the rest of my life and I only really liked to do it outside. I hated the clutter of real life to be involved, and on top of that I didn't like to be locked in.

'Why don't you want to come back?' he said, only a trace left of his Australian accent.

'Just don't feel like it,' I replied shiftily – no trace of my native brogue either. What I really meant was how great he looked leaning against a car parked up against a peeling garage door in the dark, but I could already tell – seasoned slut that I was – that it would only be downhill from the moment he produced his latchkey. He looked very nice trussed up in camouflage and khaki, but the aftershave was an indication of rather more gen-teel aspirations than those I normally enjoyed on a home visit. Going back to a squat with an ex-con was one thing. Going back to a flat with posters of productions from the RSC on the walls was quite another.

'It's only round the corner.'

'That's what they all say. I've got to be going. Got to get to Ilford.' Sheer fantasy, and we separated, bumping into each other at least three times later that night, thereby sealing the vault on our lamplit friendship.

We never met again, but I was always hearing about him. We knew lots of the same people and his name often came up. My various noms de guerre meant that our entanglement was invis-ible and so our names were never discussed in the same breath.

Until *The Judas Kiss*.

'Strange,' said Neil when I told him the story. 'He never mentioned that he'd had you and he wasn't very discreet.'

'It was before I was really me. No one remembers me from that time.'

Every line of the play had another layer to it from that day on and the whole thing felt sacred. Bille lived on in my borrowed gestures and the two most successful moments of my performance as Oscar were stolen from him.

CHAPTER FOUR

Marriage Material

The Judas Kiss is a marvellous play that has been performed once before in the UK to disastrous effect, savaged by the press in reviews that even our excellent production cannot quite bury.

The first act takes place at the Cadogan Hotel where Oscar flees after his libel action against the Marquess of Queensberry collapses. For any diehard Wilde fan the last afternoon of freedom in that poky room on the corner of Pont Street is one of the great romantic riddles of the nineteenth century. (I have slept in that room, by the way. No message.)

Why does Wilde not run when he has the chance? Does he know that his place in history is being carved as he sits there waiting to be arrested? Or does he, as David Hare infers, simply think that if he gets bail he and Bosie can still dine at Willis's that night, where, according to Betjeman (in his poem 'The Arrest of Oscar Wilde at the Cadogan Hotel'), his favourite fur coat has been left in the cloakroom? Is he immobilised by indecision (Hamlet), or carrying his cross all the way to Reading Gaol (Jesus)?

In David's play everything is possible, and Oscar sits centre stage considering his options and drinking heavily – watching the crash from above – while on either side Robbie Ross and Lord Alfred Douglas fight over his soul if not his body. Robbie, beautifully played in our production by Cal MacAninch, urges Oscar to leave for the station. Bosie, blinded by hatred and desperate for revenge, wants him to stay, to fight to the death, but neatly manages to escape himself before the police arrive.

Sloshed in a chair, it is finally immortality that Oscar is playing for – not life, and anyway the clock is ticking and soon time has run out. The last train has gone. 'Do you hear the wheels running away down the track?' he asks a distraught Robbie. 'Do you feel the life we did not live?' The two friends sit together in the fading light and wait for the police to arrive, a curtain tableau which uncannily captures the famous illustration 'The arrest of Oscar Wilde'.

The second act – even better than the first – finds Oscar at the end of the road in a crumbling, rat-infested palazzo outside Naples as his affair with Alfred Douglas finally unravels. A beached whale, his butcher and a bit of rough spend one last long night tearing each other to shreds as the Bay of Naples shimmers below them 'jewelled like the scrawny neck of some ageing dowager'.

Robbie arrives – a fictional meeting, but as dynamic as Schiller's imagined confrontation between those other two queens in his historical play *Mary Stuart* – informing Oscar that unless he leaves Bosie his wife will divorce him and cut off his small allowance. Robbie still loves Oscar and (I think) Oscar loves Robbie, but he doesn't know it. It is an enormously tragic scene. Robbie retreats and Bosie moves in for the kill. Again, Oscar is the observer at his own death. There is nothing left.

At the end of the play he rejects God – as not artistically true – and appeals to nature 'whose sweet rains fall on unjust and just alike'. The play ends with his face framed in a pool of light. He is literally fading from view laughing at himself and at life. It's the only play I've been in where you can hear the sobs and sniffs of the audience at the end.

One is prey to emotional storms during the lengthy crossing of a West End run. At the start everything is breathless and uncertain, corks pop and we pour in ecstasy onto the stage like so many sperm shooting through the proscenium into the warm dark space where the eggs lurk. We must crack and fertilise them with the playwright's (hopefully) still breeding thoughts, and it is this communion between player and spectator that helps create the theatrical close-up – that curious imagined lens – in the otherwise endless long shot of a play.

But as one crosses the yardarm of a long run that tremulous first kiss feeling tends to wane. It's day 189, and I must fake another thundering orgasm. Arteries and capillaries strain and squeeze blood to the relevant areas, but deep-vein thrombosis could set in at any given moment (75 mg of aspirin each day is essential). Eyeballs may pop and haemorrhoids burst, but the bard must sing on.

'No deeper wrinkles yet?' Get me the Preparation H.

Then sometimes something happens. Perhaps it's a kiss, an affair that suddenly blooms. Perhaps you see someone in the front row you fancy and the whole thing lurches back to flickering life. Perhaps some terrible world tragedy makes you feel safe and lucky, or a silent movie star passing through town is asleep in the stalls or – once in our case – it is Lady Olivier, half blind in a wing armchair laughing in the off-prompt box during the midweek matinee at the Brighton Royal. The performance waxes and wanes in the thrall of all these various moons.

But nothing prepares me for tonight. Before the show our author slouches into my dressing room like the school bully from *If.* I always feel a bit like a new boy with David Hare. He brings a strange vibration into a room, one I have not felt since school. A theatre is similar to a public school in many ways and it is easy to imagine David slouching around the corridors of Lancing College, perched on the cliffs near Seaford, that marvellous head of hair flying in the salty wind. Brilliantly clever, witheringly funny, unkempt in a tweed jacket and tie, flannel trousers and unlaced shoes, moving in a flotilla of henchboys, ruling the sixth form library or some such lofty institution, while effortlessly scoring straight As in all his exams.

He can be rather severe, but he is also terribly funny. The henchboys today are agents and producers. But he is also quite vulnerable, and this is perhaps what one doesn't notice at first. He is terrified of his own work. If we get it wrong it sounds to him like fingernails scratching a blackboard. He has been found foetal in the corner of a box on occasion, unable to face the play.

(During the first catastrophic run-through of *The Judas Kiss* his face quickly clouds over. By the end of act one all moisture has drained from it, and he fixes me with a diabolical glare of undisguised repulsion. It's more or less impossible to continue. The text scatters on its way from my brain to my mouth. The actors hide in the coffee nook during the break, a gaggle of geese honking in the corner of the pen as the wolf prowls the perimeter. During act two he has sunk into despondency and just looks into the middle distance, speechless at the horrors of Armageddon revealed to him in some parallel universe. At the end of the run-through the silence screams. I flee.)

Still slightly unkempt, but with curious dashes of haute couture mixed in – courtesy of his lovely French wife, Nicole Farhi – he strides the corridors of theatres in a wake of jubilation or despair. When he lets you have it, you'd better have recourse to a good tranquilliser or the sympathetic ear of your agent because he can be brutal. Like all new boys I am in awe of him on the football pitch and slightly shy if he sits next to me in the refectory. He has been careful and kind and we are doing good business, which always helps. He is also the first to pass on compliments while most of us conveniently forget them.

'Gay marriage has just gone through,' he says tonight, laughing. 'Will you be marrying Babinho?'

'Possibly. I don't know if he'd have me,' I reply as I paint on the eyeliner.

'Of course, you're against it, aren't you?' I think he has me down for a neocon.

'I loathe weddings, if that's what you mean. Gay or straight.'

'I say. Going a bit strong on the rouge tonight, aren't you?' he says, looking at me through the mirror.

'Oh. Am I?' Still too much make-up all these years later. Some habits are hard to break.

Through my open door I can hear him spreading the news up the stairs to the other dressing rooms and it suddenly strikes me that tonight our play is the most important artistic expression of the times. In the theatre seven hundred people's worlds collide each night, but this evening we are all tottering in on one of the great tectonic plate shifts as our whole interior world is realigned. This is how it suddenly feels. Just a century ago a man, Oscar, could be imprisoned and ruined – killed off, basically – simply for being gay, but tonight, as it says on the cover of the *Evening Standard*, a homosexual stands on equal ground with the rest of society and I am quite unexpectedly extremely moved. Oscar winks at me in the mirror as I apply more eyeliner.

I remember a letter he once wrote about the road to freedom for Uranians (homosexuals). He predicted that it would be long and smeared in the blood of martyrs. It has been, still is, and will be for a long time – it's not over – but right now, laced in by darling Josie to my corset, glued into my wig by the divine Helen, cigarettes and lighter courtesy of screechy Scotch Helen the ASM, hat, gloves and cane in one hand, draped in my favourite

fur, it feels important to finally be marriage material. I make for
the stage with a new spring to my step.

Sitting in the blue light of the wings in my usual seat, my
heart beating as fast as a first night, watching the technicians
and actors emerge from the darkness in that methodical slow-
motion dance peculiar to our trade, checking props, fixing ties
and collecting thoughts as the auditorium fills and the energy
gathers, I know it's one of the great moments in my life and I
have the most extraordinary feeling that the whole universe has
stopped in its tracks and is watching. (Syphilis probably, but at
the thrilling stage.) I am aware of every minuscule movement
in my body – veins gurgling, little muscles twitching, hairs
standing up and waving – but also I can feel the whole audience.
We are absolutely united. The same thought is crossing all our
minds. This is THE night to see a play about Oscar Wilde.

'It's a good one,' says Alister, who plays Moffatt the butler,
his ear cocked, appearing through the gloom, giving his nightly
appraisal of the audience's enthusiasm. The front-of-house manager pokes his head through the pass door with a nod to Mike
our company manager, who comes over to our little group.

'Time, please, gentlemen.' He is a jolly publican. The house
lights fade with that strange surge of electricity as the stage
lamps come up brown-blue and spangled pink. The audience
fall silent and the music begins.

I hurl myself onto the stage for my first entrance, a theatrical
Lazarus back from the grave. I am the crest of an invisible wave.
Its undertow is the whole history of cruelty – the pillory, the
scaffold, the red-hot poker and the burnings at the stake, all the
vileness invented by humanity to curb and control the practitioners of the unspeakable sin – it's all tumbling on and Oscar
is there in every word, razor-sharp, slashing the world down to
size, glittering in the lights and crashing against the walls of the
theatre. The trained lamps fading or flooding, the technicians

whispering into their headphones, the faces of the spectators, the whole world has stopped in its tracks and is watching aghast.

After the curtain call – a standing ovation – our Bosie and I are walking from the stage. He looks like a little child suddenly.

'That was our best yet,' I say.

'I was crap.'

'No you weren't. You were a god.'

If these moments of clarity could only last. The next night and for the rest of the run – another ten days or so – I search for the same impetus but the eclipse is over and the spark has gone. On the last night there is a party in Cal's dressing room. Everyone else has the energy to be thrilled but I feel like the walking dead. Corks fly, the reminiscences begin and I edge my way from the room. I hate goodbyes. The party echoes down the staircase as I look for the last time at that disease trap, my empty dressing room. It has taken on the dimensions of a person during this long, bitter winter. Its two shivering fridges groan a goodbye, and the downpipe behind the sink does a gurgle of victory, followed by a final ghastly smell. The last occupant, knowing something that I did not, had left me two bottles of cough mixture. They were delicious. I have left the same clue for the next earthbound star.

On the stage the stagehands are already dismantling the set. Outside a big lorry is parked to take it all away. There goes my biggest success, and that's the theatre for you. Here today, forgotten tomorrow. Another show, a new crisis, the next war. Only the building stands firm, the trees and the traces of ancient streets as I walk home through the freezing spring.

CHAPTER FIVE

In Search of Oscar Wilde

Waking up on the morning after the end of a long run is like being in heaven after a difficult death. The sheets are snowy mountains in the dawn light. Beyond their ridges the world hides, and for a moment I am weightless in ecstasy. The play is over. The thought triggers a chemical flood across my body and I fall into a dreamless sleep, smiling. I am free. But not for long. A touring actor always has a train to catch.

Every Sunday I lunch with Philip Prowse. He is the director who gave me my first job in the theatre. I was eighteen. He was forty-two. Thirty-five years later we are – miraculously – still talking. He is my greatest and most dangerous friend. He is as charming, expansive and generous as he is critical, merciless and reductive. It depends on the day. If you are feeling vulnerable, or having your period, watch out. Philip can smell blood!

He is a tall, imposing man in a mackintosh with cropped hair over a large pointed nose and surprised eyes. His long El Greco fingers – he was born with six on each hand ('she's a witch, dear,

like Anne Boleyn, be very careful', someone once said) – lie
against his chest or play with the mole on his neck while he talks
and his pièce de résistance is that his ears draw back when he is
nervous like a dog's. He is the cleverest person I know and the
best read, and if I am unable to scale the dizzy heights of his
intellect we at least have hypochondria and humour in common
and we both think he is a genius. Working for him in Glasgow
was the most fulfilling part of my career. The Citizens Theatre
lived up to all my expectations.

Normally we meet in a restaurant called Smith's near his
house in Wapping, but today – the morning after the life before,
the first day of freedom from the clutches of the West End
run – we are lunching in the station hotel at St Pancras. I am
catching the three o'clock train to Paris en route to Naples, in
the footsteps of Oscar.

He is sitting at a table in the far corner of the restaurant looking out the window. He seems vulnerable and slightly shrunken
against the glare of the huge gothic windows, waving from a sea
of starched tablecloths. One's friends always appear unchanged.
One sees them as one first saw them. Then, for some reason,
by chance, you see them as they really are, and today Philip
looks like the ghost of his former self. His face is drained of
expression.

'You look like Marie Antoinette on the tumbril. What on
earth's the matter?'

'My dear! This place is hideous.' His voice, thin and high, is
at its most perilous.

'Poor David Collins decorated it.'

'Hardly poor, dear. For a colour-blind nelly she's gone a
long way.'

'Yes. All the way. She's in heaven!'

'At this hour?'

'Not that Heaven! She died.'

'Oh really? What happened?' Philip rallies slightly. He loves a good death.

'She dropped dead, more or less. She had a biopsy on a thing in her ear. A month later she was gone. Her funeral was last week.'

'Oh no. Poor trollop. How terrible.' Long fingers instinctively reach for the lobes of his own large ears.

'One lump or two?' I ask sweetly, pouring myself some wine.

'Fuck off. Actually, those chandeliers are quite good.' He looks around the restaurant, yellow with gilt edges, revising his withering opinion in a bored drawl. 'They are! But look at the lamps. And the chairs.' Life is a series of facts for Philip. There's little point contradicting, and anyway he is usually right. Suddenly his eyes narrow to slits and his ears go back. 'Christ!' he breathes. 'There's Daphne Guinness! What's she doing here?'

Daphne Guinness is a waiter we know from our usual Sunday restaurant. She is a tall thin Eastern bloc fairy with blue hair.

'She completely blanked me in Waitrose last week.'

'She probably didn't see you.'

'Oh yes she did. I was practically screaming.'

Daphne sidles up. 'Hah gahs! Vaats oop?' We never understand a word she says, but it doesn't matter. We just glower at her beatifically, as she towers over us radiating star quality. It's true that she does more or less ignore Philip, but she is convinced we are both obsessed by her – we are not – and while a middle-aged fairy like me with a certain provenance measurable (just) in Daphne's *X Factor* world view, and worthy therefore of cultivation, she does not have the necessary radar equipment to trace the screech that Philip's long and distinguished career has left on the atmosphere.

To Daphne, blue-rinsed in drainpipes and court (jester) shoes – swishing through Waitrose with nothing more than passion fruit, brie ('And Twiglets, dear!') in her trolley – living the EU dream as she makes her selection, on nodding terms already with all the fabulous hedge fund fruit on Wapping High Street – a greeting from Philip looming over the horizon is a PR disaster and only confirms what the cashiers and local shoppers already suspect, which is that Daphne is in fact a Romanian hooker on the run from the police rather than the super-fabulous something-or-other about to make a big splash. A chat with Philip in Waitrose is not on Daphne's ageist agenda and the con-nection must be nipped in the bud, so she acts deaf and pushes her empty trolley on, hotfooting it round the corner into kitchen utensils, scanning the aisles for witnesses.

'What happened to Smith's?' Philip asks nonetheless, putting his most fascinating face forward. Daphne throws him a with-ering glance.

'Zey maak biiig faht! Zey dorn't haav wespect me.'

'Oh, surely not!'

'No wurreez. Ah'm cheel wiv eet.'

'Cheel?'

'Yeah. Cheelax!' She does a weird dance step and surges off across the room, arms flowing behind her, and Philip's face drops.

'You see. She can't even look at me. Did she just say big fart?'

'Big fight, I think.' We laugh.

Now Phil turns his attention on me. 'Do tell me one thing. Why on earth are you going to Naples? Why can't you just stay put? You look absolutely exhausted.'

'Thanks, dear. If I stop now I'll never get going again. It's hard to explain.'

'But what is the point of going to Naples now, if the film is still not going ahead?'

'Keeping going! It's the only thing I can think of.'

'There's a moment when you have to let go of an idea, you know.' Philip wants everyone to do nothing.

Yes. Having a dream in middle age is a dangerous occupation

and mine is crushing me. Several years ago – five at this point – encouraged by the success of my first book of memoirs, I turned my attention to screenwriting, my dream being to create work for myself as an actor since no one else seemed to be very keen to do so. The success of my last Hollywood incarnation was still a flickering ember on the horizon, not quite dead. I thought it could be blown back into a flame with a judicious move and a prevailing wind. Oscar Wilde in exile seemed to be the obvious choice. If the only role I was permitted to play in world cinema was the gay best friend, then I would take it all the way back to the prototype.

Since I was rudderless and in the career doldrums again I had nothing better to do but read every book written about Wilde and soon, with the help (and hindrance) of Philip Prowse, I wrote a script. Robert Fox sent it to the world's best and toughest producer, Scott Rudin, who loved it, thought it was brilliant. I remember that day very well, the intensity of happiness, the congratulations I received from all the doubters in my camp. I was walking on air, making all sorts of plans, acceptance speeches in mirrors, dispensing largesse.

However the next day Rudin told Robert that he wanted Philip Seymour Hoffman to play Oscar and here is where I made my greatest mistake. I should have said yes. Hoffman, of course, would have been brilliant and my career as a screenwriter would have been established at the highest level. However, I declined. I had written the script for myself and I still had grandiose plans. I wanted Roger Michell to be the director. Robert Fox managed to persuade Scott to let me act in the film as long as Roger was definitely involved. So far, so good. Roger then decided that he didn't want to direct the film after all but at least Rudin didn't follow him straight away into the woods. He gave me a list of directors he would accept and I approached them all.

You can't imagine, drear reader, how slowly things can move

in the corridors of power, how long it takes to get an important person to read your script. There was a list of six directors. It took nearly two years to extract a negative response from each of them. Rudin backed out – the last ember of my Hollywood career by this stage having irretrievably crumbled to ash. I was just another old freak on the dust heap, joining Mr T, Robby Benson and Mark Lester in the 'where are they now' category.

Soon I had nothing left but my script. And that was when I decided to try and make it myself. Fuck them. Fuck them and fuck them, I thought.

Alarm bells rang everywhere.

Of course I should have let go. Instead I beetled off to Germany where I had been having quite a success as a leather queen and began the lengthy process of creating an international co-production. It seemed like an inspired move. There was a lot of money in Germany, and with my new Teutonic producers we managed to find about half the budget, but in the rest of Europe we hit a brick wall. Potential backers cited a number of reasons not to take part, the most enduring one being that I was too good-looking to play Oscar. In reality I was simply past my sell-by date.

Then I had the idea of doing *The Judas Kiss*. With the help of Robert Fox, Jonathan Church from the Chichester Festival Theatre and the blessing of David Hare, we set the play up at the Hampstead Theatre and everything suddenly came to life. The play was a hit. The tide turned and I was back on the beach, surfing in on a seething, bubbling wave of success.

On top of all that, my second book of memoirs came out a couple of weeks before the play opened. It got some excellent reviews. Then with Robert's help I managed to get the BBC involved with the film, at the same time scooping up a great distributor – Lionsgate. This all happened in September.

However, on this slushy March morning I am still short of

money. It is often the last chunk that remains elusive, and everything moves incredibly slowly. Days turn into weeks turn into years – and the tide turns again. One must kick madly or get dragged back out to sea. Today at St Pancras I am waiting to hear if the BFI will back my film and provide the elusive million. Meanwhile I must keep going. Now more than ever is the time to push on although I am completely knocked sideways from the endless winter run. I have explained all this to Philip before, but we have diametrically opposed views on how things should be done, how life should be attacked.

'All that energy, dear!' He looks at me with sympathy. It's the same old conversation. 'I wake up in the morning – nothing to do – the whole day stretching out and it feels absolutely marvellous.' He's retreating into his sing-song voice now. 'I go to the shops. The movies. Watch *Coronation Street*. Make a spot of supper. I really don't think I have ever been happier.'

'Good. You don't look it. For my own part I don't think I've ever been unhappier. Anyway, I can't think of anything worse than cooking dinner. Let's go. I don't want to miss my train. Come and see me off.'

'Oh, Christ. Must I?'

He makes it as far as the giant kissing couple in bronze that dominates the station. It stops him dead in his tracks. He stares aghast up the girl's skirts. 'Christ! Look at those shoes. Bye, darling. I'm not going to wait. Have a lovely time. Call me when you get back.' And he disappears, waving, towards the Underground, while I make for the train.

CHAPTER SIX

Eurostar

Like a shark I am at my best on the move. Arriving doesn't suit me, I hate leaving and staying in the same place feels like drowning. But once I am on the tracks and the past falls behind, I experience a kind of weightless ecstasy, a sloshed affection for the world, which looks its best after all from a passing train.

Even one's problems achieve a sort of fin-de-siècle glamour. One's travelling companions are endlessly fascinating. One can't pack everything, so a large part of oneself is left behind with all the other unsuitable clothes. The future starts at the end of the line and so we sit together – but alone – in the bubble of the restaurant car, or the couchette, or the compartment – and life is briefly reduced to simple things like watching.

The train for France initially heads north, snaking round the city through a wilderness of deserted hangars and factories, which over the years have been discreetly dismantled, replaced – almost out of nowhere – by a city of glass, its dreary streets with the dreary names of the council burghers who spawned them. Ellie Smith Road, for example.

Somewhere in there are the ruins of Greek Andy's house, built on a kind of island between bridges and embankments, in that tangle of railway tracks and warehouses just north of King's Cross. Greek Andy was a perfectly formed miniature, not quite five feet tall, the star of a long-forgotten scene – the Daisy Chain in Brixton – back in the eighties. I always think of him on the Eurostar, scour the wilderness looking for the ruins of his strange kingdom. Andy had cauliflower ears and a giant cock. He kept a horse in a stable and had a garden that shook as the trains rumbled underneath. The horse looked out of the stable door during all-night parties in the summer and the trains flashed by in all directions while Andy danced like a crazed elf in a group of skinheads. The only thing missing was a cauldron. He died of Aids.

Looking for some trace of him through the window, the only thing I see is my own ancient reflection staring back. A furrowed brow, a sunken face and dribble drains falling from once-proud (but not that proud) lips caught in a permanent scowl by the changing wind. Andy is the irretrievable past, but he lives on in the memory of anyone who used to go to the Daisy Chain and takes this train. I write his name with my finger on the window.

Another lady vanishes.

This mystery wasteland gives me an odd feeling. I can't place myself in it. One needs to know the place one is leaving. It gives a context to travellers, a frame from which to focus on the outside world. The old train from Waterloo left one in no doubt as it curved along behind the river until Vauxhall, burrowing through Victorian Clapham on its Dickensian brick embankments, the slate roofs and chimney stacks climbing towards the jagged horizon of Lavender Hill, music halls, town halls, steeples and domes all soot-caked under the low London sky. One knew, looking out of the window, what everyone was doing – who they all were – as the train clattered by and one braced oneself for foreign affairs, swearing never to return.

Before that the night train from Victoria gave one an even more intense sense of self and the city as it groaned across the fairy-lit river. The giant mausoleum of Battersea Power Station loomed over the tracks, pink smoke drifting from its chimneys through the orange sky. In the distance Albert Bridge, threaded in fairy lights, was a giant farewell smile, its wiggling reflection on the river so pretty that everything else fell away. In those days I left London always longing to come back.

Now I care less. Age blunts. Everywhere has become the same place, and I got bored with the place. The new train tells me what I already know. My world has flashed past, and the new world spread out before me, covered this afternoon in a thin layer of snow, is a moonscape. On the other hand the adventure of making – or trying to make – my film is driving me on, giving me – thank God – a slightly manic sense of purpose and enthusiasm and suddenly I'm loving the chase again, following Oscar from Bloomsbury on his journey into exile. It's one of the great romantic departures and the starting point of my film. I order a drink to celebrate.

Oscar was released from Pentonville shortly after dawn on 19 May 1897 and was driven to a parsonage in Bloomsbury Square, the home of the Reverend Stewart Headlam – a loyal supporter – and the man who had posted bail for him before he went to prison. From there he would head to Victoria and the boat train. I pass that front door on my way home from the West End every day. Oscar's first steps of freedom were trodden on these particular slabs of Yorkstone. He must have got out of the carriage that morning and looked around – nothing had changed in two years, nor has it now – Bloomsbury Square through Bedford Place to Russell Square, the same black-and-white mansions, the same plane trees swaying in the same gardens. Sirens, jets and the rumble of Euston Road may have drowned out the gentle echo of the tradesmen's cob horses clopping down the street and the Reverend Headlam's house may now be a language school, but the door is still there and it's easy to imagine the house, the sound of the bell, the decoration (the reverend was a collector of arts and crafts) and Oscar lumbering up the stairs into a large dark drawing room where the friends – Ada Levenson, More Adey – were gathered, pasty-faced in the gloomy light, all on edge, wondering what was going to happen. It was seven o'clock in the morning. Ada hadn't seen Oscar since the day he left her house for the third trial – two years of hard labour ago. They needn't have been anxious. Oscar still knew how to make an entrance. He exploded into the room, younger, fitter, religious to boot – and immediately came up with a famous quip. 'Oh Sphinx,' he said to Ada. 'How typical of you to know precisely what hat to wear on such a delicate occasion. You didn't get up. You stayed up.'

That morning he was overflowing with Christian zeal and settled down immediately to write a letter to the Jesuit priests at Farm Street, begging to enrol. You have to smile. The others must have caught one another's eyes and gaped as he wrote. The letter was dispatched. A reply came quickly back – politely declining. Fresh waves of tears. Unable to tear himself away – shades of the terrible afternoon at the Cadogan Hotel – he missed train after train. He couldn't stop talking. The doorbell kept ringing. He had his hair done. A tailor came. He only got to Victoria at six o'clock in time for the last train that would get him to Newhaven in time for the night packet boat to Dieppe.

It must have been dusk – a May dusk – lying low in the carriage praying not to be recognised, pulling out of Victoria, over the river and away from London for ever. Goodbye to Kent and Sussex and finally the South Downs, chugging through tunnels and sleepy villages, past country houses glimpsed through woods, lanes banked with cow parsley and waving may – it must have been intolerably poignant through the open window, the cool scent of the spring dusk filling the carriage. Did he know, looking out, the setting sun reflected in his eyes, that he would never come back? Would the scars ever heal? Could he live with the regret? Or would he drown in his own bile? Luckily for the time being puritanical thoughts provided a kind of anaesthetic, a new world view, and the past fell away down the tracks into the dusk, a passion play in which Bosie was Judas, homosexuality the unoriginal sin and Oscar the Christ crucified. The future was reconciliation with his wife and children. Born again!

Thinking about all this I suddenly have a fabulous idea. (Not another!) If our budget is unachievable – and according to my producers it doubles each week, no matter how many corners and scenes I cut – why don't I set the film NOW, in the present day? I'm serious! We can take a handheld camera onto the Eurostar and then the TGV and forget the old expensive trains and the stations into which they steam. Why not the Normandy ferry, instead of tearing what's left of our hair out trying to find a packet ship? (There's only one by the way and it is on the River Clyde. We use it in the end.) A modern courtroom instead of the old Old Bailey. Euro Disney instead of Dieppe. Just imagine Oscar being chased from the enchanted castle by Minnie Mouse. Maybe that's going a bit far but-you-know-what-I-mean. It would be fabulous. All the characters in modern dress except for Oscar and Robbie and Reggie, still decked out in their nineteenth-century garb. The boys in trackies and crew cuts. It could be fantastic. Finally, Oscar would be a real oddity, trying to look inconspicuous as he scuttles through the modern-day Gare du Nord, his face buried in a fur coat and a floppy hat. That's the effect I have to achieve, anyway. The world stops dead as the monster passes by. Sitting on the Eurostar now I start rehearsing, calling the waiter 'dear boy' and waving my hands about as I order from the usual complicated and inedible menu, knocking back the wine, the port – a brandy, tons of cheese. Now I'm feeling very Oscar, tipsily looking out the window as we plough through the frosty Kent marshes, crossing the River Medway clustered with little sailing boats beached on the low tide. I turn my attention to the amazing-looking black man who is sitting opposite me. He is decked out in Gucci and Prada, with bangles, rings and chains, diamond-studded shades on an exquisite shaved head with delicious tiny ears begging to be nibbled. Beautiful white teeth with pointed molars peek from behind pillow lips. I glance at him surreptitiously. He glances back. Soon we are chatting.

He says he's a footballer but I don't believe that for a moment. He must be the boyfriend of some fabulous sultana or other, but I play along.

'What team do you play for?' (Don't ask don't tell, probably.)

He says something that sounds like 'Arsehole'.

'Arsehole? Great answer.' I am impressed.

'ArsenAL.'

I take another look. He does seem vaguely familiar.

Needless to say the producers are horrified by my idea. At first they think I'm joking and then they get shirty. They think I'm making fun of them. (Germans!) I explain how we could make the film for a quarter of the budget, and we could probably clean up at awards season. I am screaming down the phone – remember I'm quite drunk by now – but nobody is impressed except the footballer.

'I'd watch it,' he mouths with a wink.

Some producers are inventive rather than creative. They prefer to cook up a tried-and-tested recipe. Unfortunately the result is often a dog's dinner. This is the basic modus operandi of show business. Invention trumps creation every time. If you want to have an original thought, you had better be young. This is my unoriginal thought as I weave my way through the station to the taxi rank, my heads spinning.

Of course – I think too late – it was Thierry Henry. Damn. I should have got his phone number. Then I could make a thrilling segue into football.

CHAPTER SEVEN

Dirty Snow: Easter in Paris

Now it is Good Friday evening in Paris. An icy wind moans through the cracks in the windows. My usual bedroom looks over a little courtyard – a well, really. On the other side, one floor below, five women in white laboratory coats sit around a table. They are stitching beads onto a sumptuous wedding dress which overflows around them in a froth of silk, tulle and net, held in five places by the various pairs of hands – some small and dainty, others blunt and chubby – of the seamstresses, heads bowed and hardly moving as they work. They could be statues around a fountain as the dress gushes from their fingers. The rhythmic movements of their hands, the careful tying of knots and threading of needles, their calm contemplation as they sew is mesmerising, and I have spent many hours lingering in the dark – when I should have been out doing something else – watching transfixed at the construction of another extraordinary battleship for a battleaxe.

One of the ladies gets up to answer a telephone. She relays

some message to the others and they quickly put on pairs of white gloves and continue sewing. Soon a tiny man dressed like a Chinese peasant comes into the room and they all look up. He circles the table gesturing and clearly nervous. At one point he roughly grabs a needle from a cowering seamstress and begins to sew, talking all the time. The ladies huddle around, marvelling at the skill with which he stitches, and well they might. This tiny man with the shock of black hair – he would not look out of place sitting at the back door of a circus caravan – is called Azzedine Alaïa, the last of the great couturiers.

The master explains. The ladies nod and soon the sharp bell of the nearby convent chimes six o'clock, the end of the week and the beginning of Easter. Azzedine leaves and the ladies gather their things. Soon the lights go off, the door closes and the quiet gloom of the Easter weekend suddenly envelops me like a fog. I can just make out the wedding dress, grey and lifeless as lights go out in various other windows around the building.

Moments later a burst of chatter from the courtyard, an exodus of heels on cobbles, the shudder of the big door slamming shut and silence. In the distance the bell of Notre-Dame thuds across the river to mark the moment of Christ's abandonment by God, and now we must settle down for three days without him or – more importantly for Azzedine – his seamstresses.

As if on cue, the light snaps back on in the room across the courtyard. Azzedine returns. Alone now, he prowls around his creation, stroking it here, inspecting it closely, gasping with frustration, before choosing a spot and ripping the dress from hem to haunch. Then he sits down and starts to sew. I sit on my bed in the dark, amazed at the sheer energy of this man compared to mine.

No one knows exactly how old Azzedine is. Probably eighty. He still lives above the shop. Unlike other designers, who designate entire collections to assistants and stylists, Azzedine is intimately involved – right down to the sewing – with every garment that is made under his name. He works each night until four in the morning. He has made no compromise with the modern world of fashion, and yet his clothes are still among the most sought after and sell out the moment they hit Saks or Barneys or Harrods or Dazlu.

In a fashion landscape of copycats, frauds and sell-outs, Azzedine has charted his own course, declaring jihad on American *Vogue* along the way, which normally means suicide, but not for him. He is built for terror. He holds fashion shows when he feels like it. He has what the rest of us on the E! channel have given up on long ago – integrity. He is the real thing. His only concession to the asset-stripping culture we live in is the creation of one of his houses into a three-room hotel. I am sitting in one of those rooms tonight.

The walls are chalky white. The floors are concrete. Four windows look over the street and now snow flutters down in front of them. A long leather couch curves like a caterpillar across the floor. The table and chairs look as though they might have been taken from a children's school. In fact they are made by Prouvé, and are priceless. There is a kitchen and two bedrooms. It is the luxury cell of a millionaire monk, the chicest hotel in the world, and it is almost impossible to get a room. The prices are high except that as far as I can see, nobody ever pays. Azzedine is extremely generous.

I meet Azzedine through Sophie in the eighties. She is his design assistant and PR. She is also the best friend of the actress Béatrice Dalle. I am, at this point – 1986 – that lady's lover. (Yes, me! Look Ma, no hands!) But while Béatrice and I quickly drift apart, Sophie and I collide, soon up to our eyeballs in that childlike frenzy of living in one another's pockets and driving everybody mad.

Sophie is completely French, a strange, noisy girl, courageous and fiercely loyal. She would have been perfect in the Resistance. She is *pulpeuse* (polite word for buxom), raven-haired with a pretty, oval face marred only by a quivering witch's chin – all liberally painted over, cracks and all, with chalk-white powder and Liz Taylor eyebrows. Her head and her bosom smell of vanilla. That quivering and powdered décolleté owes something to a marvellous tricked-up bustier invented by Azzedine and is inevitably framed by giggly-girly cardigans with rows of tiny buttons over tight drainpipe jeans in a look that rarely changes throughout the years I live in Paris.

She is twenty-five when I meet her, still flushed with youthful hysteria, the younger sister in a swarm of brothers so she knows how to hold her own (i.e., elbow her way into a conversation, scream louder than anyone else, and drink). Her boyfriend is called Thierry and, like Azzedine, looks as if he has recently decamped from the circus. He has a crippled arm – acquired in a car crash as a child, in which both his parents are killed. He is a Provençal version of Montgomery Clift, a sexy, wounded bird, dark and gaunt, and he speaks, like Sophie, in that harsh nasal twang – *l'accent du Midi*. They come from the same town near Lourdes, Bagnères-de-Bigorre. He is a fashion illustrator of note and makes latex dolls in a studio given to him by Azzedine, while they live in a flat on the Rue Richer, opposite the Folies Bergère. In summer with the windows open you can hear the old music hall songs drifting across the rooftops, while Sophie and Thierry shout and scream inside the darkened room, and looking back now, it all seems impossibly far away, another life, although Thierry's studio – in which I lazed away many an afternoon – is in fact the same room I am looking into tonight.

In those days – they seem glorious in retrospect, but actually they are just the tail end of my youth – old Paris still lingers. The Place de Clichy where I live is a dusty backwater for an impoverished bourgeoisie. The house that Azzedine will one day turn into a hotel is a hive of collapsing apartments inhabited by breathless old ladies and a pair of furious queens. One by one they are dying off.

Sophie's set comprises three formidable young ladies and me. (She's not crazy on men – she's in love with them or she hates them unless maybe they're clever, useful queens – and certainly NOT silly vacant ones.) These ladies too are circus folk. Nina Hagen is a German punk singer who looks and dresses like a ventriloquist's dummy. Her black hair is a wig cut into a fringe over her wide – frazzled but shrewd – eyes, with two girly ponytails tied with gingham bows. She is bald underneath this wig and without it she is a completely different person, a rather sensible and shrunken nun with puffy eyes. But once her party hat is glued on, Nina is electric with energy. Her face is contorted with mirth or shock, and her voice swoops up and down the registers from growly bass to trilling soprano. She has a strange giant boyfriend who is as reserved as she is radioactive. He looks like Jesus but is called Franck. She speaks a wonderfully expressive gutter German, which is just as well because Sophie only speaks French. This is another thing these peculiar friends have in common. They don't understand a word each other is saying, but it doesn't seem to matter. We are in our primes – all drunk on just being there.

Rossy de Palma is the second in the group. She thinks that she speaks French, but actually at this point it is a brilliant language of her own invention. Her face is a Picasso with Edith Sitwell's nose superimposed over General de Gaulle's lips. Her eyes sparkle with humour. She is a giantess, a tree goddess from a children's book, or a fairground gypsy standing on a swirling whirligig. She is ambitious and quite tough, a marvellous Mediterranean fishwife in couture.

Béatrice is the last of the group and the jewel in Sophie's crown. Béa can do no wrong, even if she cruises the juice out of Thierry and Franck. The girls turn a blind eye. She can't help it. She must attract and be attracted, and men are zombies in her company. She is a classical French star in the tradition of Arletty and Bardot. She comes from 'le zone' – the gloomy French swamps – and is up for all sorts of things, including shoplifting and grave robbery. She is utterly thrilling even if she consumes your energy, but she can't help that either. However she is discreet, aware that she is a killer bee and is largely absent at these boozy meals, partly because she does nothing as ordinary as eat and drink, but mostly because she doesn't share the vaudevillian high spirits of the other girls in the gang. She prefers to sit at home and watch TV with her man – her latest being Fred. He thinks he controls her, and can get quite frustrated doing it. Béa loves this. She needs the frisson of violence, and the mirage of male power, although of course it is he that is being controlled – slowly eaten from inside. By the end of the relationship he will be a hollow shell and Béa – our butterfly of love, that little innocent elegant cabbage white – will one day casually eat his face, burp discreetly and flutter off through the moonbeams to pastures new.

(After Fred, she falls in love with a felon while shooting scenes in a prison, where her dressing room is a cell in which the crew have constructed a mirror surrounded by naked light bulbs. Everything about Béatrice is epic.)

We go out every night. The Palace on Sundays, the Bains Douches every other night. None of us knows how to cook. Dinner is at one of our regular haunts – The Thai trans restaurant in Rue Tiquetonne, or the Japanese next door to Azzedine's. Recently I found a stash of cassettes in a trunk. Aside from acting, I had just landed a job as a roving *Vanity*

Fair reporter and was obviously taking my work very seriously, although listening to a cassette upon which is written 'A typical night during fashion week', I wonder what kind of piece I was thinking of writing.

'Sopheee,' screams Rossy over a clatter of plates. 'Ye suis yamais yalouse.'

'Yamais yalouse???' screams Sophie, bursting into fits of nicotine-caked laughter.

Listening to these tapes – years later – is like rubbing a genie's lamp. The picture snaps up like a magic trick.

Visibility is low. Everyone has a cigarette going and the smoke curls into a cloud under which this European Union sits at conference. Each of us is screaming and nobody understands a word. Funnily enough, I am the only one who can more or less speak everyone's language – badly. (This could be the one autobiographical truth of this book.)

'Vaht ah dey telling?' asks Nina, very close to the mic.

'Rossy says she is never jealous.' My voice sounds thin and uptight, rank charm school.

'Yamais,' repeats Rossy firmly.

'Tu es com-plèt-ement-cin-glée!' shrieks Sophie (one of her catchphrases).

'Lo tomo, lo como, lo tiro.' Rossy performs a flamenco movement with her hand.

'QUOI?' Sophie.

'WAS HAT SIE GESAGT?' Nina.

'I pick the apple. I eat it and I throw it away,' I translate to no one in particular.

Nina is laughing with her mouth wide open. I can see her tonsils. She leans over to her boyfriend and there is an enormous crash, the noise of a glass breaking. More hysteria.

'Baby! Rossy is never jealous. You should be with her.' Jesus looks towards heaven.

'Moi non plus! Je ne suis pas jalouse,' screams Sophie, endlessly competitive.

The table explodes. She is the most jealous person we all know. Thierry raises his arms in despair. Franck/Jesus pats him on the back and the two clink beers, while Nina and Sophie high-five and laugh till they cry. Rossy wraps her branches around the table and no one has noticed Azzedine, who has come into the restaurant and is now crawling under the other tables towards ours. Suddenly his two hands shoot up from the tablecloth and clasp Nina's breasts and all the girls scream (including Thierry). He climbs out, pulling the cloth with him so that the whole table goes over. Bottles, glasses, nems and butterfly prawns all fall into Sophie's lap. She screams.

'Tais-toi, Sophie! Tu es hystérique,' commands Thierry.

'J'y crois pas,' says Sophie, and the recording ends.

I hang out most afternoons in Azzedine's atelier waiting for Sophie to finish work. Azzedine sews at a table in the corner in a pair of spectacles while Sophie and Eric, a good-looking Algerian boy – Azzedine's other assistant – sit at another table, also sewing, or snoozing, or talking lazily on the phone among the piles of swatches, the boxes of belt buckles and lace. I love it there. We mull over the day's news. Sophie is an easy tease and is soon screaming.

Azzedine looks up from his sewing. 'Tais-toi, Sophie,' he says, but always wants to be filled in. He knows everything that is going on in Paris without moving from his fortress. The news comes to him on the wings of fashion editors at lunch and society ladies, and supermodels over fittings. Azzedine's is the chicest lunchtime destination in fashion. That meal is eaten in a tiny makeshift kitchen across a rooftop along a plank. Tina Turner or Julian Schnabel in pyjamas can be seen teetering across it, supplicants on a pilgrimage to their mountain sufi. A huge black man cooks in the small room with peeling blue walls and there is a makeshift door through to Thierry's studio.

One day at lunch, Jerry – who knows everything, but don't let me start on him, it's too late to bring another character into this drama in a teapot, especially one as complex as Jerry – and I are having lunch at Azzedine's when Jerry says that they are doing an American remake of *Priscilla Queen of the Desert*.

'Now's your chance, girl,' he says mockingly. 'Get Azzedine to make you a dress. Go in drag to the Thai restaurant on karaoke night. I'll get a camera from work (Jerry works at a pro-duction company) and we'll film it and send it to the director.'

I know he's just saying this to wind me up. But then I think – well, actually, it's rather a good idea.

Much to Jerry's surprise I get straight to work, and tell Sophie to ask Azzedine if he will make me a frock.

'Mais tu es com-plè-te-ment cing-lé,' she says as usual.

Amazingly, Azzedine agrees, and soon the whole thing has become a major fashion moment. I have to rush over for fittings. There are even rumours of a shoot for *Vogue Hommes*. He sews me a brilliant body stocking, with vast jelly breasts and wide amazon hips. He produces a pair of size 11 Manolo Blahnik stilettos and Jerry and I get a fabulous black wig from an Arab shop in Le Goutte d'Or.

On the day of the shoot we get ready at Jerry's flat. He has made a little film set at the end of his sitting room with a couple of lights and a glitterball. I sit on a chair. Sophie arranges the dress and the hair. Some make-up queen friend of Jerry gives me a last liberal stroke of jungle-red lipstick. A freak from Jerry's work operates the camera. Jerry proclaims 'Action,' and we all collapse laughing. Then I act some scenes from the movie with Jerry reading the other part – in a frankly patronising kind of Candy Darling American accent.

My other best friend is Lychee, and she arrives with her white fur coat that I want to wear for the show. She's not happy about lending it to me.

'I work very hard for this coat, bitch.'

'Are you coming?' I ask her.

'Bien sur que non,' she snorts. 'I can't stand burlesque.' She drops the sable coat on the floor and stalks out. (This is the coat, incidentally, in which she will be murdered in a couple of years.)

Then we all bundle into three taxis and drive to the restaurant. The place is packed. Jerry has asked everyone we know.

'How could you do this?' I hiss.

'It'll be fine. You need a warm hand on your opening.'

I am rushed backstage (the toilet) where I am separated from my gang, which is hell because we've only been having a laugh up until now, but suddenly I'm on my own and it's all getting rather serious as I find myself squeezed into a tiny room with four murderous Thai transsexuals getting ready, and they are not happy.

'What happened, girls? We were all such friends when I was on the other side of the camera – so to speak.'

Like Lychee, they are put out by my amateur drag, and so they go on limbering up, stretching their legs sitting at the sink, studiously ignoring me. Maybe they're just jealous, I think to myself as I check my two sets of eyelashes in the mirror (a Donatella invention). I can hardly keep my eyes open under their weight. My hair is a wild gypsy mane backcombed and sprayed – shoulder-length. I am wearing a pair of antique jade earrings courtesy of Lychee's mum Perle, who thinks I am going the same way as Lychee and is distraught.

'Prends ton temps,' she pleads as she hands over the jewels. Perle speaks impeccable French with an impenetrable accent, and so her elegant turn of phrase has the added charm of surprise. Her solemn eyes, her physical poise, her attention and affection make her an extraordinary foil to her wayward child, the infamous Lychee.

Jerry has never met Lychee's mum before and is fascinated.

'What was she saying?' he asks later in the taxi.

'"Prends ton temps", obviously,' I snap.

'Why is she saying take your time?'

'Why do you think? Because she thinks I'm going for the chop.'

Jerry giggles mischievously. I always knew it would be a mistake to take him to see Lychee's mum, and now he's never going to let it go.

'Well, are you?' he asks. 'It's quite a thought. After all, things aren't exactly moving very fast as they are.' He prods me in the ribs and I can't help laughing.

'She's right,' he says after a little while, in a silly voice. 'Prends ton temps, Rupert.'

My dress, by the way, is a beautiful black knitted wool stretch sheath with tassels and is heavenly. Azzedine has made stockings for my boobs, and they look like the real thing peeking and wobbling about under the crocheted front of my frock. My waist is about seventeen inches wide and I can hardly breathe, but it looks sensational, accentuated by Azzedine's fake hips. Of course the girls are jealous. My shoes are Manolos. My make-up is impeccable if obvious. I have lifts woven into my hair so my skin is tight and my eyes are Asiatic. The look is fierce, I say to myself, trying to get up a bit of energy, but I can only think of how much I wish I had rehearsed my number more. Jerry appears laughing and waving a packet of coke and we squeeze into the minuscule cubicle and do a line.

'Prends ton temps,' he sniggers as I try to bend down over him crouched on the loo to the cistern where the lines are chopped out.

'Do you mind if my make-up guy comes in?' I ask coyly as we exit the loo. This is the last straw and the girls squawk like rooks in a winter tree.

'Good luck, girl,' says Jerry, beating a hasty retreat.

The show begins.

One by one we are called down to the scaffold. Sitting up here drinking a beer through a straw, listening to all those wailing Asian ballads and the raucous standing ovation after each number, I wonder if it might be better to escape through the tiny window over the roof and just take a taxi home. I have rarely felt so nervous, and am just about to see if I can actually fit my legs in the dress through the hole when my time comes.

The owner – a plus-size amazon called Nibbles – puts her head through the door. 'Allez, Rupert. C'est à toi.'

I put on my fur and edge my way down the tiny staircase, hyperventilating. The crowd catch sight of me and go crazy. Sophie is crying. Claude Montana is there, for some reason. Jerry starts the music and as I climb up onto the tiny stage my heel rips through Lychee's fur coat. It can be heard over the music and everyone gasps. They all know Lychee. Now my shoe is caught in the coat, so I unload the fur earlier than planned and the reveal of the dress is rather undermined, but I soldier on. The stage is three feet long and about a foot wide. My head reaches to the ceiling in the heels, but nevertheless I vamp madly from one side of it to the other. Bent double, I can hardly breathe, and my vision is sparkling and flaring. I know that any minute now I am going to puke and fall over. The corset is too tight. I've drunk too much beer. Looking down, the floor is miles away. The room is spinning round and round and suddenly I get the song mixed up. I launch into a verse, but Tina doesn't join in. The audience is delighted. Their screams are coming and going as I veer towards blackout. I feel absolutely desperate, back and forth, back and forth but the show must go on and it does, and I receive a standing ovation even though I have not been very convincing, but even the other girls seem to have buried the hatchet and are clapping by the side of the stage.

I don't dare bow because I know I will never make it back up, so I just stand there trying to get my breath back, bathing in the applause (not), then stagger offstage and make a run for it – on all fours up the tiny staircase to the dressing room. As soon as I get there, I puke.

The next thing I know I am half-naked on the floor with my wig beside me. Nobody is about, just Nibbles humming as she takes off her make-up. A pigeon coos outside the tiny window and the echo of a motorbike buzzes into the distance.

'What happened?' I ask.

'You pass out, honey. All your friends have gone.'

'Where's my fur coat?'

'Relax. It's right here. This Lychee coat. Right?'

'Yes.'

'I seen her in it.' Nibbles strokes the coat lovingly, with awe. 'She gonna be werry werry cross,' she sings. 'Look.' She shows me the rip in the lining. I nearly faint again.

'Oh, Christ!'

'You want me to tell her? I seeing her tonight in the *bois*.'

'No. Leave it to me. Thanks, Nibs.'

I put my wig back on. I don't have any civvies to wear so I just put the corset in a plastic bag and Nibbles helps me zip up. I climb back into my Manolos and hobble downstairs. The restaurant is empty except for Claude Montana sitting with a boy. They are eating silently.

'How was I?' I ask, slumping down. Claude's eyes twinkle.

'You were great, baby. For a second I really believed you were a man.'

'Thanks, Claude,' I say, opening my bag. No keys. 'Where's everyone gone?'

'The Palace.'

'What cunts.'

It is dusk on the Rue Tiquetonne. I am walking home with my plastic bag. It's starting to rain. I flag down a taxi. It slows, sees me and then speeds off.

'Fucking queers. People like you should be electrocuted,' shouts the driver.

'Nique ta mère,' I shout back. The taxi screeches to a halt. The driver explodes from the car and bounds towards me. I take off my shoes and run.

Jerry edits the tape and we send it to LA. It is really good, and quite mad and I feel sure that I'm going to get one of the parts. A few weeks later, however, I get a message back from the director via my agent. 'Thank you very much, but it's just too obvious.'

The movie tanked. Not even Patrick Swayze, Wesley Snipes and John Leguizamo could save it. Or maybe they ruined it, actually. But that's show business for you. Even the trans roles are taken by straights.

Sophie leaves Paris one day and never comes back. She and Thierry have not been getting along, but everyone is surprised to hear that she is not in fact returning to work. She soon resurfaces in New York, spotted in the foyer of the Chelsea Hotel with Steve, a beautiful model. I leave Paris at the same time. Lychee has been killed, and I want a change.

'Find me an apartment in New York,' I ask Sophie over the phone one night.

'No problem,' she says. She never does. Instead she becomes a very successful fashion designer in her own right. She wins the CFDA, also the Woolmark Prize. She gets rave reviews in the *New York Times*. She even makes clothes for Mrs Obama. It's a fairy tale until, one fateful day, she sends out a press release saying that she would never dress Melania Trump, at which point everything falls apart. She loses all her contracts, and has so many death threats she has to go into hiding in Canada. She now lives in Montreal, where she has launched a successful online fashion business.

CHAPTER EIGHT

A Good Friday Disagreement

Remembering all this, I walk up Rue Charlot towards the Place de la République on my way to visit Lychee's mother. Lychee has been gone for twenty years, but it could be yesterday. Nothing much changes here, and Easter and Christmas have always been dead times. Everyone disappears. There are no Regent Street decorations, no binge-drinking office parties, no Easter Bunnies in bras and panties. Just the wind moaning round the corners of the old houses, leaning in, closed up and hard-faced under the orange street lights. Rows of cars are tightly packed on either side of the long thin street, empty tin cans that only add to the feeling of desolation and abandonment.

I may have left the play behind but I am still haunted by Oscar. Or maybe I am haunting him.

Oscar arrived in Paris in February of 1898 and wandered the streets for two years ('the circle of the boulevards – the worst in the inferno'), moving from hotel to hotel, spotted everywhere, often alone, on the bridges, on the bateaux-mouches, at the side altars of churches, staring up blankly at the saints in their niches. Tonight I am shuffling with him through the high studded door and the thick musty curtain of the Armenian Church in Rue Charlot, dark and high, smelling of damp and incense and collapse. Hundreds of candles flutter and swerve as the door creaks open.

I light one for Oscar.

The church is about a quarter full – families in little clusters stand in the empty pews. They are well turned out and sombre, celebrating the moment of ultimate sacrifice – they are the victims of genocide themselves, and this memory seems to be written across every adult face in the candlelight. A little girl stares at me from the folds of her mother's skirts. A black widow prays under her veil, black beads wrapped around overworked fingers. A man sings a solo from his seat. It's a dirge, a howl almost, and the congregation picks up the chorus in a strange close harmony, part barbershop, part Byzantine. At the altar the priest presents the host to the congregation, who cross themselves and bow.

('It isn't true,' whispers Oscar in my head.)

The priest wears a jewel-encrusted turban and a marvellous cape. He is flanked by acolytes swinging smoking thuribles. The black widow, supported by two men, staggers to the altar for communion. She kneels, receives the host and is carried back through the billowing smoke to her seat. Christ and Oscar have died and the news feels fresh and important in this run-down church on the empty street.

They have a different way of celebrating Easter a little further down the road at one of my favourite bars – a dungeon called Le Glove. I can hear the thump of music as I go past. Things are starting early. Inside another curtain – this one is leather – four respectable middle-aged men sit on high stools drinking beer. They are naked. It is crucifixion night, and downstairs in the fourteenth-century catacomb of this most eccentric of dives, also smelling of damp, candle wax and carbolic, and a few other things as well, the night is already getting under way.

I cautiously make my way down the old stone staircase into a low curving tunnel held up by ancient beams over an undulating floor. Arches lead to cellars on the left and right. Like the Armenian Church, this underworld is lit by candles in bottles disfigured by years of hardened wax. The place is haunted by the living. They wander around – mostly naked – like zombies, bending over to stare into some black chink in the wall only for a hand to shoot out, wagging its finger. Or beckoning. All is quiet, just the odd moan, a slap and the faraway thump of the music upstairs.

In a large vaulted cellar with a well in the middle, a pear-shaped man is strung to a cross blindfolded. A younger (middle-aged) hangman in a leather mask – just a pair of blood-shot eyes peeking through over a waxed moustache – nude and chunky, with a cigar clenched between his teeth, is flogging the Christ figure half-heartedly, although the older man is making a good deal of noise. I can't help laughing. The aggressor suggests a break and with great decorum undoes the manacles attaching his victim to the beams, undoing his blindfold at the same time. The older man gingerly steps from the cross as if he is getting off a train. They withdraw to the nearby well where two large beers stand next to a loo roll and a bottle of poppers.

The older man, bald and gaunt with a snub nose and squinting, octopus eyes, double-takes when he sees me. 'Ooh, hullo, dear. Fancy seeing you here.'

If you want to avoid the English, stay at home (Oscar talking again).

His friend turns and offers me the whip. I politely decline.

'Remember me?' asks Christ.

'No. I'm afraid I don't.' He leans in close, skeletal, all eyes in the guttering candlelight, as if he has just seen a vision.

'It's me! Carlotta, dear. From the Inland Revenue.'

'Oh my God. I haven't seen you in years. Not since . . . '

'Don't, dear. We must look forward. This calls for a celebration. Shall we adjourn to the bar?'

Upstairs we order beers and clamber onto skanky stools. There is an old photograph of Dalida on the wall, and the barman is nude with a barbed wire necklace.

'No. I went wrong in the head, dear,' Carlotta explains, and her friend nods his head gravely in agreement. 'To-tal col-lapse, dear.' He bangs out every syllable. 'This is Jean-Charles. Do you speak French? Of course you do.'

JC and I shake hands while Carlotta explains that we knew each other 'dans les années soixante-neuf, dear!' shrieking like a hyena.

Actually we met in the eighties. She came on the scene during the summer of love. She was ugly then and she's ugly now. She fiddled the books for party favours at the Inland Revenue, was made redundant and then tried to strangle a bit of trade – who did not press charges, but after that, according to legend, she killed her flatmate and has never been heard of since, although not entirely forgotten. She has her place in the gay legends, and still comes up in lazy conversations in those odd gaggles of reminiscing queens. 'Darren saw Carlotta.'

'No!'

'Yes. She lives in Düsseldorf. Working in a dry-cleaner's.'

'Laundering money, probably.'

Now I will be able to add another verse to her story. Carlotta has died. Carlotta has risen. Carlotta will come again. 'And how, dear,' she says with a huff, and I can tell she is itching to get downstairs again.

'But there's so much I want to ask you.'

'I bet, dear,' she says uncertainly. 'I don't want to lose the cross. Are you here for the long haul?'

'What do you mean?'

'Doors close at midnight, or you're here till the resurrection.'

'Not likely.'

'Lah-di-bloody-dah as usual. Donne-moi la pipe, JC.'

'Ah ouai. Si tu veux,' replies that man, unzipping a fanny pack and extracting an evil-looking glass pipe. He squints inside it then puts it in Carlotta's mouth.

'Yes, dear. I used to do drugs in the eighties. Now I do them in any temperature.' She giggles guiltily.

JC runs a lighter under the pipe and Carlotta sucks the skin out of her face. She takes the pipe from her mouth. One, two, three, and she exhales a cloud of evil smoke. A Saddam Hussein lookalike appears through the leather curtain and she suddenly tenses.

'Here we go, dear. I'll say goodbye now. The gag, Jean-Charles! This one's the real thing. Ciao, darling. Say hi to everyone.'

Carlotta scuttles back downstairs.

'Dépêche-toi,' I hear her hissing as I beat a hasty retreat. I am not ready for my crucifixion. Not yet. I make for the leather curtain with a new energy, and gulp for air as I hit the street.

Lychee's flat has not changed since the night she disappeared twenty-five years ago. It is the perfect courtesan's abode, a first-floor mezzanine in an eighteenth-century house near the Palais-Royal – the traditional quartier for ladies and gentlemen of the night. The apartment's windows look over the courtyard. There is a traffic phrase in French that one sees on signposts which reads *au fond dans la cour et à gauche* – to the end of the courtyard and turn left. Lychee, explaining to friends where she lives, modifies the phrase and it becomes one of her famous lines. Substituting the word *cul* (arsehole) for *cour* (courtyard), a pilgrim seeking direction is told to get to the end of her hole and turn left.

Lychee has been comfortably brought up in Vietnam. There are doctors in the family 'and rice fields ... ' her mother Perle will sadly remark later on in her occasional evaluation of all the loss her family has suffered since fleeing Saigon in '75. Despite this valuable start in life, as soon as the family hits Paris everything changes. Lychee – née Tuan – starts saving for a new pair of breasts, while at the same time perfecting her knowledge of the French language of the gutter, which after a couple of years on the scene, if not the game, she speaks brilliantly. It is one of the secrets of her success.

Lychee's flat (at the end of the courtyard and to the left) actually comprises four low rooms that give on to each other in a row. Pretty quick out of the stable she starts making good money and the flat is completely redecorated before she moves in. The kitchen is the latest chrome galley. The walls of the whole place are lacquered in chalk white over pale wooden floors. There is a black velvet divan, a glass-topped dining table with a matching suite of chairs. There has never to my knowledge been a dinner party.

Against the wall there is an upright piano with music by Bach on its stand. Lychee says she plays it every day. Actually she can only play chopsticks. But she weaves a marvellous character for herself since joining the world's oldest profession. Peach-lit in her china-white flat, she is a princess from Macao recently marooned, gracious, educated, artistic and a real slut in bed. Top or bottom, as it happens. This interesting versatility is due, or thanks to, a rule laid down by her mother when she originally embarks on her new life as a lady. Breasts only! Leave the rest alone.

'She was going to change back, *tu vois*,' sighs her mother one day, years later. Fat chance. There is no going back. Lychee is drunk on it all. She is in her prime, and it's too strong for her, but it must be said that when she moves into this flat, which has everything a working girl of the highest calibre could wish for, including a two-way mirror between the sitting room and the bedroom through which she can observe her 'michton', she enters into the most exciting period of her life. She is a legend in the *bois*, and a star of the Parisian night, the last real dem-imondaine. She models for Thierry Mugler and even makes a record. She is a stunning beauty and one of the funniest people I ever met.

Her work divides her into two areas. In the Bois de Boulogne she is a venerated she-man warrior in a white fur coat, ruthlessly stalking her corner of the street – which ends up being a whole roundabout in those giddy days right after the prime hits its peak. She is Titania, queen of the fairies, holding Bottom on all fours in a deadlock in her secret thicket – a cave under the dank-smelling rhododendron bushes, littered with all the billets-doux of the trade – soiled paper tissues and spermy condoms. There she fucks the living daylights from a man, quite possibly stealing his wallet at the same time. It is a marvellous game, and she is fascinated by the weird freaks she entertains.

But at the end of her hole and to the right is where her other character lives. In her apartment she is a royal courtesan from the belle époque. While she is still breathtakingly beautiful, this role is her greatest achievement. She entertains rock stars, police chiefs and the odd guy she just fancies on the peach satin sheets. She adores sex. 'Je suis amateuse,' she laughs. 'Mais aussi très professionelle.' She has tons of cash. These are the days of huge crispy five-hundred-franc notes. They are scrunched up in her handbag and the pockets of the sable coat, and stuck down the back of the black divan.

But soon it all gets to be too much. She is on a roller coaster and can't get off. She gets too high too much, and suffers various smash-ups and punch-ups. She finds a boyfriend pimp, half her size, macabre, creepy. He drives a vintage Morris – one of those half-timbered Tudor vehicles – and he slashes her across the back with a cut-throat, and is probably the one who eventually kills her.

At a certain point she only has to look at a motorbike and she falls off. After six years on the game she is a chipped china doll. The masculine side of her face emerges as she is forced to come off some of the hormones that keep her pretty. Actually she looks great like this – a new breed. She has the personality and allure to carry it off. She even lets stubble grow on her face. Her jaw gets broader, and she soon looks like one of the Vietcong she so earnestly fled all those years ago. The lacquered walls of the flat become jaundiced, stained with smoke. Too much has been spilt over the black velvet divan, including tears and other human fluids. The cupboards are stuffed with shoes and dresses and dildos. The shutters have not been opened in years. There are burns on the pink satin sheets, and the piano has a huge layer of dust over its lid. Like its mistress, it has been out of tune for a while. Lychee – a realist – sounds the retreat and abandons the place to stay in the relative peace of her mother's. The flat waits empty until after she dies. Then her mother moves in.

A noise of shuffling feet and keys, and the door opens slowly. It takes twenty-two years. They have gone by – in a flash, actually – since the morning Lychee is found, wrapped in her sable coat, dumped in a ditch on the edge of the park at Versailles. Perle is ninety-three now. I have not seen her for a year. Since then she has had a fall. Still, I am shocked when the door opens and she appears dressed in pyjamas with bare feet. Her hair is dishevelled and her eyes are dim. She is painfully thin. She leans on a little table with wheels, and reaches for the furniture as she staggers in slow motion across the room to the sanctuary of the black divan.

When I first meet Perle in 1983, she is an elegant lady in embroidered silk trouser suits with mandarin collars. She has beautiful, manicured hands and her wrists are wrapped in gold and jade bangles with dragon's head clasps. You can tell she has suffered, but she carries herself with the dignity of an émigrée rather than the desperation of a refugee. She has survived two husbands, and her son has become a woman. Lychee's father is killed by the communists in 1972, and Perle marries a second husband, a French colonel, so that she can escape Saigon in 1975. He is charming in Vietnam but vile in France, and throws her children out of the house. (Actually this banishment is just the opportunity little Tuan is waiting for.)

Nevertheless, Perle is a dutiful wife – she has no choice – and she nurses him through agonising cancer until finally he dies. The colonel never knows that Tuan has become a girl until he asks to see her on his deathbed. Revenge is, as they say, a dish better eaten cold. That day, Lychee goes to the hairdresser's early and wears a beautiful Chanel suit. She looks every inch a lady as she sits down on the edge of the bed.

'Daddy. It's me, Tuan. I've come back.'

The Colonel dies the next day.

Perle adores Tuan. Despite signs to the contrary he is the man of the house, and in Vietnam there is absolute deference to the leader of a family – come what may – so Perle never complains about Lychee's exploits but stays close, always there to pick up the pieces. Many club freaks will remember lounging on Lychee's bed after a long night out, watching TV, naked and lazily smoking. The front door opens and a vision appears – a beautiful Vietnamese lady. She doesn't say a word but makes everyone tea, does some housework and leaves. Lychee (high) ignores her as the door clicks shut again and she is gone.

Now Perle is clutching her makeshift Zimmer frame. 'It's easier to get about,' she says as I help her sit down. She can still walk, but only just. The flat is decrepit. The place has fallen in on itself. There is a big fridge against the wall in the hall, but otherwise nothing has moved. We sit down on the black velvet divan, side by side as usual. She takes my hand in both of hers. They are ancient now, the nails unpolished. She is still infinitely correct, and always begins our conversations with the same well-mannered preamble. How grateful her family is to mine. How constant a friend I have been since Tuan's death. How much they owe to me.

'Don't be silly, Perle,' I always say and she laughs. It's a bitter laugh. She presents me with the usual boxes of chocolates 'pour Maman', and bottles of ginseng powder for myself. We look at pictures of us all taken years ago and study Lychee's fashion sketches.

'Look,' says Perle, indignant. 'So much talent.' And she shakes her head.

Once a month a Vietnamese taxi driver takes her to Lychee's grave, which is in the Père Lachaise Cemetery two rows away from Oscar. They drive right up to the tomb. Perle used to get out of the car and change the flowers. Now she just sits in the back and looks out.

On top of the piano the final remnants of her life in Vietnam are collected. They look down onto the black velvet divan where Perle more or less lives now, her medication lined up on the coffee table in front of her. A picture of her own mother watches, printed for some reason on a large round plate. She is a strict matriarch with a beehive and traditional dress. Lychee's father, Perle's first husband, good-looking in a shirt and tie, laughs in a framed photograph with his brothers, all killed by the communists. Perle will never go back to Vietnam, and only to Père Lachaise feet first. She has reserved a place above Lychee.

I leave her sitting on that black divan, the battlefield of so many of her child's conquests and defeats. She is sitting up straight, correct till the end. This time she doesn't walk me to the door. In the old days – last year – when I get to the courtyard her voice calls out from the window above. ''Upert!' She waves, a romantic schoolgirl wooing. Now the shutter is closed.

CHAPTER NINE

Night Train to Rome

After the Easter weekend in Paris I continue on my journey towards Naples, arriving at the Gare de Lyon for the nine o'clock train to Rome. I have dinner in the station restaurant, Le Train Bleu, named after the old night train to Nice. The restaurant has hardly changed since the station was built, and nor have the toilets. Up until a few years ago they still featured those two terrifying footprints on which the evacuator must squat, trousers down, ominous hole to ominous hole, the perfect antidote to haemorrhoids, apparently. They have been replaced. But they are still magical loos, a time warp. All the travellers' excitement (if not excrement) of a hundred and fifty years clings to the walls.

The restaurant comprises four large, high rooms with ornately painted ceilings and huge fan windows that look out over the interior of the station, the tracks disappearing through its open mouth into the night. Once, the adventurer set forth in a romantic haze of steam and shrieking whistles across the continent to all the destinations featured in the elaborately framed murals that decorate the restaurant walls – Prague,

Vienna, Bucharest, Istanbul, Algeria. Now impoverished immi-
grants from those places lurk in the shadows, stuck like ghosts
in the terminus, listening distractedly to the disembodied
lady's voice echo through the station, calm and authorita-
tive, preceded by that demented electric harp arpeggio, the
'bing-bong' of France, announcing trains to less thrilling destinations, Lille, for example.

Nonetheless, sitting in the restaurant looking out at it all one
suddenly feels the vastness of the continent, the heart-stopping
adventure and romance of solitary travel. All alone one is fea-
tureless, weightless. It's a marvellous feeling, more profound
than the neon-lit departure lounge at the airport, identical to
the arrivals lounge at the other end, with the same old clouds
in between. People seem to live more in the station. We all
look pasty, worn out, tonight. Chandeliers missing the odd
bulb illuminate the rooms with a relentless glare. We sit around
tables with starched cloths, on ropy old banquettes, scraping our
cases over the unpolished parquet. It is an image of collapse,
gilt-framed. Moody waiters wrapped in white aprons present
laminated menus and later, overcooked food served from silver
tureens to an odd clientele, an uneasy melange of foreign pop
stars and fashion folk dressed to the nines, travelling families in
tracksuits surrounded by luggage, and ME.

The train to Rome is called the Thello. It is a sorry sight. Its
requisitioned carriages caked in mud drip and belch. Shabby
couchette girls stand on the platform like bedraggled hookers
or graduates from reform school. They look uncertain, as though
they had only started the job tonight. Actually they are simply
bracing themselves for the barrage of complaint that is their
nightly penance, because this train is careering towards the
Third World, which now includes Italy. The girls hold giant
pass keys like corkscrews and grimly lock us into our carriages
before we leave.

With David Hare and Robert Fox – the two cornerstones of my 'dream'.

And the dream was made flesh(y) and rather well endowed.

The enthralling Freddie Fox.

Kieran O'Knightley (moi) on a vaporetto
with a mystery man (Babinho).

Making friends with Merlin Holland at Oscar's tomb.

Aunt Peta observes my christening.

Already quite leggy with my mother and Aunt K.

Two legends – Johnno and Joan Collins.

Accessing Ozzy Osbourne
in *The Musketeers*.

Me as the Ornithologist. With Chris O'Dowd.

The death of Soho.

The Cimitero delle Fontanelle in Naples.

'I am in mortal combat with this wallpaper,' said Oscar. 'One of us has to go.'
Brian Morris had sleepless nights worrying about it. This was the eighth version.

Colin and me in the old days.

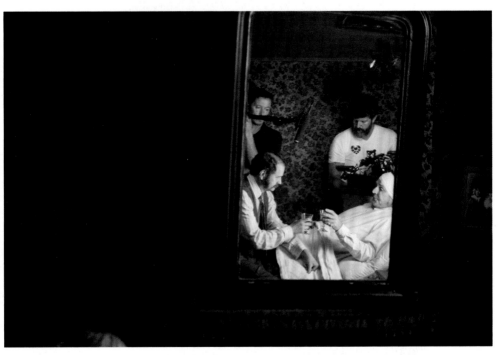

And thirty-five years later.

With Emily Watson and Tom Wilkinson in *Separate Lies*.

Emily having a nap as the Queen Mother
at Chatsworth.

Tom administers extreme unction.

Philipp Kreuzer and Katja Kuhlmann watch the action while Colin Morgan checks his messages.

Willy Moser, our unpaid unit photographer, and in a cameo as a toilet attendant (also unpaid).

Trains.

Sébastien Delloye and David Colby – our producers – snuggling up.

The witch of Capri. She never made it to the final cut.

With Caterina D'Andrea in Naples.

And Raffaelle Gargiulo.

The two incredible Neapolitan ladies who played the
housekeepers at the Villa Giudice.

A grumpy group in Wallonia.

If there were an Oscar for best extra, this lady would
have won it.

A Bohemian in tissues.

Four brilliant actors.

Béatrice Dalle.

André Penvern.

Matteo Salamone and Benjamin Voisin.

Sébastien's green screen packet boat.

Edwin on the low loader.

Gianni, our costume designer, in a good mood.

A director at work.

Assertive.

Defensive.

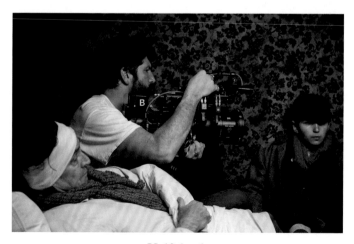

Half dead.

There are nasty odours seeping from the loo. A group of shapely black ladies from New Orleans are horrified and squeeze past with handkerchiefs held to their noses. That's when we discover we have been locked in.

'Laurellee, I cain't open this door.'

'Say whaaat, Mary Jay?' The ladies take turns rattling at the handle. Any minute now the whole door is going to come off its hinges. 'We been locked right in, baby,' says the matriarch of the group in a thick Hispanic accent. Screeches of indignation. Suddenly the door opens, revealing a scruffy couchette girl holding her corkscrew. The look of horror on her face at the sudden apparition – five furies waving fifty long fingernails – is the high point of the whole trip.

'Whaddya-all lockin' us in for, miss? We ain't slaves,' says Mary Jay.

Uh-oh. The couchette girl sensibly pretends not to speak English. She jabbers away in French and Italian, and within seconds the whole thing has escalated into a screaming match.

I step in, cool, calm, an Englishman abroad.

'Is rules,' bleats the couchette girl on the verge of tears. 'Now is open.'

She attempts to storm off down the corridor but it's not that easy. She must squeeze past her assailants who look down at her as she goes, nostrils flared, hands up, nails out – jungle red, shocking pink, stars and stripes – ready to maul her, should she come up with any more trilingual cheek.

Laurellee has an amazing bosom. It stands out from her body in two glorious smooth hills plunging into a mouth-watering gorge. It is held aloft by a cunning bra under a skintight sheath that just covers her nipples. I am negotiating a passage between this magnificent balcony and the door to my couchette, trying to mind my own business at the same time.

'You look familiar. Ever been in Noo-Awe-Lee-Ans?' she

asks, pointing a long diamond-studded fingernail, searching my face for clues.

Four words are all I need to explain. '*My Best Friend's Wedding.*' They all swoon satisfactorily and I swish off, hoping to avoid having to break into song. A few minutes later a chorus of 'I Say A Little Prayer' rings out along the corridor. I thump on the wall. 'Keep the racket down.' Screams of laughter. Later I pass the open door of their couchette and the chorus bursts out again, 'For ever, for ever, you'll stay in my heart'. Now it's my turn to laugh. They are all squelched into their bunks. Laurellee will need a shoehorn to get her out. We get chatting. 'Will you look at this room, Rooper. It's worse than prison.'

'At least the toilet isn't in the middle of the room. Have you done any time, darling?'

'Excuse me! I'm a hygienist.'

Laurellee and Mary Jay are sisters. The matriarch – their mother – was born in Havana and Susie is their cousin. They are high-spirited and funny. 'Sassy. That's da word you lookin' for, Rooper.'

'And broad.' Gasps. 'I mean, you're sassy broads, non? And I'm down-low. Isn't that the word you "Africin Americins" use to describe us perverts?'

The girls honk with glee. 'Oh, you're a hoot, Rooper. And we're Cuban, thank you very much.'

Their indignation intensifies as we hit the restaurant car, an old carriage from the Eastern bloc of puke-coloured Formica with a bar at one end over which another surly girl presides. The menu is pizza. The girls squeeze onto a table. I sit at another with the matriarch, Rosario. We all have a glass of wine swaying in unison as the train lurches and shrieks through the suburbs and out into the dark countryside. We talk about the usual things – what Julia Roberts is really like, how's Madonna – and then move on to more interesting topics: what it's like to be black and gay. 'Do you like black guys, Rooper? Be honest, now!'

The girls are all straight, and are horrified by lesbians, but they don't have much time for their men. 'They got their brains in their dicks,' says Mary Jay.

'Yeah, and your Gerrard got a small brain,' retorts Laurellee. Like most American travellers, they have 'done' Europe in nine days. They fly back to Atlanta from Rome at the weekend.

A couple of ragged youths appear and sit at a table a little way off.

'Are they speaking in Russian?' asks Mary Jay, horrified.

'More likely Bulgarian or Romanian. It's difficult to tell.'

They have piercings and backpacks, long hair and baseball hats. Soon a breathless girl joins them.

The American group have ordered pizzas, and now five hepatoid jellyfish are dumped on their table. Laurellee takes a bite and nearly pukes. But the girls are philosophical, determined to have fun and are obviously planning on making a night of it, so I make my excuses and return to my cabin. Luckily I bought a picnic from Fauchon, which I guiltily (always guilty) spread out on a napkin and settle down for a queeny moment of travel bliss. I am reading *Middlemarch*, contemplating the marriage of poor Dorothea Brooke and having some caviar on toast, when the door opens. It is one of the Eastern bloc boys from the restaurant car. He apologises and shuts it again.

Just after midnight we arrive in Chambéry. It's snowing. The train breathes a huge sigh. Snowflakes dance around the orange lamps on the platform.

The Eastern bloc kids have got off. They are in high spirits. The two boys kick snow at each other while the breathless girl walks behind them pulling a large case. They pass my window and see me watching. One of them presses his face against the pane and sticks out his tongue as the whistle blows and the train creaks into action.

I sleep fitfully. The noise of the train, suddenly deafening as we speed through tunnels, lures me in and out of the dream-scape. Empty stations late at night merge with my father on an elephant, lights flashing across a wall, a gunshot followed by squealing brakes. Somewhere we stop in the middle of nowhere. Sudden silence. Just the groan of tired metal and a muffled voice. 'Where we at?' After an eternity or five minutes we move, laboriously gathering speed and I slide into more restless dreams, turning this way and that, wound up in the sheet.

At dawn we are already in Italy, clattering through sleepy towns and misty fields. The tracks are fringed with wires draped over pylons, black against the pale sky with tiny clouds stacked up as far as the eye can see. As the day intensifies the fields turn gold and the clouds blush and shrink. The buildings are pink and yellow and the train's shadow jumps up at them when they come too near. Winter is a northern memory now, and clumps of mimosa wave by the tracks. The sunshine throws a rather stark light on the squalor of my couchette and I search my body for lice.

Soon we are nearing Rome and the interior squalor is mirrored by the appalling suburb of the Eternal City. Just forty years ago the *campagna* of Rome was beautiful, unspoilt farmland of rolling hills and woods, villages and ruins. Now it is a jungle of ugly apartment buildings in endless shades of beige. As if to shield themselves from the terrible reality that engulfs them all, the windows are shuttered.

At Rome, I step onto the platform to discover that a drama has been playing out during the night. I was obviously sleeping better than I imagined. The Atlanta contingent and some of the other passengers have been robbed. Passports, money and jewellery have disappeared. They are understandably hysterical, particularly since the policemen who have arrived on the scene in their tight, sexy trousers and shiny boots speak no English. These boys in powder blue are Italy personified; failed footballers in man drag, all good-looking, all brainless.

Possessed suddenly by the spirit of Hercule Poirot, I solve the crime all at once and in three languages as it suddenly occurs to me what has happened. The boy who opened my door was the criminal, with his accomplices the breathless girl and the other pierced boy. They must have had a pass key. I should have realised, but was too wrapped up in Dorothea Brooke and *Middlemarch*. ('Chi è questa Dorothea Brooke?') While the passengers were in the restaurant car, he and his colleagues robbed the whole train and then got off at Chambéry with the booty, making a rude face at me in the window as they went past. This face I describe to the police in detail. They must have had an accomplice among the couchette girls, which isn't hard to imagine since they are all such swamp bitches. I suggest lining them up and strip-searching them then and there on the platform, but the police appear to think I am joking. I give them my cell phone number and email address, kiss the ladies from Atlanta and run for my connecting train to Naples.

CHAPTER TEN

The Kingdom of Rubbish

From the ridiculous to the sublime – the Thello to the Frecciarossa, no speed to high speed – the train that connects Venice to Naples in six hours is among the fastest and most modern on the tracks today. I buy a first-class ticket and find myself in a huge compartment with only six seats and a separate space for board meetings. The seats recline and drinks and food are served by a Neapolitan fairy who speaks to me in Italian but switches to the impenetrable language of Naples while addressing my travelling companions, two businessmen in suits and braces, jewel-encrusted watches and thick, knotted ties. They look like brothers with matching pink potato faces, except that one has hair while the other has a beaten pink cranium. This one is rippling with genetically enhanced muscularity. His brother has grown over himself, oozing from his shirt and straining the resolve of his fly buttons with the rigid hump of his paunch.

The three of them talking patois are a sort of operatic invocation, the opening trio – servant and two masters – of the Neapolitan opera that is about to unfold. Part French,

part Spanish, Christian and Mohammedan, the whole history
of Naples is woven into the local dialect. Its inflections and
pronunciations, its sybillant s's, its reworking of words and its
languid attack are the residue in language of thousands of years
of invasion and cross-fertilisation. It has a louche sexuality and
a slightly aggressive humour that regular Italian (with its lack
of nuance and its game show vocabulary) will never manage to
achieve. The brothers are decidedly straight and the waiter is
not, but they're easy and intimate with each other.

On the other hand, the two men visibly flinch when I take
pictures, and there is a crescendo in the music as they weigh
up whether to break my legs and throw me out the window or
simply shove me down the quick-action pump loo. I immediately apologise and they are wreathed briefly in smiles before
returning to the business of murder.

The train shrieks and groans towards Naples across a vast
plain ringed by mountains – once the most fertile farmland in
the world, now a sprawling concrete suburb. Vesuvius towers
above, seen first from the north, in splendid isolation. It never
gets any nearer. (Even when you are climbing it.) The train
curves round towards the bay and the volcano remains aloof –
another planet observing the dreary urban scrub upon which
a cluster of unfinished skyscrapers bake in the sun. Someone
has tried – vainly – to create Dallas on the Divina Costiera.
These towers of broken mirrors and squat, windowless apartment blocks look more like the gates to hell than the American
dream. Actually they represent the usual Naples nightmare,
half-finished (until the laundered cash has had time to dry) and
then neglected. Their mirrored windows present the cracked
reflection of a city locked in combat between its ancient culture
and modern corruption. Instead of being a smart new business
centre, these blocks are instead a giant hive full of the world's
most fascinating hoodlums.

A traveller must be supple and know how to adjust his dreams to reality and keep moving forward. Approaching Naples after a long night, red-eyed and tetchy, there is no feeling of romance, no sign of Sophia Loren or Sacha Distel and 'Where Do You Go To My Lovely?' Just a lot of irritating graffiti, really the most tragic graffiti in the world, endless identical squiggles on the sidings along the tracks, and then the station, another – this time slightly more successful – attempt at creating the illusive modern city.

It is actually great fun in the huge hall. Neapolitans love seeing each other off and tend to do everything in large family groups. Three generations may be there to meet the train. There are brilliant gypsies, tramps and thieves, using all the latest techniques. With balletic precision the pickpockets work in pairs, one, late for a train, crashing into you while the other neatly undoes your watch – also late for another train. Limbless beggars look daggers from their skateboards, spitting curses when ignored, and wide-eyed Romanian girls pretend to find gold rings on the floor. ('I left no ring with her. What means this lady?') Amazing-looking women – all shapes and sizes – are funnelled into skintight jeans and boob tubes. They are waiting for the men to park the car. The ladies of Naples are not afraid of weight, and wobble about like huge quivering jellies on six-inch clogs. Builders' bums and breasts are displayed with pride as they scream down diamond-studded cell phones clutched in baubled, water-retaining claws. The ancient and the sick hobble through the hall with pasty faces and liverish eyes. Healthcare has more or less ground to a halt in Naples. Everyone backs off when a priest or bishop swishes over the horizon on his pilgrimage to first class.

It is a warm day, about two o'clock now, and I wait for a taxi behind two powdered Japanese ladies in a long line. A scrawny youth runs across the piazza towards us, barging through the crowds, nearly knocking down an elderly woman. The Japanese ladies gasp. A second youth flies after him shouting, catching up fast. The violence of the chase ignites the atmosphere and everything blurs around them. As they reach the road the second kid lunges like a goalie, grabbing his prey by the hair. They fly through the air and crash to the ground, bouncing to a halt almost in front of the taxi rank. The assailant – a clump of hair in his clenched fist – bangs the other's head three, four, five times hard on the concrete before staggering to his feet, winded almost but walking away, merging into the crowd.

In the taxi queue we tourists stand, frozen with horror and fascination while everybody else swings back into action. The boy starts to pick himself up. He is in a daze, either high or semi-conscious or both and is about to start screaming when two other boys appear, running from the other side of the piazza. They don't slow down when they get to him and their first kicks knock him along the pavement towards the street. He tries to crawl off but there's no escape. They kick him hard in the stomach, in the balls and in the head, screaming all the time, their arms waving in the air, footballers scoring a goal. It has, as a piece of ballet, its roots in the beautiful game.

The Japanese ladies carefully lower themselves into the back seat of their taxi, looking straight ahead, barking questions back and forth while through the window behind them the attack reaches a climax. The two men walk away while the poor boy lies crumpled and motionless. Nerveless, I climb into my cab and he slowly begins to move, the miracle of life dragging him from the floor. His face is pulverised. Teeth hang from his broken lips. Somehow he manages to stand. He screams at us in the taxi queue, pointing a broken finger. 'Fucking Neapolitans. Death to all Neapolitans.'

'Bulgarian,' spits the driver with disdain, and off we go. He has conveniently forgotten, amid the excitement, to put on the meter.

There is actually a fixed rate for a taxi taking one in to the centre of Naples from the station. But you will never pay it, and certainly not on your first trip into town. For your initiation to the infernal city you will be relieved of at least forty-five euros for a trip which normally costs thirteen. The second time you might make a fuss. You might scream and shriek, 'Prezzo fisso!' or 'Sono solo quindici!' but there is very little point. They will pretend not to understand and then babble on regardless and with growing intensity about holidays of obligation, Sundays, evenings, this route or that route and then accuse you – either with tears in their eyes or murder – of accusing them of being a cheat. Then, destination achieved, they will pretend not to have any change and so you are fleeced anyway.

The rear-view mirrors of Neapolitan taxis are inevitably slung with swinging rosaries and holy medals. Pictures of Padre Pio and the Pope are stuck to the dashboard. Drivers endlessly make the sign of the cross and kiss their fingers as they pass a spot by the sea or a bend in the road where some brother or sister or cousin or football hero lost his life, but apart from this endless religious posturing the Christian value system holds no sway in the kingdom of Naples.

In such a way I discover this insane city, on a crisp spring afternoon under a bright blue sky. The town is camouflaged in freezing shadows and warm pools of light. The sea is slate – fading to black as the night swoops in, cold and dripping with condensation. I am staying at the Excelsior in Santa Lucia, on the corner of that street of songs. Built at the end of the nineteenth century, it stands on its own like a huge slice of wedding cake. Inside a marble hall, a sweeping staircase, a deserted lounge with mirrored doors. On the roof, a beautiful garden overlooking the port of Naples and Vesuvius, one of the

most intriguing views in the world. One's mind literally drains
of thought looking at it.

It is sometimes difficult to adjust one's fantasy about a place
to reality, and at first I experience what the weathermen call
a spell of low pressure. Modern Naples doesn't scream Oscar
Wilde, and initially I am disorientated. What am I doing here?
Why did I come? For about three days I stay in my room, collapsed, watching through the window as the volcano changes
colour with the hour, sometimes disappearing from view alto-
gether – just a line over the pale bay, at others crystal clear,
almost magnified in the cool spring light. Sometimes a pretty
cloud sits on top, a pink tutu at sunset. At its foot cargo ships
crawl across the bay, and under the full moon the green lights
of coastguard boats skim blinking through the dark water. I love
being a beached whale on a large hotel bed covered with trays
of food and books and newspapers and the TV on. The rooms
are large and high with tomb-ish bathrooms, original hotel furniture and terraces looking over the small Borgo Marinaro and
the Castel dell'Ovo, a Roman fortress like a vast honeycomb
rising out of the water. (The last Caesar was incarcerated and
died there.)

The old Bersagliera restaurant is built into the side of this
small harbour. Nothing much has changed since the nineteenth
century. Gangs of little boys in swimming trunks jump screaming from rowing boats into the dirty water while their sisters
sunbathe in bikinis (aged six) on the quay. It is a quiet part of
town, no cars on the street, only the sound of flapping masts, a
few seagulls and the chug of the odd boat heading out into the
bay to interrupt one's morning meditation on the terrace of one's
room, swathed and impotent in a thick hotel dressing gown with
horrible hung-over breath. (White wine and vongole blowback.)
The view takes in every romantic notion I have ever had, and
sitting glassy-eyed in front of it I vaguely plot my next move – a

book, a play, a film – charades, really – or maybe just a waddle into the old town.

The hotel is always empty. Occasionally there are riveting functions where tiny men in dark suits and dyed hair – a thousand little Berlusconis – ignore their exhausted women in evening dress, all reflected and multiplied in the mirrored doors around the dining room, drained by the blinding light of the chandeliers. Any minute now a vast wedding cake might be wheeled in and men with machine guns will jump out and we will all end up dead. But I doubt it. No such luck.

I am following a lead concerning the location of Oscar Wilde's home in Posillipo, the hillside village that looks over Naples. Oscar and Alfred Douglas eloped to Villa Giudice in the summer of 1897. According to Bosie – reflecting and possibly reinventing years later – it was a kind of rat-infested castle, with a portico of columns and a marble staircase leading down to the sea, only accessible by boat or a rough track coming up the hill from Naples.

Since then it has been lost in the deluge of construction. Numbers and names have changed. The 'rough track' is in fact Via Posillipo, built by the Bourbons in the second part of the nineteenth century, and it hasn't changed. An amazing feat of engineering, the road is carved through the cliffs, spectacularly bridging deep wooded ravines on vast arches hewn from the local rock, a soft stone that looks like crumbling honeycomb or toothless gums.

Shortly after Oscar's day large apartment buildings began to appear along the street, finally engulfing the villa in that confused twenty-first century heap which is Posillipo today. The house was located by Richard Ellmann (author of the famous Wilde biography), but since he died no one seems to have been able to track it down. By the strangest coincidence, the man who runs the Munich film studio that is producing my film about

Wilde is married to a Neapolitan girl who knows the lady who lives there today. A strange coincidence in a long line of strange coincidences, but Naples is like that, operating exclusively through friends whose wives have cousins who know the sons of the lady who lives at Oscar's house.

My German producer is called Philipp. He is a strange, awkward character, meticulous in a pale pink shirt and blue corduroy trousers. Up until now I have had him down as an enemy in the executive structure of my film. So we are both on edge as he leads me through a grille on Via Posillipo into a kind of garage built into the hillside at the back of which an old lift – the type that usually shudders up and down the stairwells of genteel apartment buildings in Paris, with little double doors and windows – takes us down at least three storeys to an underground cavern lit by rusty lanterns, dripping with humidity like a horror film, wonderfully cold after the infernal heat at ground level, where we are greeted by a pink apparition moving through the gloom.

Kiki is a beautiful lady in her sixties – quite small, impeccably dressed, polite but reserved, with Faye Dunaway's dazzling smile. Introductions are made and she heads off down the kind of tunnel one runs along in nightmares, never reaching the end. It is endless, freezing, with weeping walls of sheer rock and a delicious smell of damp. She chats to Philipp as she trundles along and their voices echo through the mine.

'And how is dear Christina?' (Philipp's wife.)

'She is on a new murder case so she couldn't come.'

'Peccato! What a shame.'

Finally we arrive at an old marble staircase. Could this be the same one Bosie mentioned?

'Yes. Of course,' Kiki says simply as if it was only last week, and she leads me down the marble steps into a long dark cave. Canoes and rowing boats are stowed against the walls.

The waves seethe through its mouth past the rusty teeth of an old padlocked gate. The light outside is blinding and I am nearly swooning.

'These caves were made by the Greeks.' (Also last week.) Her voice echoes through the vault. She sails back up the stairs like Alice in Wonderland and is off down another endless corridor through a low door. 'Attention the head,' she commands – too late – as the poor producer cracks his forehead really hard against the roof. He reels slightly but staggers on, clutching his face, as if nothing has happened.

(This is the great German spirit – knocking oneself senseless, then keeping going. I feel suddenly reassured.)

Finally we arrive at Kiki's door. He is gushing blood but chats on.

'I don't think we can, Kiki. What a shame. Christina is not back . . . ' etc.

They go to the bathroom to fetch a sticking plaster, leaving me alone at the very same spot where Oscar Wilde – the Christ figure in my life – compounded the tragedy of his disgrace by eloping with the very man who ruined him, Lord Alfred Douglas. 'I dare say what I have done is fatal,' he wrote to Robbie Ross, his friend, from this room. 'I love him as I always did. With a sense of tragedy and ruin.'

The second act of *The Judas Kiss* takes place in this house and I am terribly moved. We have arrived on the main floor of the palazzo. There are four long, high rooms connected by double doors. You can see one end from the other. Windows look out over the sea, framing Vesuvius and the Amalfi Coast across the bay and the waves crash gently against the walls of the house.

Kiki was born here and was a concert pianist as a child – a prodigy – and the place is a time warp. Huge gilt mirrors hang on the walls. They are leaning in and the world is slipping in their reflection. Now she sits at a grand piano and plays the slow movement of Ravel's Piano Concerto in G while I watch and the lights begin to flicker across the water in Sorrento.

'The Bay of Naples jewelled like the scrawny neck of some ageing dowager,' David as Oscar in *The Judas Kiss* echoes in my head and I laugh out loud at the sheer brilliance of the line and the play. Kiki sways at the piano, possessed. Over the next few months we become great friends and she gives me wonderful private concerts at the full moon, playing all the concertos of her childhood repertoire, brilliantly whistling the orchestral parts. A putto holding a bunch of naked light bulbs is perched on the piano and throws a pool of light over her. A dramatic shadow – fingers and all – leaps up and down the wall of the long dark drawing room. It's all rather dramatic. Kiki is the Shirley Temple of the classical world, and as I laugh to myself at this notion Oscar Wilde is suddenly there. I feel him completely. I am not on drugs.

Friendship blossoms around Kiki and my visit to the villa. Something is set in motion and things with Philipp get better. Now he introduces me to a pair of location scouts called Alberto and Arturo (Arturo is also a friend of Philipp's wife. They used to be human rights lawyers together in Kabul. Kabul? Everyone is very casual about everything around here.)

Each day they collect me and we move around the city contemplating the hidden treasures, tumbledown villas falling into the sea, beautiful lakes with classical ruins at their edges, the craters of all the various volcanoes – one is a tropical forest, another a weird salt lake replete with bubbling mud and evil-smelling fumes. The gates to the inferno are located here by Dante. They show me a mile-long Roman tunnel with an amphitheatre at one end. Antiquities are treated with little respect in Naples. Temples are squeezed between garages and office blocks, knee-high in condoms and loo roll. But there is something stunning in this casual relationship. The ruins are still breathing. I remember a time when you could cruise in the Colosseum. (Those were the days/nights!) There are grand Bourbon palaces with studded fortress doors under towering crested entrances. Double sets of staircases can be glimpsed in their romantically sagging courtyards, like the laces of old stays. In the church of Sansevero is the most beautiful statue of Christ in the world, lying slightly arched under his shroud, on black marble cushions.

Kiki takes me to the Cimitero delle Fontanelle, a gigantic network of caves made by the Greeks that became an impromptu dumping ground for corpses during the great plague. Three hundred of the five hundred thousand inhabitants of the city died. In a typically Neapolitan twist, they were nursed and buried by the city's prostitutes, and their skulls are still there piled against the walls, their thigh bones converted into pretty altars with miraculous powers.

I fall in love with Naples. (I visit the Cimitero again with Anita Pallenberg during a torrential storm at the end of the summer. We go there to get a bit of respite from the heat, taking cigarettes and books, but the storm begins. It is terribly dramatic. The thunder rolls around the cave louder and louder. It feels as if the end of the world is happening. The rain is a thick dirty sheet of water over the entrance. We are stuck on the inside of a waterfall. The deluge gushes into the cave frothing into the open mouths of the skulls. We are quite alone and no one seems to care. We wonder casually if we are going to be drowned as we wade to a dry spot for a fag. It would have been the perfect end.)

I think looking for locations must be the best part of making a film. Everything is in the future. The trip starts and all my worries evaporate. The budget, the cast, the unconvinced producer – all the insurmountable odds fall away in the face of the location, this dilapidated, forgotten city, exquisitely poetic, a world apart. Naples is Aladdin's cave. Round every crumbling corner I have an epiphany, and quite soon I have turned into one of those dippy geek movie bores – staggering about pretending to be a camera, bent double, squinting ludicrously through a hole made with finger and thumb, following imaginary characters down the street, humming the soundtrack. Or else I am the star (five minutes, Mr Everett), sitting alone in a restaurant trying out lines from the script, bickering with a non-existent Bosie or staring out to sea in a climactic close-up, eyes brimming with bitter tears. (Also humming the soundtrack.)

So much has been written about Oscar's time in Naples that his footprints are strangely fresh. It is exciting being a hunter, tracking my prey ever deeper into the city and under my skin. I move my camp from Naples and the Excelsior to a small hotel in Posillipo – Hotel Marechiaro, a converted villa high above the sea. Its owner died a few years ago and his daughters keep the place as a hotel. It is a large white house on the main street surrounded by high walls at the top of the hill just below Capo Posillipo. In the courtyard there's a fountain and a gardenia tree covered in white flowers, their petals strewn romantically across the grass. The garden is a labyrinth of pathways and little lawns, box hedges and bougainvillea with a tunnel of vines leading to the swimming pool and a summer house overlooking a kitchen garden. Six rooms with dizzying tiled floors and old family furniture look out over the sea towards Capri glimmering in the bay.

On a whim – predictions of a freezing July in England and a feeling that I am discovering something huge – I decide to stay for the summer. I move into the pool house. A special rate, up front, in cash.

Big mistake, because on the afternoon I hand over the money to the Signora, literally while she is counting the bills in her long, slightly grasping fingers and giggling at how she has never seen so much cash in her life – the movie collapses. AGAIN.

My phone rings. Robert Fox from London. We have lost a substantial percentage of our funding. Actually we never had it. We are back to square one. There goes our September start.

Signora is still counting and clucking as the phone call finishes, and I am tempted to grab the cash and make a run for it. Instead she presents me with the keys and escorts me to the pool house. We chat along as we go – as if nothing much has happened. She is telling me about her father's death and I punctuate the story with the appropriate gasps and gushes, but I'm not listening. Alone finally in the room – it's already hot – I fall to the floor with its trippy tiles like a nineteenth-century actress in a melodrama and lie there for several minutes.

From this strange perspective – a ceramic landscape seething with fruit and veg disappearing into the distance – I have time to reflect. Show business is a fickle mistress. One moment I am dollying around the corner contemplating a fabulous scene by a Roman ruin starring me. The next I am back in the doldrums and have lost the will to breathe.

The BFI distribute money from the national lottery to first-time directors, among other things. Since there are only a handful of sources for money in the UK, it is fairly vital to try and score some from the BFI. The man in charge is called Ben. Apparently he is gay, which as far as I'm concerned is ominous news. Over the last two years he has never responded to my countless entreaties to meet. Everyone says this is normal and that we must be patient and Ben is very busy and you're not the only fairy on the Christmas tree, Rupert, but I know – I can feel it – he is George Hall and the BFI is the Central School reincarnated, the same face in a new hat – and he's going to say NO.

Sure enough, in a short crisp email Ben proclaims that while he himself is a huge fan of Oscar Wilde, he cannot help me with my project. The very next week, to compound this frosty slight he writes an article in *Sight & Sound* (blind and blaring) saying how he is looking for more gay-themed films and that there are no new gay directors coming forward. While I personally find the idea of any film having 'a sexuality' pretty tragic, or of a director being known primarily for being homosexual reductive, at the same time there's no denying that there couldn't really be a gayer film than mine. I am completely gutted.

'Haven't I paid my dues?' I sob to the nearest tile, a pineapple sitting on a banana.

Soon the heat begins to come in strange burning waves and the night air is stifling; no oxygen, just the suffocating scent of gardenias. I have breakfast early – after another sleepless night – at a pagoda swamped in ivy at the bottom of the garden. I sit alone at a round table, beautifully laid with a linen cloth embroidered with forget-me-nots, and want to kill myself. The hotel is empty but for Giorgio and Lana, the charming but invisible Filipinos who run the place. Sometimes I hear their voices from the kitchen as I pass the main house, or I see Giorgio standing with a hose far off in the garden, waving. This is the only contact I have with the outside world. By the second day of July all the shops have closed and the local people have fled for the beach. The village is deserted.

I begin to lose my grip. I am a people person, and there's no one here. Soon it is so hot that any movement leaves me breathless. In the darkened pool house I turn the air conditioning to full blast. Its drone is pleasantly numbing. I lie on the bed, inert. The light streams into the room through a half-opened door. Vines and flowers wave lazily outside, their shadows trembling against the wall. I sleep during the endless afternoons and sit up late at night, often until breakfast. I score weed from a good-looking boy who lives nearby. He says he smokes all day and I can call him up at any time. I'd given up but it could have been the wrong moment, and I think I might start again.

As soon as I do I find that in fact almost everyone here

smokes pot. You have to, and anyway it was one of the great exports from Bourbon Naples in the eighteenth century, after all. This is the kind of thing I'm learning from the boy next door, who has made smoking his raison d'être. He constructs and smokes in an endless movement; fingers like spider's legs around the paper, talking as he rolls with legs crossed, looking at me through almond eyes, licking the rolling paper with a long muscular tongue. I would make a lunge if I had the energy. But I don't. This day-for-night existence has left me undead, a zombie. There is no breeze, no movement at all, just the odd moped buzzing up the hill and the occasional gust of hot wind – a ghost passing, perhaps – that billows the lace curtains strangely for a second.

One evening I trip in the bathroom, nude, narrowly missing crashing my head against the bidet. As I get up I catch sight of myself in the mirror above the sink. I AM Oscar Wilde. Added to which, at this rate I may not have to use the fat suit for the movie.

Each night at nine I set out for dinner in one of my favourite restaurants.

I've spent half my life and money on restaurants. From the age of eighteen to fifty-two I have more or less eaten three meals out every day. Restaurants are to me what women are to certain men. I love nothing more than to eat alone in one and watch the world go by. In such a way I have perhaps avoided all the drawbacks of a solitary life. Alone, sloshed at a corner table one feels strangely connected. Get help, I hear you scream.

Ordering countless meals over the years I have developed various enduring friendships. Virtual, perhaps, but infinitely pleasurable. The tablecloth is the no man's land and is a bubble of good manners. One of us, with a pen and notepad looks down indulgently at the other, perusing a well-known menu. In the pauses – the rabbit or the chops? – life is shared.

My favourite Neapolitan restaurant is Cicciotto on the sea wall at Marechiaro, about two miles outside the city on the bay. Candlelit tables on the cobbles flicker under the stars cradled in the ruins of a Roman temple bricked into a high wall. It's a scene from another opera. Across the bay Pompei twinkles from under the skirts of the volcano while in the sea below boys dive for squid, their torches flashing under the water. At about half past ten they appear, climbing the stairs from the dock in wetsuits, spears over their shoulders to sell the fish in the restaurants perched on the sea wall. It's quite romantic. The last ferry crosses the bay on its way to Capri and the lights on that island begin to glimmer. For some reason, it's a sad view.

Not that one has much time to look. Eating alone can have its drawbacks, and I am more or less taken over by the Cicciotto family soon after my first visit. In due course they will find me a flat, score me a free kitchen, two widescreen TVs and they never let me pay for dinner. While a generous reduction is much appreciated, not paying on a regular basis has its drawbacks. It means that in some shape or form you will have to do the washing-up.

The Italians are childlike fans and expect total reciprocation. They all want to do photos. The Cicciotto brothers feed me to them and I graciously concede. After all, I haven't had this much attention in years. These two brothers (one extremely good-looking, the other less so) run the place along with their father, who wears a sailor's cap, has one tooth and is partial to a sing-song which I adore, while their mother and sister man the coffee shop in the square above. Quite often three generations of the same family can be observed screaming at each other through the kitchen window, or in the case of Ciro's in Mergellina, sitting behind the same table in the restaurant next to the cash register operated by a miserable cousin. There, the old matriarch in a tight chignon surveys her kingdom like a bird of prey, charming and ruthless in satin, flanked by her three sons, the ruins of classical temples themselves, in their fifties, still with killer looks. In complete contrast to the Cicciottos, they never give even a free breadstick.

Dora's in Chiaia is owned by an ancient pirate with an eye-patch and the hugest hands I have ever shaken. The waiters are also from a pirate movie, Matey and Smee, and the tiny restaurant even has portholes. Dora herself is dead, reduced to a sign now, blue joined-up writing blinking sadly as you come round the corner from the front. Lunching with Piero Tosi one day – the world's greatest costume designer, eighty-four years old – I am telling him about my exploits in Naples. 'Sempre viva Dora?' he asks in a faraway voice, the name itself, spoken for the first time in years, conjuring up a host of flickering images in the ensuing silence – long lunches with Visconti, dinners after rehearsals at the opera, and I can almost see the lady herself in Piero's eyes, large and lumbering in a white apron, like her husband. At Dora's dinner for one – with 'una piccola presa d'amicizia' – is extortionate but excellent.

Dora's is at the top of one of those tall, thin lanes, long and straight, swamped in shadows under a glaring strip of sky, in the old city. The houses are scribbled over with dangerous-looking balconies swathed in cables and washing lines, all held together by a thread and a prayer. For this purpose (prayer), little stupas to the Madonna line the walls of the street. Families living in one tiled room (*barras*) can be glimpsed on the way up in the evenings, breathtaking portraits sitting at tables, bathed in the blue light of some nonsensical television game show, flickering and echoing through the open doors while their daughters stand outside in hot pants smoking and talking on cell phones, draped provocatively against the arches of crumbling courtyards next to walls plastered with dog-eared posters announcing the death of some hag. In the long, hot afternoons operatic washing blows romantically over the street, the occasional pair of pants landing on the ground in front of one, an autumn leaf falling, accompanied by a shrill Neapolitan aria bouncing across the walls above.

Over the hill from Villa Marechiaro lies the ugly side of Naples, although it has its own charm like everywhere else. Parco Virgiliano is at the crag of Capo Posillipo where Oscar Wilde – abandoned by Bosie – contemplated suicide. I on the other hand contemplate moving here. The sea murmurs far below, seagulls are small dots wheeling and squealing, pine trees cling to the steep cliffs and the rest of the world is a remote dream, half remembered. From here you can see the island of Procida (where the plot was hatched to kill Julius Caesar) and further off Ischia, a long shadow rising from the sea. A two-mile beach falls away to the right, behind it a vast abandoned factory complex caked with toxic waste. A gigantic tottering hangar the colour of dried blood dominates this hopeless testament to Italian corruption. (Donald Trump should take it over and turn it into a beach resort.)

Beyond all this lie the cities of the plain – Fuorigrotta, Scampia, Capua, Pozzuoli – a beige and yellow patchwork quilt stitched with asphalt that has grown up over the orchards and vineyards and hamlets of not-so-long ago, smothering some of the richest farmland on the planet, but the Neapolitans don't care much about nature. The craters of minor volcanoes rise from the urban mist in ridges like frozen waves, crested with houses.

Above it all a network of suspended highways explodes from tunnels through the hills onto the kinds of flyovers last seen in *Wacky Races*, stretching high over the plains on spindly stilts converging into a dizzying spaghetti junction underneath the cliffs of Vomero. On a hazy day this place reminds me of Rio de Janeiro. Another city on a vast bay, a kind of magnet drawing cargo and cruise ships into its clutches, crowned by exotic mountains carved through with tunnels.

The Carioca and the Napolitano have much in common. They live in kingdoms of their own, with secret dialects, dangerous sexuality and their own unwritten constitution. They are dramatic and direct when they feel like it, foreign even to their own countrymen, uncontrollable by the state. They charge you too much or too little – rarely the correct amount. Business and pleasure are conducted through a network of friends whose cousin's sister has a shop which sells exactly the thing you want. Naples is the (much) less dangerous of the two cities, unless you include the taxi rank next to the Hotel Excelsior. There one is constantly on the verge of a heart attack in the sweltering noon sun as one is taken for a ride again and again, but not necessarily to the destination you had in mind.

As a result, I have decided to walk everywhere, or take the bus. My favourite is the 140 from Capo Posillipo down into Naples. It's a rickety old orange thing covered in graffiti, and thunders down the steep winding street, seemingly out of control, shooting out over hairpin bends, screeching round at the last second. The view of Vesuvius and Naples swings in and out of sight through the windows like the back projection in an old spy movie, real but unreal, and headlong collisions are narrowly avoided and largely ignored. It is more exciting than a ride at Universal City or Disney World. Delicious matriarchs with varicose veins and short, rust-coloured hair cluck together unconcerned over their shopping, while boys off to the beaches slouch against the handrails in shorts and flip-flops over girls in hot pants and boob tubes – screaming and flirting – as the bus hurtles on, flying out of one pothole and crashing into the next. A rude boy with gigantic curling lips holds forth – some amazing story about what happened yesterday with all the demented Italian gestures flung in – to his enthralled audience, a comic opera bringing the house down again and again as the bus shudders to a halt and another ninety-year-old man grasps at the rail and hauls himself aboard. It is a theatre all of its own.

After a month at the hotel I decide to take a flat in a palazzo nearby, underneath one of the Cicciotto brothers, and suddenly the blue gouache Naples of my dreams snaps to black and white. Just trying to connect the electricity requires the patience of a saint. The company is called ENEL – pronounced ANAL.

'Yes, Rupert,' says a rather unattractive new queen friend, squeezing my arm. 'No worry. Together we will go to your place and make ANAL. Is easy!'

Well, exsqueeze me! The misunderstanding is cleared up, thanks largely to my English hairdresser Jamie's Neapolitan boyfriend Danillo, Danillo's mother and father, their brother and sister-in-law and Danillo's cousin Mauro. They arrive en masse in a van, screaming orders and now I have gas, electricity, a kitchen and a Samsung TV. Thanks to Kiki and her friend Bubi I have a seventeenth-century bed – good start – a divan, four chairs and a bookcase. Downstairs in one of the converted stables off the main entrance to the palazzo an old couple run a haberdasher's. (They have been working there for forty-four years, married for forty.) They are reupholstering the divan and the four chairs.

My kitchen unit is a gift from Fabio, whose father owns a huge furniture empire. I don't quite understand at the time but I think I may have agreed to take part in their Christmas commercial – only local TV, just a *comparsa*, an extra I am assured. Who cares? A free kitchen is a free kitchen, and pretty soon I find myself sitting on a black leather three-piece suite in their vast store screeching into the lens: 'Cinquanta percento riduzione.' Then I am in a fabulous kitchen, washing up. 'Ciao! Sono Rupert Everett e questa cucina – (scream) CINQUANTA PERCENTO.' It's very chic. Now I am on the local telly every night.

Finally the place is beginning to look as I had imagined it on that reckless day I signed the contract, the flat of a maiden aunt from a good family appropriated by a disgraced queen in exile. To that end, four original photographs by the Baron von Gloeden are arriving next week.

The apartment is in an eighteenth-century palazzo belonging to a marchesa aged ninety-three. She lives on the piano nobile with two Sri Lankan maids who wear pale green nylon uniforms that crackle with electricity when you approach. They are called Nicky and Lucie and they spy on me coming down the main staircase through a tiny window inside the marchesa's flat. The marchesa's nephew is a lawyer with silver hair called Aldo – extremely good-looking, with one of those curious snatch bags which straight European men of a certain era (seventies) have dangling from their sausage hands. He arrives for each meeting with a different lady colleague from the office. Together we have signed the contract over a glass of Orangina in the marchesa's drawing room. The poor marchesa, still marvellous-looking with shining eyes in deep sockets and a dazzling smile, is under the weather this summer due to the tremendous heat and the aftershock of a stroke she had last year. She was born here, and observes the street from the same window at dusk each night, barely visible, the last echo of another world. (The *viale* running down to the sea carries her name. Her family were given the palazzo by the Bourbons.)

Tonight she can hardly lift the pen, but she gallantly wills her spidery signature to be formed on each page of her nephew's long and totally incomprehensible contract. We are probably both leaving everything to him.

I leave the Villa Marechiaro to begin my new life as a Neapolitan, and little by little the shock recedes and the colour edges back in. Now I have a ringside seat to watch the next episode of the European meltdown. But more importantly my feeling for Wilde deepens with each day.

It is suddenly November, and the city looks tired under a black sky by the gunmetal sea. The streets are cold and wet. The rubbish looked better in summer but smelt worse. Now it is flattened and soaked. I wonder how Oscar felt here all on his own as winter set in, and my sympathy plumbs new depths as I slink through the same freezing shadows on the same thin steep streets. They creep up and tangle you in gloom. Even today there is something tragic and trapped for the marooned English queen in the Neapolitan winter when the sea and the bougain-villea have faded. For Oscar, all past and no future, trudging up the hill in the autumn wind towards Parco Virgiliano, it must have felt desperate.

There is still a spot in that run-down park with its overgrown lawns and broken benches where the suicides jump. Looking over the cliffs towards the islands – death ships in the autumn dusk – Oscar saw the ghosts of the dead, Neapolitans who had thrown themselves onto the rocks in despair. They beck-oned him to join them and according to a letter he wrote, he nearly did.

'Could you imagine spending the afterlife in Naples though?' someone asked him. 'No. The cooking is really too bad,' Oscar replied.

I have a terrace which looks out to sea towards Capri. Today that island is a black hat covered with a cartoon storm. I am about as close as I ever want to get to that clusterfuck of rich bitches and paunchy gigolos. From where I'm sitting it can still be the magical island of my dreams, the gay haven between the wars, with Gracie Fields singing Neapolitan ballads at the piano.

My flat is beautiful, but no one told me about the disco across the road every Friday and Saturday night. Cars rumble past with basslines thumping, doors slamming, girls screaming and men braying. After one such sleepless night I find the peak of Vesuvius dipped in snow at dawn. Lucie and Nicky observe me from their secret window above the main staircase, giggling as I pass by. All eyes turn as I climb onto the street through the Judas door in the palazzo's gate. The people in the café are cagey but fascinated. The old men who stand all morning by the garage regard me with blank faces as if I was a visiting Nazi. Ladies – always my friends – giggle and preen. After they have been through the A to Z of show business they get down to serious issues.

'Perché? Why are you here? You LIKE Naples?' They are horrified. No one understands.

Naples is my 'move'. It has taken me somewhere – sharpened and deepened my understanding of Oscar Wilde. And after all Italy is the only place where I am still a star, an old movie queen vaguely glimmering in the firmament, my hits as far off as the Crab Nebula but still shining over Naples through the shadows of space. Over a century divides Oscar's visit from mine – everything changed in between – but as far as this place is concerned we both came at the end.

Once, not long before, the kingdom of Naples was one of the great cultural and economic centres of Europe. They did everything first. Then came Unification and the south was pillaged by the north. Naples still lives in the shadow of that time and has gradually been reduced to its present incarnation – a kingdom of rubbish. Alberto and Arturo take me to the villages of garbage that are piled up outside the city. As high as apartment buildings as far as the eye can see – all over the surrounding countryside, in fact – the compressed, unprocessed rubbish of Russia and Northern Europe waits to be sent on to Africa.

Naples today is the fault line between Europe and the Third World, a city on the verge of collapse, buckling under constant pressure from all sides and eaten from within by its own plague bacillus – the Camorra. The Mafia. According to rumour ISIS have already moved in. Across the thin strip of diseased sea, men from Africa risk all to paddle and claw their way to Italy's mythical streets of gold. There are none in Naples, and no friendly face of welcome either. One false move and it will all descend into chaos. That's how it feels.

And so, the view from the terrace is frightening and dizzying, beautiful and tragic. In the winter shadows the city seems almost to be drowning. But in the summer months the magic revives and everything jerks back to life. The energy of the Neapolitan is unquenchable in the jolly faces in windows, voices bouncing across courtyards, the cheerful insanity of the street, the clouds of exhaust belching from cars held together by rosary beads and sticky tape and the sun flickering through it all, across the collapsed grandeur in the magic hour before night falls, wrapped in a warm breeze smelling of night-flowering jasmine and overflowing drains. Tonight a tarantella band plays down in the street.

It reminds me of a line from a play I once saw in Glasgow. Diaghilev in a fur coat sitting on the Lido in Venice, under a full moon. It's 1914. The end of an era.

'I wonder if anyone will ever realise how wonderful it all was?' someone asks, looking out to sea as the lights fade slowly. CURTAIN.

PART TWO

CHAPTER ELEVEN

Purple Moments

The first half of this book was written while making a film remained a wonderful dream. The second half has been written on waking from the nightmare of having made it.

Flash back briefly, drear reader, and the year is 2010. In the game of snakes and ladders, my film and I are back to square one. After the excitement of the first stage – conception, birth and cot death by Scott Rudin – it is now a freezing, fluey January and my career seems to be in hibernation. Hollywood has zipped up behind me, the script has been rejected by all the usual suspects and I am back in the theatre – thank God for Dr Theatre – not getting great reviews at this stage, aged fifty, bitter, desperate and becoming more complicated by the minute. All the various atrophies of middle age are setting in and the future looks as drizzly and grey as the West End winter.

In this legato moment a definitive move is suddenly masterminded by David from Miami. It is he who makes the fatal introduction to Jörg Schulze. David is one of my closest friends. If you have been kind enough to graze through my previous rose-coloured rambles, you may have noticed that he was my neighbour when I lived in Miami. He became my partner in crime on the American charity circuit. We have much in common despite the fact that we are completely different. Example. We are both blind, but I wear glasses.

He was extremely good-looking in the early years, an homme fatale on various scenes – Paris in the eighties, New York in the nineties – and for a time life fell into his hands. Like me, he curdled slightly at the turn of the century, and that was when he got tattoos. He (and they) sagged slightly in the new age. So did I. Now he is a silver fox, rugged but giggly – high on helium, low on self-esteem, living between Düsseldorf and the Dordogne. He is funny and erudite with extreme views which always make a splash, and that's the way he likes it. David is a performer.

Drunk on all his new German contacts in the screen trade (he was editing a magazine for the Berlinale and it went to his head), David proclaimed loftily one evening at the end of 2009: 'Listen. Your script is dead in the water' – a muffled gasp from me – 'but I think I could sell it here in Germany.'

It seemed like a good idea. No one had managed to sell it anywhere else, so I agreed. He took it to a few of his new friends and ended up making a deal with a camera hire company from Berlin called Cine Plus who were 'getting into making movies'.

I was not convinced. 'Well, I suppose it's better than selling it to a car hire company.'

Their head of production was a man called Jörg Schulze, who I talked to on the phone. He had a rich voice – 'I loved the script, yeah?' – and said things like it was a 'perfect fit' and that he could definitely find the money to make the film.

'I don't think it will be that easy,' I cautioned. 'I've been everywhere. You are my last resort.'

'Are you crazy? You're Rupert Ewerett, yeah!'

'Was. Not any more.'

Jörg laughed delightedly. There's not much point telling the truth in show business because nobody listens. Jörg was no exception.

However, for the time being he was dynamic and dominant on the phone and conjured up an image of Eastern bloc machismo. I imagined him wearing pointed boots and tight trousers, draped in scarves like Doctor Who.

In reality he was an exuberant giant with flapping shirt tails and a new-potato nose that pointed upwards towards a pair of watery blue eyes. He had German colouring – sandy skin and hair. He smoked endlessly, and over the years could always be found standing outside the rooms in which we huddled, staring gloomily at the weather in a cloud of smoke like a cartoon villain. He reminded me of the long-suffering producer in *All About Eve*. He spoke good English but was unable to pronounce the letter v, and he confirmed every sentence with 'yeah'. There was something touching about him. He had a child's enthusiasm – a dangerous trait in a producer – and it veered towards fantasy.

His best friend and partner was the head of production at the Bavaria studios in Munich ('Bawaria, yeah'). His name was Thorsten Ritter. As Jörg was large and dishevelled so Thorsten was small and neat, with tidy brown hair and sensible shoes. His eyes were kindly and amused and he spoke flawless English. Together they reminded me of the Two Ronnies. Or the Two Wonkies, as we came to name them.

The third wheel in the group was Jörg's assistant, Katja. She WAS from the old Eastern bloc, a pretty girl with a sandy complexion who spoke perfect English, Spanish and French. She too was full of enthusiasm and merry laughter but I could tell she was as tough as old boots.

This was my new dream team. They appeared laughing and waving over the horizon. They adored the script and loved nothing more than a long night out discussing it. It could be a marriage made in heaven.

The only snag was that none of them had ever actually made a film. A lot of people are producers these days. From Cecil B. DeMille to the star's plastic surgeon, everyone's producing, but to actually 'make' a film, to navigate it through the rapids and the whirlpools of the business, is a different matter; and although the names Jörg reeled off sounded riveting, and while I nodded sagely with approval at each new incomprehensible title, I had never heard of any of them. Which of course isn't saying much.

But I didn't care. At this point Berlin was my second home. I loved it there. As soon as I touched down at Tegel (the airport on the outskirts of the city) I felt young again. It reminded me of London in the seventies. Bankrupt. Sexy. Anonymous. I lived in a wonderful run-down hotel off the Ku'damm and indulged the midlife crisis of my sexual identity to the hilt, looking ten years younger in the red-lit dungeons of Berlin, flying high on God knows what, a praying mantis in black leather waiting to pounce. In such a way – without moving a muscle – I dreamt up every frame of my film. It would be the strangest, greatest German film ever made. An effortlessly European affair that divided naturally into three languages. It felt important to be starting the journey here in Berlin with Jörg and Thorsten and Katja.

With David now in the role of Carlo Ponti, we arrived at 9.30 a.m. one October morning at the offices of Cine Plus in Berlin to go through the script. The jolly trio was sitting around a table in a glass box of a boardroom as funky agency types swam by outside. They had brought in a 'script expert' to solve some of the problems they had with the structure of my film. He was a tall man with a gunmetal crop and red eyes framed by rimless spectacles. Unlike the others, his English was unfathomable.

'Script Doctor Goebbels!' David whispered to me as we all sat down. It only takes five minutes in the presence of Germans for the English to reference the war. (This should have given me a hint.) Dr G thought the script was 'bvilliant', but that it fell apart halfway through.

'Oh really?' I tried to look reasonable. 'In what way, exactly?'

Ludicrously I picked up my pencil, ready to rewrite on the spot. He looked at me over his bifocals as if I was a naughty student.

'Ah sink zis Boosie ees nat so essential, ya?'

'Non,' I replied. 'I mean ja. Very essential.'

'I think in Naples is the weakest part, yeah?' pitched in Jörg.

They were moving in. What they meant was 'we'll never get to Naples on the budget', but it took me years to be able to translate their brand of banter into my own and by then it was too late. In the meantime I knew that the trick was to remain calm, and a sudden picture of my father seething about 'bloody Jerry' on a ferry packed with Germans in the sixties flashed across my mind. I managed to keep glittering – at least on the surface – and anyway I had been warned.

'They've got bees in their bonnets about Naples,' David had said.

'Well, many people would agree with you,' I said, trying the expansive approach. 'But of course my story is ABOUT Bosie and Oscar and the end of their relationship.'

'Mmm. Yeah. Maybe. Maybe we can change a leedle,' giggled Goebbels.

'Certainly. What do you think we should do?'

'Maybe we can cut this section?'

'Cut Naples?'

'Yeah. Good idea.'

And here was where I realised – or thought I realised – that no one in the group had really understood my screenplay.

'Telling me samesing?' asked the good doctor with infinite patience. 'Vher zie virst ekt ind unt zie segund ekt begeen?'

What on earth was he talking about? He repeated the question in German and David translated. Apparently Goebbels couldn't understand where the first act ended and the second one began.

'Rules, rules, rules!' I screamed inwardly. What did he want? A red velvet curtain swishing up and down? However, I nodded with sympathy and explained. 'I should have made it much clearer. The second ekt begins at the station in Rouen.'

'I can tell you now,' said Goebbels, making snipping gestures with his fingers, 'ziz zeen hitting cutting-womb floor.'

'I see,' I replied crisply.

The problem seemed to be that although everyone in the room – with the exception of Script Doctor G – spoke faultless English, there was a cultural gulf that made things difficult to explain. Nuance is central to the English language, whereas German is fairly direct.

'Remember their word for a UFO is a flying-under-teacup,' David had said. 'They are very literal.'

Apropos, Goebbels asked: 'What exactly are these "purple moments" Oscar talks about on page sixteen?'

'It's like being blue,' explained Jörg.

'Blue?'

'Is when he feels werry depressed, yeah?'

'No. Actually it is just a frilly way of talking about sex?'

'Frilly?'

We were all going to need a lot of patience.

I tried to explain that the film was meant to be amusing as well as tragic, but this is an unusual concept in German so we decided to have a coffee break. Germans huddled in one corner, murmuring to one another, English queens in the other, cackling about some latest antic of Madonna. The problem is that things are either funny or tragic in Germany but rarely both. And anyway, from the English standpoint humour is not the Germans' strongest suit. The language simply isn't built for it and neither are they. They are tremendously discreet, with great resources of loyalty and terribly thorough in sex. They don't gossip about other people, and I could tell they were shocked at lunch when David and I tore our mutual friends to shreds. We tried to explain that it wasn't really serious, just another form of affection, but Thorsten looked concerned and Jörg was a bit bewildered.

Trying to explain the tone of my film took up the rest of the day.

'Actually "purple moments" are a perfect example of humour in the film – such as it is. It's not meant to be laugh-out-loud funny, but when you watch Oscar holding forth hopefully there will be a smile on your face because he is quite grandiose and theatrical, a bit of a clown, with all the tragedy of the clown as well.'

They were furiously writing everything down.

'There he is with his trousers down in a rancid old knocking shop with a young hooker with whom he has just finished having sex, and he talks about the event as being a purple moment sullied by green notes.'

'Ach so! Wat are zees green notes?' Goebbels.

'Money.' I was shrieking slightly and David nudged me under the table.

'Ahh.' They all looked blank.

'Does that mean we don't like him? He must pay for sex?' piped Katja.

'We all pay, sweetie.' I was getting waspish, and now David kicked me.

'We do like him, but he isn't just a hero. He is also an idiot.'
Bemused looks.

'Look at the way he pushes himself towards ruin. As well as being brilliant he is blinded by his own success.'

At the end of the day everyone seemed happy and we all went out for dinner where we got legless on gin and tonics. They had huge Wagnerian reserves of energy while I was half-dead. At about midnight I made my excuses and went to a leather bar to calm down.

The next day I returned to London.

Looking back on all this, they had a reasonable point. They wanted to create a sympathetic hero. I wanted to recreate a historical character. Was Wilde sympathetic? He certainly wasn't heroic. At least not in the normal way. That's why I loved him.

A month or so later, Jörg and Thorsten appeared in London for dinner and a catch-up. We were back at *Pygmalion* in the Garrick Theatre, so I got them tickets and arranged to meet them in J Sheekey's after the show. They behaved rather oddly at dinner and never mentioned the play. Not one word. I asked them if they had got the tickets. They said yes. I waited modestly for them to say how fabulous I was as Henry Higgins, but they just carefully nibbled at their breadsticks and slugged down the first gin and tonic. Now we were off piste.

The usual couple of well-wishers wheeled by and congratulated me. The two Germans looked up at them like little children as the accolades rained down. I thanked them profusely and returned my attention to the table, my face a cheerful question mark begging for an answer. Nothing. They were blanking the whole experience. It was very strange. Perhaps they spent the show in the bar. Perhaps it was a race thing. Maybe in Wagnerworld it was rude to talk about normal everyday things like being excellent. In lazy old Luvvieland lying is essential. It is so much easier to say how wonderful someone is even while inwardly you are resolving never to see them again. But I couldn't have been that bad. Or could I? A strain fell over the table like a shadow.

On the other hand, they told me some interesting stuff about the German funding system although it all sounded like double Dutch after two shows in that rattling theatre. (The Piccadilly line rumbled past under the stage.) There were four places – states – in Germany that awarded money to movies. One was called MMD – Mitteldeutschland. This was the worst one for our purposes, having been completely flattened in the war and then rebuilt by the Soviets (i.e., no architecture to use as a set). Another was Bavaria, which was quite good. They had a big studio and a lot of over-restored architecture. Berlin had the famous Babelsberg Studios, although the money you could get out of them was limited – Berlin being a bankrupt state. The best subsidy was from Cologne, also flattened but extremely rich and with a great studio.

It took me months – nearly a year – to understand this whole formula. That night in the low lights and the clatter, the desperate drinking to keep going and the weird suspicious feeling about the play, I never really listened to what they were saying. Jörg had a peculiar meandering way of talking, his head buried in his drink, and it all sort of washed over me. It was after all a matinee day and I was half-dead. Did he want some MDMA?

'MMD, yeah, but we don't weally want them. We are going for two million from North West Australia.'

'Great,' I said, wondering who on earth they could possibly know in Australia. They hardly seemed to know anyone in Germany. But I just nodded sagely as if it was all totally normal, and only months later did I gingerly ask Jörg how everything was going in Australia and had they sent the cash, and he looked puzzled.

'I don't know anyone in Australia, yeah?'

'Really? But you said they were going to give us some money.'

'No.'

'Yes. North West Australia or something.'

'Ahh. North Rhein-Westphalia. This is the area round Cologne.'

At this point we all laughed.

CHAPTER TWELVE

Berlinale

I was in Argentina a few months later when Jörg called me and said that I had to come to Germany for the Berlinale.

'But I just got here,' I replied.

'We have a lot of interest. People are crazy about the script. We have a lot of meetings set up.'

'Oh well, in that case . . .'

I had rented a flat in Buenos Aires from an old lady and I was trying to settle down and write a book. The place was all black with a very needy cat and it was getting on my nerves, so even though I had to cancel my trip to Ascension on a cargo ship, I was happy to have an excuse to get out. The film was the most important thing in my life and within a week I was back in London on my way to Berlin.

Film festivals can be hellish affairs. If you are hoping for a dose of old-world glamour, forget it. It is the one ingredient palpably absent on the modern-day festival circuit. Power is the thing that counts. The powerful flex while the powerless grovel, and the rest of us juggle our way up or down. All this is played out out in theatres and halls and hotel lobbies, at dinners and screenings, at breakfast meetings and focus groups. The stars run by, draped in borrowed jewels, followed by flotillas of their 'people'. The public watch – breathless – through the keyholes of a thousand cameras bristling behind the velvet rope dividing the red carpet from the vagabond world and the whole thing goes on year after year, season after season and nothing ever changes except the faces get bigger (fillers) and the movies get smaller (budgets).

At least the weather is temperate at Cannes and you can pop into Venice from the Lido but at Berlin, what can you do? Freeze or fornicate in the February drizzle.

One thing not to do at a film festival is business. Nobody concentrates. Everyone is looking over their shoulder. This was where I first met Philipp Kreuzer, the man who later banged his head on the doorway to Oscar's house. At this point, he was the other head of the Bavaria studios – in charge of production and the man who was meant to set up all our meetings with distributors. He too was like an overgrown schoolboy with an unbroken voice, and glasses covered with fingerprints.

My initial feeling was that he had no interest in my film. Bavaria wanted big American films – not mine. Philipp had left everything to the last minute but luckily for him I was the only one who noticed. Thorsten was too polite and Jörg was driven along on the crest of his own wave. He would soon discover where enthusiasm ended and reality began.

Before our first meeting with 'the most important guy at Canal Plus', he pumped me up like a boxer's manager in a B-movie. 'This is a really important meeting, yeah? Canal Plus is the perfect fit, yeah? He already loves the script. It could be great.'

We followed Philipp blindly through the sleety streets as he scuttled like a crab – left and right – from one festival acquaintance to the next, weighed down by a heavy Third World shoulder bag full of festival paraphernalia. We were running to keep up, crashing to a halt like a gaggle of geese, me and David, Jörg and Katja, as he stopped to greet some passing executive of interest. Introductions all round, goodbyes all round, honk honk honk, all in a split second and off we charged into one of those grim towers near the space needle, up the escalator into a dreary canteen where he explained it 'would be a great place to have our meetings – quiet, private'.

We squashed around a greasy Formica table cluttered with squeezy bottles of ketchup and mustard and were served tea by a grumpy waitress. We were the unlikely characters of a nursery rhyme – the cook, the queen and the candlestick maker at sea in a pea-green canteen. Philipp was right. It was very private. The place was deserted. We could have been on tour in the north of England. Snow was now falling outside, discoloured like divine dandruff.

Our man from Canal Plus was late and Jörg broke into a muck sweat, his eyes swivelling back and forth scanning the horizon. Philipp made frantic calls on three different phones. He dialled. He listened. They rang. He dropped them. He pecked at one with nibbled fingers, firing off messages while his face observed another with a kind of perplexed horror, his eyes gigantic through the thick lenses of his spectacles. It was the mesmerising ritual of a show business shaman summoning the spirit of Canal Plus into the room, and finally a tiny creature appeared waving from the escalator. He WAS wearing a Doctor Who scarf.

Panting and apologising he collapsed at the table, uncoiling himself from the scarf, talking all the time – the plane, the luggage, the hotel – while the grumpy waitress dumped a cup of tea in front of him and we all fixed sympathetic smiles with caring groans on one of our faces. The vibration of panic subsided. I liked him immediately. He had sharp intelligent eyes and an easy smile. It would be the best meeting of the trip.

He said straight away that he hadn't had time to read the script but that it sounded exactly what they were looking for. Jörg wiped his drenched face with a napkin. Inwardly furious, I nevertheless managed to be slick, smiley and spontaneous as I described the film for the fifteen-thousandth time and he sounded pretty enthusiastic, so we arranged to meet soon in Paris and he rewound himself back into his scarf and down the escalator.

We never heard another word.

The fact was that nobody had read my script.

'But Jörg. You told me that everyone had read it.'

'Yeah. Me too. I thought they had, yeah?'

'Yes, and hang on – you said they all really loved it. I have come all this way here for nothing.'

'Oh, no. The meetings are going weally weally well.'

Three bald men appeared through the snow from the land of MDMA – Mitteldeutschland. At another gruelling reception, their blue shaved pates were sprinkled with snowflakes that melted as we talked and slid rivetingly down their faces. They asked me if I had spent much time in East Germany, and I told them about the time I went for a picnic in a little village where everyone was sitting naked around the village pond. They laughed heartily. You could hear their bones squeaking. 'Yes, we like to be very natural.'

'And what was amazing was that everyone was shaved,' I replied.

My Germans' bubbling faces briefly froze but these former communists beamed proudly.

'Zeez eez ecksaktly so,' one exclaimed, slapping me on the back.

Encouraged, I enlarged. 'Even the grandmothers – legs akimbo, not a hair in sight. You could almost see their tonsils.

I loved it. If everyone from an English village had to sit around the pond naked and shaved, that would be the end of the village. They would all have to move out the next day.'

They instantly pledged a million euros. In the taxi we were all ecstatic, rewinding moments of the interview as though they were goals in a great football match. It was quite sweet and somewhat intoxicating. We had scored, finally. 'It was great when you said ...'

'But what about when YOU said ...'

'I loved how you ...'

What no one explained to me was that for the million euros half the film had to be shot in Leipzig.

The head of acquisitions from the French distributor, Gaumont, sat at a table in a crowded foyer. He was hunched and morose with long, thin hair and a wonky nose, a French cartoon in the jovial *Biergarten* atmosphere of the festival. Sitting next to him was his young subaltern, as good-looking as his boss was ugly, tall and dark, proficient in eight languages with perfect frosty manners, a university beauty all set for world domination.

They looked up at us with undisguised boredom as we squeezed through the crowd, our come-and-buy-me smiles fixed to both ears, and settled down at their table, cracking jokes, bringing with us – we hoped – that unstoppable energy of success that was going to knock them off their feet. It didn't. It just bled into the noise.

To start with it was more or less impossible to hear what anyone was saying. At a glance the man – François – seemed typical of his breed and profession: arrogant and disdainful. As he leant forward slightly, a hand cupped to his ear, I thought how funny it would be to slap him really hard. That would get the meeting going.

The French in cinema are fairly nationalistic at the best of times, and there was little sign of any entente cordiale. In fact, they are suspicious of their British counterparts, mainly because of their easy access to the American market. But the poor French are disdainful of everyone, the Italians for their flakiness, their featherbrains and their inability to shoot natural sound and the Germans for their lack of style, their bluntness and their superior business sense. (We won't even go into the Belgians.) And of course, they exasperate the rest of us, too, by being so superior and for boring us stiff all these years with their dreary *cinéma philosophe*.

In short, none of the old war wounds had particularly healed. François had – obviously – not read the script and left all the talking to the good-looking sidekick. I got down on all fours and launched into my bubbling, effervescent pitch, shouting to make myself heard. The assistant listened concerned while the old fossil scanned the horizon for a waiter. Philipp and Jörg leant into the table with gleaming eyes ready to take the ball and dribble it home, but there was no sign of a goal or even goalposts for that matter.

The conversation broke down and drifted into silence. We looked at each other for a long moment. Was anyone else going to say anything? The noise around us was suddenly deafening so we got up, politely made our excuses and left.

'Well, that didn't seem to go very well,' I said.

'I think they were weally weceptive,' reasoned Jörg.

'Oh, God,' I thought. 'This is *Alice in Wonderland*.'

I saw the young assistant on the Eurostar a few days later and greeted him.

'It was great to meet you both the other day. Thank you.'

'No problem,' he said, walking quickly towards the barrier.

'Do you think we could meet again after you've read the script?'

'We're pretty busy right now.'

'Does that mean no?'

He stopped and threw me a withering look. 'No,' he said with an upward inflection. I was about to ask if no meant yes or no, but there wasn't time. He'd gone.

What I could tell immediately from these disastrous meetings was that absolutely no one was interested in getting into the 'Rupert Everett business' as they say in the States, and I didn't really blame them. Only my Germans loved me, I thought as I gathered another frothing round of bevvies and crisps in my arms and negotiated my way through the crowd towards them sitting round another table at another bar after another meeting littered with empty glasses and overflowing ashtrays. You could still smoke in Berlin that year. They were wide-eyed with enthusiasm and exhaustion. They were possessed by the whirl of festival activity, and the moment they dropped me off at the hotel each night they marched in formation to screenings to parties to bars to late-night huddles in hotel rooms ending at dawn, staggering back to pick me up for the first breakfast meeting at the space needle canteen at which they sat – matching the pea-green walls – in hung-over silence. They hadn't slept for days, and I felt a surge of warmth.

'You get what you want in the form that you deserve,' someone once said.

I got Jörg. I left Germany without a single deal.

CHAPTER THIRTEEN

Merlin

But the film refused to die. It seemed to have a life of its own. Something always happened at the last moment to make me turn back.

This time it was a phone call out of the blue from Merlin Holland, Oscar Wilde's grandson. If you become obsessed by a dead poet, and if in the course of time you become familiar with almost every aspect of his/her life like a terrible stalker, then making contact with their surviving relatives is a thrilling victory, particularly if they are orbiting the star as close as two generations away – the only son of the only (surviving) son. The sins of the father are still being visited on Merlin Holland and he couldn't fit more perfectly into the role. (I also have a literary crush on James Joyce. Unfortunately his grandson Stephen is much more cagey. Was. Dead now.)

Hearing Merlin say his name on the telephone – one evening shortly after Berlin, out of the blue – the world stood still for a moment, my vision blurred and my body jerked around uncontrollably in a strange writhing spasm, a sort of petit mal. It was as if someone was walking on my grave.

Speaking of which, he declared: 'Oscar's tomb is going to be surrounded by a wall of glass. So many people are kissing it that the stone is being worn away. We are having a small ceremony, and I would love it if you would come and read a passage from something.' His voice was melodious, comfortable, strangely intimate, exactly how I imagined Oscar's to be. I wondered how he got my number. I hadn't even performed in *The Judas Kiss* at this point, and I felt it was a sign. Oscar, like Christ (as usual), was sending his only grandson.

Merlin proposed that we meet in Paris for a dinner at the Irish Embassy and that we go the next morning to the Père Lachaise Cemetery and present the new glass box to the press and the world.

All the doubts I had about making a film fell away during the conversation, like a draining bath. Such as it was my creative energy was released again.

The tomb at Père Lachaise, built by Jacob Epstein, is a strange, ugly block of stone. I knew it very well. My friend Lychee ended up being buried two rows away from it. Her funeral – two months after her death – had taken place on a freezing February morning in 1996. Perle, strangely dignified in her grief, suddenly came undone and howled that morning – a dry scream – as Lychee's slim coffin was lowered into the ground, surrounded by squinting club freaks – all the colleagues – in fancy dress, shivering in the cold wind. It was a horrible moment, and I remember looking away and seeing the weird sphinx on Oscar's tomb. It seemed to be flying away from the scene into the pus-coloured sky.

Since that day, we passed it a few times, Perle and I, as we hobbled along the great alleys of the cemetery for a birthday or a deathday, winter or summer, and we always stopped by Oscar's grave on the way back to the taxi rank at the gate.

'Et le film?' Perle always asked sweetly while I looked dejectedly up.

The Epstein tomb is a stone filing cabinet. The sphinx seems to be crammed into it – like an S&M trick – ready to slide out of its drawer and fly off. It towers over the rooftops of the more conventional resting places of the *voisinage*, minarets and sentry boxes, a collapsed villa on one side with rusty grilles, a romantic lady on the other draped over her marble husband's slab. Others watch with dead bronze eyes from their plinths as everyone hurries by towards the star attraction.

Oscar's body was moved to Père Lachaise in 1909 from a burial ground in Bagneaux. The tomb was unveiled just before the First World War in that hot August of 1914 by Aleister Crowley (of all people). Its huge testicles were a bone(r) of contention and its nudity was initially covered with a kind of period thong, a metal butterfly that so infuriated Epstein that he boycotted the inauguration. In 1961 these huge balls were removed by vandals and disappeared, only to reappear later as a paperweight on the gardener's desk in the cemetery potting shed.

Oscar's tomb is the most popular destination in Père Lachaise, above Jim Morrison, Marcel Proust, Chopin, Piaf and Colette and its base is covered with the lipstick prints of a million kisses. It is a beacon for lost dreamers, a straw to clutch at for outcasts and the clinically depressed, and there is a strange energy around it.

We met in the bar of the Hôtel Regina on the Rue de Rivoli. The Regina has been in the hands of the same family for generations. Despite the current proprietor's rigorous attempts to renovate this hotel, it is firmly locked in its marvellous art nouveau bubble and no number of jazzy acrylic rugs or stonewashed tables and chairs can disguise it. The bar reminds me of Graham Greene, dark-panelled, down at heel; its red velvet banquettes – scuffed and singed – have seen better days. Two glum barmen preside in white jackets, and across the road the Louvre

is glimpsed through the heavily draped windows between the
smear of headlights and tail lights and the shadows of passers-by,
looming and shrinking under the lamps of the arcade.

Merlin didn't disappoint. He too seemed to step from the
pages of Greene. Well preserved at nearly seventy with a mass
of hair – faded ash – pillow lips and kind grey eyes, he had the
perfect manners of an Old Etonian and the dress sense of an
Oxford don – sensible, economical, in a colour chart of porridge
and heather. At the same time he was quite unequivocally the
grandson of Ireland's most flamboyant poet.

My first thought was that he was a spy. There was something
contradictory about him, coiled and hidden. He was self-effacing
and yet he made a great impression entering the room. Perhaps
it was the weight of history on his shoulders – three generations
of shame howling around. He was as tall as Oscar with large
hands and feet, but the feet were not flat. Actually he walked
slightly on tiptoe and sometimes spoke as if he were peering
over a fence. Seeing him was seeing a vision. I felt like a whirl-
ing dervish who had spun and spun and finally the miracle
had occurred.

His wife Emma was his polar opposite. A formidable woman,
younger than Merlin, she seemed slightly frustrated to be
swamped in the long literary shadow. She had possibly spent too
long watching it eat up her husband's day. She had been Merlin's
son's nanny and the two had fallen in love in the full glare of his
first marriage, always a complicated scene to stage (no shadows),
but they had denied themselves in those early days – whispering
on staircases, holding hands under the kitchen table – and only
regrouped fifteen years later. It was romantic and valiant and
they had paid a certain price. It was written on their faces. Exile
was the obvious choice and now they lived near Chalon in the
heart of French Burgundy country.

Emma's eyes had a mischievous glint and I immediately

adored her. Poor thing. There was a lot of work involved in living with a myth's last link, and of course there was no money in it. Merlin's work for his grandfather was conducted on strictly charitable terms. Wilde was in the public domain, and while he clearly possessed Merlin, his wife had long ago been exorcised.

Suddenly I remembered something.

'I don't suppose the name Peta Everett means anything to you?'

Merlin turned sharply. 'Why?' he asked.

'She was my aunt.'

There was a pause as the glum waiter put down the drinks. Lights turned green on the street outside and there was a sudden roar of acceleration. The room shivered.

'Peta Everett is the reason I saw my father for the last time.'

Time stood still. I nearly fainted.

Flashback.

At first we called her Aunt Pat. Then briefly she was Petronella before finally settling on Peta in the sixties.

'The name's Peta,' she said firmly when being introduced at home, while my father muttered 'Crippen' behind her slightly hunched back.

She was his only sister and, quite frankly, a source of embarrassment in his blinkered military world. For as long as I could remember she lived in Hammersmith in a huge service block called Latymer Court, at first in a penthouse, then in a smaller flat and finally in a bedsit. In her glory days she worked for Revlon or Mary Quant.

She was extremely glamorous – a Marlene Dietrich for Hammersmith in sheath dresses, a pale honey-coloured beehive and gigantic swooping eyelashes, which I used to watch her put on when she came to stay with us at home. It was a horrifying and fascinating operation as she lifted her eyelid, her pupil straining to look up at the black creepy-crawly covered in weird white glue that was balanced on the tips of her long fingernails and artfully stuck above some stumpy lashes of her own. Their weight pulled her lids down and immediately turned her eyes into tipsy slits. This was acting. They completely changed her character. Suddenly in the mirror Aunt Pat was sultry and knowing – 'The name's Peta!' – not that I knew exactly what knowing was at that stage, but I was aware that some extraordinary change had come over her. She became a different creature as she trowelled on layers of delicious-smelling make-up, heavily pressed with powder by a divine coral puff with a frilly back.

'Can I have that?' I apparently enquired aged three. The powder cracked around her eyes into a thousand tributaries, the dried-up rivers of tears, as she laughed. Her dressing table was covered with bottles and pumps and curlers and coils. It was enthralling to the little boy already cross-dressing and my lifelong love affair with 'slap' dates from that time. She dressed in a way we had never seen in Essex – my mother made her own clothes on a Singer sewing machine – but Aunt Pat was an exotic bird flapping in on a wave of 'unsuitable' scent.

Although genteelly impoverished, she was incredibly extravagant. She once came all the way from London in a taxi, and this was the last straw. Her behaviour was pronounced 'extraordinary'. Presumably ordinary was our aim. War was silently declared and we – her two nephews – were brought up to ridicule her. Actually she was the only one in our family who had any fantasy and actually challenged us to think, to look outside our own little world, whereas the sixties went by without either of my parents really noticing. She was a voracious reader.

Another thing – and this I only discovered later – poor Peta was a fallen woman. She had given birth to a baby boy, sired by a married brigadier during the war and her mother, my grandmother, Marcella, the strictest of Irish Catholics, insisted she deliver it in Ireland and leave it with the nuns. This probably accounted for the restless changing of names and later, the heavy drinking. She couldn't face herself.

If she never recovered from abandoning her child she made up for it by indulging my brother and I in a way the rest of our family never did. Five-pound notes were extracted from alligator skin bags and proffered between long red fingernails to screams of horror from my parents. Ten bob was the maximum in our rationing-obsessed world. My brother wanted a mouse. She turned up with two of them in a smart blue cage. (One was brown.) I wanted a make-up kit. She took me to the Leichner shop in Covent Garden. I still have the make-up, delicious sticks of crimson lake, peach and ivory and a proper box with shelves and my initials. I wanted a Pekinese and my father was horrified. Peta appeared with a white one. It promptly died but she was not to be thwarted. Another arrived.

She probably did it all to tease my father. She wanted him to be the bachelor she had known in Malta in the early fifties – they had been a team on a certain scene – cheek to cheek in Valletta as the band played 'Sugarbush' and the young royals swayed on the dance floor, but my mother put an end to all that and those two women never got along. Once she gave me a packet of cigarettes. I smoked the whole lot in one sitting and then was sick all over the house.

'Quite extraordinary,' said Mummy on all fours, scrubbing.

After that, Daddy and Pat were at constant loggerheads with Mummy egging them on from the sidelines. Then, quite suddenly, she became Peta. 'The name's Peta!' It must have been 1967. Because at about this time I was sent away to school and she wrote to me every week. Her writing was like a cardiogram and her letters full of good advice for a lost child. As time went on she held her drink less and less well. The beehive deflated at lunch and the swooping lashes fell into the soup. My mother found one on a pillow like a squashed centipede. How we laughed as we showed it to everyone. She died reading a thriller and wasn't found for weeks. My father was the only mourner at her funeral.

One of the 'most extraordinary' things was that she had apparently been a friend of Oscar Wilde. By the time I was old enough to know that this was a physical impossibility I was already in the first stages of my teenage revolution, dressed in Indian shirts from Kensington Market, high-heeled boots and long, centrally parted hair, screaming at everyone.

'Aunt Peta wasn't even born when Oscar Wilde died,' I sneered.

'Something else we're wrong about?' sighed my mother, exasperated.

I endlessly goaded my parents for this idiotic mistake, but soon the story was forgotten and I couldn't have thought about it since I was seventeen. Until tonight.

'My mother was called Thelma,' said Merlin in the same lilting tones that made his grandfather a famous talker. 'She used to do the queen's make-up and then she went to work at Revlon, where she became friends with your aunt. When my father was dying – I was up at Oxford at the time – my mother sent for me. I arrived at our flat in Earl's Court to find your aunt having dinner. At the end of the meal my mother said, "Take Peta downstairs and put her in a taxi, would you?" We lived in the Boltons at the time, so I walked her round the corner onto the Old Brompton Road and hailed a cab. Instead of getting in, Peta turned to me and thrust a ten-pound note into my hands saying, "Go and see your father in the hospital, now."

'So I did. And he died that night. When I got home my mother was furious. She thought Peta had seduced me.'

We laughed. Someone opened a door and a cold wind came in with a group of noisy Americans.

'Imagine. If I had waited until the next day to go to the hospital it would have been too late. He died in the night.'

I was speechless. Wilde's grandson had seen his own father for the last time, thanks to Peta Everett. This was important news and took some digesting.

The Irish Embassy was on the Avenue Foch, a stunning hôtel particulier that still boasted its original furniture. We were led through the gilt and cream reception rooms, one after another, through huge double doors. The house groaned and creaked like an old galleon and smelt of polish. At each door the Ambassador lit a glittering chandelier and the room sprang to life, blood-red carpets and ornate mirrors in stand-offs with one another, reflecting dizzying worlds of endless doors.

The minister of culture was a leprechaun and Merlin was a giant. In the candlelit dining room their shadows leapt up the wall behind them. The minister held Merlin's hand and sang an Irish ballad. The angel flew past in the ensuing silence, pulling Oscar behind it through the ether. It was terribly moving. Emma watched with a faraway smile at the end of the table. We caught each other's eye and winked. Neither of us was in a party mood that night. But we sat and watched as the raconteurs threw out their nets, the wine gurgled and sploshed into the glasses, the candlelight fluttered prettily and the waiters leant in from the shadows.

Aunt Peta and Oscar Wilde was a file long closed in my brain. Buried. Exhuming it, by chance, from the depths, all the trapped chemicals of that time came bubbling to the surface, burning through my veins, down to my fingertips, like a flash bulb exploding, catching Merlin in a kind of blinding double exposure. I could see him clearly all those years ago. The street corner I knew well and the October night in 1967 was the middle of my second term at school.

I closed my eyes and the conversation echoed and slid towards it. Heels on pavements, wheels through puddles and the broken reflection of Aunt Peta in the orange street light, the mani-cured fingers searching for the tenner she could ill afford in the black alligator skin bag. Looking up at Merlin, in full Marlene mode, the eyelashes under the light sending shadows down her cheeks of a hundred little fingers, flirting, her mouth reaching towards him.

'Go to the hospital now. The name's Peta.'

And there was Merlin, twenty, spotty, freaked, those big lips feeling their power – who is this woman? – getting in the cab and looking back at the solitary siren in the pencil skirt walking away towards Earl's Court, humming the latest hit by Lulu, perhaps 'To Sir With Love'.

And I am somewhere there, perhaps not on the Old Brompton Road itself, but there, in her mind. She may have written me a letter that day. Or maybe she was going to write me one the next day.

Laughing, toppling from the dream, I found Merlin looking straight at me – or was it Oscar?

'Were you having a nap?' he asked.

'Not at all. I was just thinking of my aunt.'

That night in bed I couldn't sleep. The feeling of amazement congealed and a terrible anguish set in. I hardly dared to take stock, to go back all that way into my dealings with our inconvenient aunt. Suddenly I realised I had never even thought of her for years, not even when my father – her own brother – died. I had completely erased her. Had I asked her to any of my premieres or first nights? I couldn't remember, but I am sure I didn't. I tried to locate her in some other dimension – in the space behind the eyes or the periphery of vision – but there was no answer. Out of the blue I suddenly remembered her telephone number. Riverside 4285. We had turned our backs on her and now she had turned hers on me. Walking off into the night down the rainy streets of purgatory. Click click click.

Sleepless nights don't suit me, and I was quite moody and deeply hung-over the next morning when we all met at Père Lachaise, bundled up against the cold. It was one of those bright winter days, blue skies and freezing shadows, smelling of bonfires. The tomb was encased in a rather chic bulletproof window. I thought it added something. There were about a hundred journalists and an equal number of freaky fans, a gaggle of French diplomats and park officials and it felt like the graduation I had never achieved. The outcasts of '59. I read from 'De Profundis'. Merlin made a speech. The Irish minister was very funny.

Somewhere under the ground Oscar listened in his box. Were his fingernails as long as Straw Peter's? Did he have a hard-on, like Byron? And where was the urn containing Robbie's ashes? Together for ever in the dark, the pot and the box and the dead times, observed by the odd intruding rodent.

After it was finished there was applause – a strange hollow sound outdoors – more shades of sports day. I drifted off and found myself back with Lychee. I sat on her grave and told her the whole story.

'Et le film,' she said.

Suddenly I didn't feel like going back, so I sloped off past Piaf via Chopin and had couscous in a restaurant near the gates to the cemetery before heading back to London. Since that day Merlin and I have become firm friends. He located some extracts from his father's diary in which he (Vyvyan) wrote that Peta was coming over.

'She and Thelma are off to see the spooks (spiritualists). Peta drinks too much. But I suppose we all do.'

Apparently Peta and Thelma used to table-turn every Sunday afternoon. Who was she trying to contact?

'How extraordinary,' said my mother when I told her.

Merlin sent me a picture of Thelma. She was the same sort of creature as Aunt Peta, only the beehive was black.

One thing was sure. I had to make my film, no matter what.

CHAPTER FOURTEEN

(No Story is Complete Without)
Roddy McDowall

It's difficult to explain to a civilian why we in the 'profession' whine about show business so much and yet here we all are, hobbling along on our Zimmer frames years later, rushing for the bus to the next audition. Why are we so bitter?

Julie Andrews once bleakly remarked in an interview that while you may love show business with all your heart – dedicate your life and soul to it – show business will never love you back. It waits for the moment you are down and it kicks you carefully in the teeth. It is a dismal forecast and only goes halfway to describing the weird relationship we performers have with the strange profession that we never willingly relinquish.

Becoming a star is an addiction and a mirage, a pretty picture at first, but quickly stained by the thick hairspray of power and paranoia that slowly dulls our features, freezing them into our favourite 'fuck me' grimace and calcifying the central plumbing system so that, after a bit, the hot water starts gushing from the cold water taps and general disorientation sets in.

With the first twinkle of stardom we exist more on the silver screen than at home behind the kitchen sink. (For example, NEVER ask a movie star to say I love you. They just can't. They have given it their all in close-up on a sound stage dressed as an Apache. In real life the sacred phrase is a long shot at best in black and white. And don't say I love you to one of them either. They can't cope. The fourth wall will tumble down like the tabernacle veil. They will either reply 'OK' (Madonna) or 'Thank you' (Michael Douglas).

Once you have tasted your first blood – the blood of nubile fans – and their fresh knickers are sailing through the letter box every morning with the post (or in my case, at one point, my own records smashed and daubed in the shit of a mad anti-fan who later got help and wrote me one of those torturous Step 8 letters saying sorry); once you have felt the power of your (lack of) personality projected onto a screen, backcombed and backlit, your view of yourself and the world around you changes for ever.

It's a hall of mirrors. Your eyes – either empty and bewildered or just two greedy raisins in real life – are suddenly the shadowed and glinting windows of a tortured soul in the judicious beam of the 'inky dink', that blinkered lamp – no longer used – that once launched a thousand shits. These eyes burn like coals and bore through the footlights into the very heart of the spectator – and once you have felt all that, there is no going back. In the wonky mirror of everyone's eyes you believe it's all you, all that depth – but actually you are nothing much more than the undead waiting for another fix. Only Klieg light will bring life to those dead pupils.

Hopefully at this point you become a star, and time briefly falls away in the waves of endless adulation that even has your own mother treating you with caution. You are in equal measure omnipotent and a victim. Everyone loves you but they're out to get you, too. Everyone wants a piece, but who cares – as far as you're concerned it will last for ever. Sometimes it does. Either way you are totally immersed and will never escape. Movies, movies, movies. You know it all, who is doing what, why it's all happening and where. You are in total control. And then it suddenly snaps, and everything falls away. It's a game of snakes and ladders, and you are back to square one.

You may not notice at first because the main wonky mirrors are the gang of your own goons, Mummy included. But one day you discover that people actually laughed at that great performance you gave in *X*. They always thought you were mediocre, screechy, shallow. Cute maybe, but talentless and tricky. And now? Oh no! You are twenty-five or thirty-five or forty-five and washed up. The fabulous character you have developed in the eighties is suddenly a clunky old battleship in shoulder pads disappearing over the horizon, while a new day – one in which you have no role, not even a cameo – is already rising in the east with its cold sharp light, no inky dinks this time; just digital with a bit of bounce if you're lucky. (Note to self. Don't get technical.)

So you widen your net to survive. Italian films. TV. Voice-overs. Supermarkets. Teaching. And of course, rehab. Rehab is the downbeat in this syncopated rhythm, and why not? Your face in a mirror hoovering up a delicious line is the only one that reminds you of the misunderstood anti-hero you once were. Now you reject everything that is happening. But it's still your whole life even if you never see a film; you hate the theatre and TV stands for tired vaudeville.

This is the worst circle of the inferno. You are undead. The years shriek by. You may grab onto a passing vehicle and briefly be catapulted to the top, or the middle like some cartoon fish that is suddenly caught on the jet of a fountain and shoots sky-high, but it's a balancing trick that requires the whole universe to be in tune. The tune changes and you're back with the bottom feeders moping around the pond floor. Before you know it (or have time to find a reliable surgeon), you're fifty.

They say that sometimes ghosts don't realise they're dead and wander around screaming because no one is paying them any attention. Well, in show business you may have been dead five years before you finally twig. You howl around the corridors of power while the elect march straight through. Then one day you catch yourself in a mirror and there is nothing looking back.

The new you, suddenly in sharp focus, a black and white blob limping from the crash, held together by steel pins, a hacking cough developed from ten years of gasping with disappointment, will need to re-educate those crushed limbs into new life, another start – or succumb to that flickering existence of haunting, of sometimes being seen in a certain kind of light, at dawns and dusks, *Dancing with the Stars* and daytime soaps, flashing on and off like an old bulb. And so you live more and more in the past; but how far back can you go?

Personally I love watching silent films. There is something miraculous and inspiring in those flickering images, pockmarked and fading: the silver close-ups, the jaunty acting, the running in and out, hands on hips, fingers wagging, all speeded up, all observed by the static blinking eye of the Hollywood pioneer – God observing himself through his latest manifestation – the camera. It's true what they say. The camera steals the soul (none of us has any left by the end), and while I don't much care for the silly stories with their tiresome captions, I love the old silent movies for the life that is sucked through the lens and somehow branded on the celluloid.

These frozen moments are forgotten in cupboards and attics only to come alive again years later when the light burns through them at Roddy McDowall's screening room in the valley. (Dead. They're all dead.)

One summer night in the early eighties, sitting in the cool dusk after an early supper between Luise Rainer and Gregory Peck, their upturned faces bathed in the film's flickering reflection, the anxious present fell away, just for a moment, as all the fun and innocence – the whole smell of Southern California at the turn of the twentieth century – came tumbling into the room. I sat between these two gods, bored and twitchy – much more entranced with my new friends in the Brat Pack than by these marooned fossils.

'How effortless it all seems,' sang Roddy dreamily, the smoke from his cigarette curling through the projector's beam.

'It wasn't,' replied Luise, curtly.

'But you know what I mean, dear.'

'I'm not sure that I do, dear.'

'Well. Someone invests the money. Not much. Someone else knows the actors. Someone knocks together a set. Around the corner, actually, on Fryman Canyon. The cameraman owns the machine. The film is shot on Monday and finished by Friday.'

Luise Rainer was not convinced. I looked at my watch.

'Maybe. But you know, dear, this was all before my time. I am not THAT old,' she said with a laugh, patting Roddy's hand.

'Even later,' mused Roddy, 'when things became more regimented, Orson only called Marlene on the morning of the shoot and suggested she play the role of the gypsy in *A Touch of Evil.*' Thrilled, that lady rushed over to Paramount, where Travis Banton lent her some wigs and a costume before driving to the Mexican border, arriving on the set and jumping straight out of the car into one of her quirkiest performances. Her best, actually.

(Things have certainly changed since then. Today's siren would need hair and make-up, script approval, a deal memo replete with back end and perks – trailers and transport, assistants and dog walkers, gardeners and their brothers – all negotiated before getting out of bed.)

'The camera certainly stole her soul,' I ventured.

'Stole? She couldn't give it away. I don't think she was getting a lot of offers at that point. She was quite hard work, you know. She turned people off,' quipped Roddy.

'Do you know Barry Navidi?' Greg asked Roddy.

'Over at Fox? Nice guy.'

'I'm pitching an idea to him tomorrow.'

'Aren't you a bit old to be pitching ideas at the studio?' sniggered Luise, to squawks of disapproval from the room.

The debate continued as the night closed in. Luise looked bored. Gregory Peck had a tendency to go on a bit and his wife wore a huge hat that seemed to slip down her face until only the lips were left.

Roddy went around the room turning on lights, and Gregory's melodious ideas were the only noise.

According to him (he spoke slowly and deliberately, a beautiful voice that nevertheless sent one into a coma) film-makers suffocated by the sound stage and the back lot set off for the furthest frontiers of the world – 'like modern day explorers'.

'Whaddayamean? They were getting away from their wives,' broke in the ever practical Luise.

Either way John Huston, Humphrey Bogart and Katharine Hepburn went up the Congo on *The African Queen*. 'And then it all went too far when Francis (only Christian names and first words) lost his marbles in Manila making *Apocalypse*.'

'Really?' We were all bored, and Luise started gathering her things.

'At one point someone tried to fuck a chicken. I can't remember who.'

'You mean some kid? That's not so very unusual,' scoffed Luise.

'No, dear. A chicken. Of the cluck-cluck variety.'

Now she got more interested. 'Really? Who?'

Looking back – all of us looking back, me now on them, them on the whole thing – I am full of regret. Although always polite, I was inwardly dismissive of these beached whales. I would regale my young peers the next morning with stories of colostomy bags gurgling and wigs slipping, missing the main point – the touching elegance of their struggle to keep going. Little did I know; within the flick of a lively old rug I would be in the same position as they – only much less idolic/idyllic.

But perhaps regret is what gives memory its divine kick, its phosphorescent quality. Looking back now, that June night glows like the stage in a darkened theatre. Silently the curtain comes up and the last bittersweet act of a forgotten drawing room comedy is a dot of light from a back seat in the gods.

Roddy helped Luise into her car. They were having lunch at the Polo Lounge the next day to discuss an idea. I went back to a bed on the landing of my friend's house in Hollywood, for another sleepless night longing for something to happen. Nothing did, not then. That's life. Things come and go on the tide. Even immortality is not for ever! I'm still waiting. Still pitching, like them, making grandiose plans. I am a toothless old chihuahua from the circus in a neck scarf and captain's hat.

That's how it feels as this year – 2015 – begins. I am full of doubt. Am I strong enough to pull Oscar Wilde through the cat flap and onto the screen? Is my script good enough? Is this a desperate last-ditch ego trip or a divine intervention? Either way it has hijacked the rest of my life, not to mention my career, which has definitely hit the 'where are they now' category. The unseen waves seethe and recede. The one I'm on is taking me further and further out, past the windward isles around the cape, next stop Perdu.

CHAPTER FIFTEEN

Kieran O'Knightley Goes to Venice

My nom de plume when travelling abroad is Kieran O'Knightley. As you can see I am a complicated animal these days – a long-toothed, lesser-spotted show business queen – and I have developed a tendency to shun the world. (I met everyone and they all turned out to be the same person. Then I got bored with the person.)

Unfortunately I have also developed a fixed taste for the good life, but the tiny principality of show business in which I am still crown princess produces a spiral of diminishing returns, and so I have taken to skulking around the world off-season – and on a tight budget. When everyone else is busy doing fabulous things – taking the kiddies back to school, going to Clouds for a winter top-up or simply churning out one fabulous film after another – I am on the night train to Venice with a picnic from Fouquet's and a tramadol. (Don't take this train, by the way. It is a disease trap.)

Miss O'Knightley attacks the ski slopes of Kitzbühel in early January – term time – and only heads for the hills again in August to join tribes of Orthodox Jews in St Moritz while all the other religions head for Mykonos or Syria. She takes her summer holiday during the Christmas rush. She travels by train or cargo ship, and has never been seen printing out her own boarding pass at the airport. With a melange of judicious timing and casual name-dropping, she has learnt over the years to score remarkable deals at all the best hotels. This winter I have set my sights on the flat black Adriatic.

The afternoon before I leave – it's early in January and the *Charlie Hebdo* massacre happened this morning – I am plodding down Frith Street with a heavy heart and I notice that the coffee shop on the corner of Old Compton Street has closed down. There is a note on the door.

'Susie says goodbye and Happy 2015' is written in sweet swirly rain-stained letters. She continues in neat block capitals. 'After 25 years my lease is not being renewed. I would like to thank all my customers for their loyalty and support throughout those years – the good and bad times we all shared. Soho is not the hub of characters it once was. However it is onwards and upwards for all of us. I am sure our paths will cross again. Saying goodbye would be too hard and bittersweet. Love, Susie'.

I read it twice, standing there in the rain as people rush by. This is how dementia begins. Frozen in front of some inexplicable piece of bad news, unable to make the next move. But that's Soho for you. Here today, gone tomorrow, mourned by a few remaining ghouls shuffling past Susie's in the rain on a January night. We are in the hands of extremists – at home and abroad.

It seems apt somehow to be going to Venice, the wedding cake of all wedding cakes, a Disney World cleared of all Susies, and perhaps the metaphor for our own sinking Europe.

I travel from London to Paris on the Eurostar bristling with policemen – where I must step away from the gloom for a moment to celebrate one of the most amazing bottoms I have seen in years. It really cheered me up. There is a future. Am I allowed to do this, I wonder, or am I being reductive, racist and sexist? It is the bottom of a glorious muscle-bound attendant. He is sweet and slightly sissy with a delicious cockney French accent and eyes in the back of his head. (You'd need them with an arse like that!) Like Marilyn, he seems to have been sewn into his uniform. His trousers strain at the seams. They can hardly contain these flexing cheeks, and my seat can hardly contain me as I topple out time and again watching him striding up and down the aisle. In the old days I would probably have hung out by the toilets in the hope of joining the Mile Low Club. But today is the first day of the end of the world – or at least that's how it feels – and so I am more in tune with the slim gloomy tomes of Jean Rhys sitting on my lap.

Paris slides by wet and deserted, street lights and traffic lights glittering in the rain that for once really does feel like a flood of tears. The city looks crushed, collapsed. I have a hushed dinner with Tom and Sabrina Stoppard, Sabrina's sister Miranda and her husband Keith Payne. The girls – twins – are sixty, and they planned the weekend months ago and none of us knows quite what to make of the fact that their big day should fall at such a dark time. I have known them since I was a teenager, so it's wonderful to be with them forty-five years later, but it is a sombre occasion, as if war had just been declared and we already know the result. The waiters at the Voltaire – normally the most fun and convivial creatures; they've all been there since I first set foot in the place in the late seventies – are white-faced and tight-lipped as they flit back and forth through the swing door to the kitchen. There are none of the usual witty asides. Conversation is murmured. The Louvre looks sad in the drizzle. The others are going to the Je Suis Charlie march at the Place de la République in the morning but my train is at noon, so we say goodbye and I walk across the bridge past the Tuileries where we all used to cruise in the old days. Now the gates are locked. Looking at the Louvre, I think of Louis XVI running through the deserted palace looking for Marie Antoinette running from the other side looking for him as the noise of the oncoming revolution echoes through the empty marble halls. That's how it feels tonight.

Venice is deserted from 5 January until Carnival. St Mark's Square is a vast drained swimming pool in need of a good scrub. Empty gondolas bob about on the canals like rows of open coffins. Beady boatmen keep a lookout for winter trade from the nearby bars. The big bells boom from the pointed towers, reverberating through the night as my water taxi takes me round that amazing corner – under the antique lamp that swings in the breeze and twinkles on the water – to the Grand Canal shrouded in mist, the lights smudged on the green water. There is an icy breeze but I stand erect at the back of the boat and we bounce about in the wake of a passing tug. The scent of salt and diesel is delicious.

We pass under the Rialto Bridge and someone shouts, 'Hi, queen!' Am I being recognised? This is an increasingly rare occurrence nowadays and I am unsure how to react. I look round. Yes.

'Ciao, Kieran!' screams a chubby Italian, waving.

How delightful. Should I jump into the water and swim over to thank him personally or should I snootily look away? I settle on a regal wave. The boatman observes through eyes like slits. Another twenty on the bill.

The Gritti Palace is one of the best hotels in the world. Actually I think it could be the best. It remains luxurious and discreet – an almost impossible combination these days. It is quite small and beautifully furnished like the inside of a jewellery box in gilt and glass, damask and marble. Unlike most of the grand hotels it has survived the obligatory refurbishment with its dignity more or less intact. The staff are from the old school, with brilliant manners, neither obsequious nor aloof.

The concierge remembers the first time I came to the hotel in 1983. 'You haven't changed,' he lies sweetly, winking.

Actually I look as if I have spent the night in prison. On the other hand, I have negotiated a rather generous deal for a single room looking over the square, so imagine my delight as I am shown to the most expensive suite in the hotel. In the game of snakes and ladders I have thrown double sixes.

'Since you are writing your book,' says the manager, throwing open a door on the first floor of the palazzo, 'we thought you might like to stay in our Somerset Maugham suite.' I grovel like a rabid Pekinese and immediately decide to stay for an extra week.

Two high coral and cream rooms hung with elaborate chandeliers look out over the Grand Canal through pointy windows. During the day the sunlight bounces off the water and shimmers on the ceiling and the chandeliers gleam. The room literally trembles with life, and that is one of the strange things about Venice. The place sometimes feels more alive than the people, the past more vivid than the present.

The bathroom is a grey marble mausoleum with a glass door to the loo. I nearly knock myself out walking into it on my first night. There are delicious bath salts by the tub, vases of roses and bowls of nectarines. It's a foamy sarcophagus, and I feel strangely immortal lying there for an hour listening to the noises of the canal – the vaporetto grinding through its gears, the water slapping and gurgling against the walls of the hotel and the odd snatch of 'O Sole Mio' from the half-hearted tenor with accordions that pass on a cluster of gondolas crammed with Chinese tourists in slow motion along the canal.

The bar downstairs is empty. Just me, the barman and Jean Rhys. I am in heaven. Once you have got used to being alone in a hotel there is no going back and each new arrival is viewed with undisguised horror, but tonight I sit in splendid isolation in that hall of mirrors, just the barman in one corner, me in the other and all the ghosts in between – Garbo and Gershwin, Coward and Cocteau – trapped and watching through the glass walls.

In the old days the Giglio gondola rank was a little cruisy. Not any more. There is a little wooden cottage where the gondoliers stand about, grumpy and flubby in their striped shirts and straw hats, making noises like primates – oyee, owoo – at their colleagues on passing boats. They show little enthusiasm as they haul the tourists onto their gondolas, and less when I ask how much it would cost to do some pictures (for this book) with a good-looking punter. (I fancy a Madonna-Like-A-Virgin moment.) My offer doesn't go down very well. The old gondoliers strut around indignantly – oyee, owoo – then come up with an insane price. (Probably the good-looking gondolier is living in Las Vegas and has to be flown over.)

Harry's Bar is the first port of call for all visitors to Venice with enough money but less imagination, and tonight is the last time I shall ever go there. It is unchanged since the twenties – except for the price. You are neatly fleeced from the moment you walk through the door. On the other hand, the waiters here are much better than the gondoliers. They are charm personified. The bar itself is judiciously placed right by the door so the first thing you see is the handsome barman beaming at you and proposing a cocktail. 'Americano, Negroni, Bellini?' Ker-ching.

With a drink in your hand you are handed along the line by another pristine and smiling waiter towards 'your special table', and soon you are gushing superlatives and ordering everything on the menu just to keep up. The place is brightly lit. The waiters all wear white jackets, bow ties and black trousers. They look marvellous clustered in groups by the bar against the canary silk walls. The place is small, intimate, a throwback to a gentler time – you think – until you realise the pasta you ordered costs nearly fifty euros. Not only that, but when it comes there are only about thirty strands of spaghetti on the plate (1.50 a strand). However, it is all beautifully presented and you may as well give yourself to the flow.

You order a glass of wine. A carafe appears. Your salad is gone in three chomps. Just in case the spell is broken, Mr Cipriani himself is wheeled in from the freezer – ancient and pristine in a dark suit and white hair. He reminds me of Mr Visconti, the war criminal from *Travels with My Aunt*. He leans politely over every table shaking hands and finger-fucking us all into submission. The bill for pasta and a mixed salad is 160 euros. Thank God polly pound is strong.

I stay in my room in the morning trying to work sitting at Somerset Maugham's desk but he isn't being enormously helpful. I don't think he approves of Jean Rhys. I stare at the busy canal, vague and directionless. A weird lethargy sets in. I stumble out at lunchtime to wander the city, down the streets where lean illegal boys from Ethiopia and Somalia brace the cold in front of the fashion houses – Gucci and Louis Vuitton, Versace and Prada – selling counterfeit handbags. These bags are spread out on the ground in front of the real thing – a gleaming mirage in the shop window – and the boys stand between them, silent, waiting. One moment of eye contact is all they need. Otherwise they are invisible. Local ladies swathed in furs walk through them. Relations with the police seem to have reached some kind of entente. A few years ago they were constantly on the run. You could see them grabbing all their stuff – three hundred pairs of shades – and sprinting off. Now they can be seen late at night sauntering home through the mist, strange tall figures, six handbags on each arm, queens who have dropped in from another planet and got the protocol wrong.

I listen to an amazing conversation in a nice little restaurant near the Rialto called Paradiso, only it isn't so Paradiso tonight. It's a tiny place on a thin dark side street with a seventy-year-old head waiter. I think he must be an aristocrat fallen on hard times. He is incredibly nice and calls me 'caro', which is sweet. The place is empty. Just me and an electric fire until an American family arrives and then an English couple from the home counties. He is corpulent in corduroy trousers and a scrubbed pink face and she is a screechy stick insect, and the old man puts them at the table next to the American family, who are eager to strike up a conversation.

They start off with me. The man catches my eye, we smile at each other and I continue with my book. (I'm on *Voyage in the Dark*.)

'Your face looks ree-allee familiar,' he says when I look up.

'I'm Kieran O'Knightley, the actor,' I reply politely and dive back into Jean.

'Tell us some of the things you have been in.'

Now there is absolutely nothing worse than being a celebrity who has to trot out his own CV. There is literally NO glamour. Nevertheless I cheerfully list my credits and they respond to each title with a puzzled shake of their wretched corn-fed heads. It would appear they've seen nothing of my work until I mention that I once wrote a travel book called *Rambles in the Balearics*.

'I love Rambo. Did they make it into a movie?'

'Alas, not yet.'

The English couple observe furiously. Undeterred, the American gentleman turns his attention to them. Introductions are made. Brandi. Ursula. Our kids. Trett. Jonathan. Common ground is located.

'Je suis Charlie,' declares the American daddy, winking and raising a clenched fist.

'Je sniff Charlie,' the pink-faced man replies languidly, before barking with laughter. The Americans join in, unsure. The stick insect senses danger.

'Actually I always loathed *Charlie Hebdo*,' expands Jonathan.

'Oh really? But don't you love freedom of speech?'

'Not really, no. I suppose you know why it's called *Charlie Hebdo*, don't you?'

'No.'

'Well, when De Gaulle died they came up with another of those ghastly unfunny-if-you-ask-me covers and the government stopped them from printing it. So they changed the name of the magazine to *Charlie Hebdo* – after De Gaulle. There's freedom of speech for you. Freedom for who?' He's bellowing now.

'Whom, darling. Freedom for whom,' corrects Ursula, nervous.

'Fuck off, darling. My wife is a world-class ball-breaker,' barks Jonathan, splashing wine into his glass.

'Well, we don't want to go to France any more,' says the American man.

'Then you absolutely mustn't,' agrees Ursula. She's in a Noël Coward play.

'It's become very difficult for Jews.' Trett.

'You think it's easy for Muslims?' Jonathan.

The patrician maître d' has collapsed on a chair by the kitchen and makes faces at me. Some more guests arrive – Italians – and the place suddenly feels electric.

'Don't get me wrong,' continues Jonathan, oblivious. 'No one deserves to be shot. Ghastly. But it was bad form doing another cover. That really was pathetic.'

'I completely disagree,' says Trett.

'You would. You lot are the reason we're in this pickle.'

'Don't listen to him. He doesn't know what he's talking about,' squawks Ursula.

And it goes on. A communal bottle of wine is ordered. The two men become competitive.

'This is just plonk.'

'We like it.'

Ursula and Brandi grow rigid as only good wives can. The Italians murmur. Jonathan's face turns purple. He is approaching his John Galliano moment, but the maître d' has other plans and the bill is placed firmly in front of him.

'Oh. Did I ask for that?'

'I did,' snaps Ursula.

In the tiny loo I am accosted by the old waiter, white-faced and quivering.

'Signor O'Knightley. Mi dispiace. Thees is not good people. Come again tomorrow and we give you something special.'

CHAPTER SIXTEEN

February: Fifteen Million and Rising

O n my return I discover that the film has collapsed again. I
am a winterworld Don Quixote, slumped on a train criss-
crossing Europe for the Christmas season, Brussels, Berlin,
Stuttgart and Naples chasing that buxom windmill – Oscar
Wilde – waving at me from the edge of the horizon, cantering
on, over the hill and not a sign of life, tipsy on mulled wine at
another outdoor Christmas market or staggering from another
Wagnerian meeting on my way back to the hotel. Each start date
is a mirage that melts into the next start date. And I charge off
yahooing towards it.

'We definitely go in April, yeah?' says Jörg.

We get an office at the Bavaria studios but then Jörg's boss,
Frank, pulls the plug.

The problem is that a line producer from Munich called
Stefaan Schieder has budgeted the film at fourteen million
euros. No one can believe it, but since it is unclear whether we
have even raised nine million yet, the one thing we all know is
that we are standing on the edge of a cliff. Money has been spent

and it's too late to stop. Equally it may be impossible to go on. There is a black hole-ish feel to meetings and long silences with dramatic sighs on phone calls.

At the suggestion of Robert Fox, I bring in a marvellous legend of a line producer called Redmond Morris to take over. It isn't a good idea. The Germans are furious. He is too grand for my film and possibly a little too *pulpeux* I think as I climb behind him – gasping – up the six flights of stairs to the office in Munich that Jörg has rented for us all to go through the schedule. After the fourth time down that staircase Redmond tumbles, grey and sweating, from the building. 'There are some films,' he gasps, 'that just don't want to be made. This is one of them.'

We scout the locations – Germany, Belgium, ending up in Normandy – a strange caravan, standing in a row contemplating the remains of another belle époque hotel converted into flats. My mother's gardener Steve has been lent to us to drive my enormous BMW. He's part of a new economy drive, and to that end David has come in his own car with Katja and Brian Morris, the designer. We are all dirty and exhausted, in used underwear and frayed tempers. We've driven for hundreds of miles squashed together, and we fall out of the cars, knees and backs buckling in front of the Hôtel des Roches Noires in Trouville for the last visit of our (not very) grand tour. It's a clear and freezing February dusk, and for a moment my spirits rise. The tide is out and the beach is huge behind the hotel. The sky is streaked with thin black clouds and a watery sun leaks onto the horizon.

'This is where Proust stayed,' I say in a know-all-ish kind of way, but no one is particularly interested. Seagulls wheel and squeal above and one takes a shit on my head.

'What do you think, Redmond?'

When he finally speaks, he stutters as usual at the cliffhanging part. 'I'd say f-f-f-fifteen million and rising.'

'Jesus Christ!' groans Steve, who is grilled by my mother over any expenditure larger than five pounds.

At the airport we say goodbye. Redmond is going back to Ireland, Steve and I are taking the ferry to Newhaven.

'I wish I could have been more help,' he says guiltily. 'But my advice to you is to let it go. You don't want to make the film badly just for the sake of making it.'

'That's true.' I can feel tears welling up in the backs of my eyes.

Redmond – by chance – went to the same school as me and for some reason this makes me feel more pathetic.

'You see, the whole thing is wrong. Germany. Belgium. Your film doesn't take place there. You should be making it in some castle in France near a town that could double for Paris, with one location visit to Naples for exteriors. There's nearly two million in travel and hotels.'

He smiles at me. 'You're not going to listen, are you?'

'I can't. We're too far in.'

CHAPTER SEVENTEEN

The Ides of March

In March I go for a meeting in Brussels with another of my producers – Sébastien. He is responsible for the Belgian side of the film. Tall, thin and aristocratic, Sébastien reminds me of Chopin. He has a beautiful wife – older – like a sweet powdered Pekinese and during the meeting I think of him playing nocturnes to her under the full moon.

Unbeknown to me, I am coming down with pneumonia. For the time being it just feels as if I am walking around in a fog. In a moment of deep treachery – or is it fever – I suggest a palace coup against the German producers.

'Why don't you take over the film?' I ask Sébastien.

There is a moment of silence.

'Sure,' says Sébastien evenly. 'It's not a problem.'

You get what you want in the form that you deserve.

I return home and am sicker than I have ever been in my life.

CHAPTER EIGHTEEN

April and the Ornithologist

Low, long and suburban, in oatmeal pebble-dash under a slate roof, The Nare Hotel – five and a half stars and counting – crouched over a huge Cornish beach. The dining room was all windows, and the magnificent view stretched out in all directions observed glassily by an ancient clientele at candlelit tables draped in pink and white linen, puffy clouds hovering against the dusk.

The whole thing was like an upmarket rest home, or a residential hotel from the old days. The heating was on at full blast. A grandfather clock chimed cosily in the hall. The room rate included breakfast, dinner and afternoon tea. Scones and cake were served in the drawing room at four thirty with clotted cream and canned conversation.

The owner was a blond called Toby – ex-navy – and the place was run with military precision. Everyone had their table. We all murmured 'Good evening' and 'How was your day?' as we were seated with great attention by the sweet Romanian and Slovakian waiters, a crew cut brigade in tartan cummerbunds, white shirts and waistcoats. Their sergeant majors were a couple of young Englishmen – queens, I presumed, but you never knew these days – and above them in the chain of command were two lady generals, Barbara and Alex, in navy-blue suits, a formidable duo in their sixties.

At the table next to me sat a man hell-bent on communication and while I studiously buried myself in a book each night, on the other side a series of couples were at first charmed and then exasperated by the endless chatter in dreary flat tones, Northern and knowing, about local walks and gardens and of course the weather. Everyone knew there was a film being made in the vicinity and the words Judi Dench could be heard breaking on the waves of conversation that lapped against the pink linen beaches of those twenty or so candlelit kingdoms. It was a gentle soundtrack with discreet crescendos and sudden silences, the angel passing overhead perhaps, or even the grim reaper, accompanied by a rhythm section of cutlery on china, corks discreetly pulled and the crash of the ocean breaking on the rocks below. *Judi-pop-boom*. The tables and their patrician guests turned to silhouettes as the night drew in and the vague lights of faraway cargo ships moved slowly across the vast space.

In the gloom Barbara made bananas flambé on a portable kitchen unit for a table of geriatric generals and their wives. She was from war-flattened Cologne, and the old wounds had healed with strange scars. Her son died fighting for England in Afghanistan and they all knew.

'You're absolutely marvellous, Barbara,' one general said with feeling, fixing her with a fierce glittering eyeball.

'Yes. We all think so,' confirmed his tight-faced wife.

'Bravo,' agreed their friends, and they were right. She was an inspirational woman and her warmth flooded the room. With a Germanic sangfroid she liberally doused the pan with alcohol, the flames leapt to the ceiling and the guests recoiled in delighted terror. It was romantic and sad, an old-fashioned play of some sort with an indigo backdrop and a printed moon, a drama about the end of something, the struggle for life in some cases, or for the wheezing blob at the corner table just the death rattle of a dull career. At least that's how it felt after three days on standby, washed up on that beach in the freezing Cornish spring.

The film was a Hollywood extravaganza and had taken over the area. The roads were blocked. The hotels in St Austell were full of us and at night cranes with bright lights illuminated the tumbledown coastal village that was our set. It was as if a spaceship had landed and the film crew were the aliens in their quilted coats and woolly hats, their tight trousers slung with walkie-talkies, hammers, rolls of gaffer tape and all the tricks of the trade. They seethed across the night-time village talking their strange language, drawing bushes and lamps, make-up ladies and hairdressers towards a nucleus of blinding light where a scene was being prepared on a tree stump. Two actors stood in the glare – prisoners marooned by the swirling Martians – and the director sat hunched under a black canopy dressed in black, a nutty black pope from the Crab Nebula.

Tim Burton was thin and anguished and I liked him immediately. He may have had a kind of locked-in syndrome because he seemed unable to communicate in the conventional way, but it didn't matter because he exuded a touching empathy and an infectious enthusiasm that made everyone want to turn somersaults. He certainly didn't want to sit down and have a gossip, which was rather a relief in a way because I had run out of things to say. Instead he dashed around on the balls of his feet, an elf in black drainpipes, arms outstretched, long bony hands waving directions. During the day he smothered his face with sunblock so that he looked like Marcel Marceau or

The Scream by Munch. He WAS from outer space, but like all the great aliens he came in peace. He was also one of the last auteurs. His vision was absolute, unsullied by the meddling of the desert hags in Hollywood. Due to a long string of hits he was able to realise his aesthetic in the grandest possible manner, and this time I was a part of it.

Unfortunately, a very small part.

It all started when my new agent Sue told me that I had been offered a role in his latest film, *Miss Peregrine's Home for Peculiar Children.*

'I'm really pleased,' she said. 'I've been working on this for a while.'

This is the kind of sentence with which a show business agent often peppers sparse news. Well, for some reason (and-I'm-not-blaming-you-Sue), I got it into my head that the character I was being offered was called Mr Barron. How I would have known the name Mr Barron if no one had said it to me is anyone's guess, but anyway I gloomily set about reading the script one night in bed. My long-suffering boyfriend, Babinho – lying beside me – was more excited than me.

'Trust me,' I groaned. 'It's going to be one line.'

'Maybe not. Maybe Tim Burton loves you.'

'I very much doubt it,' I snapped and Babinho sighed, returning his attention to the great god Face Booky flickering from his iPhone.

Well, I couldn't believe my eyes. Mr Barron was a rather good part. Actually it was a very good part. Someone had edited the script – it was too long – and it was obvious they had cut out a lot of his dialogue, but some of it could easily be replaced and then, well, next stop Hollywood. Someone once said there are no small parts, just small actors. I disagree. You can bash your head against the brick wall of a bad part and no one will notice, whereas a good part in a good script is like driving a Rolls-Royce over a cliff. There's bound to be an explosion of some sort. You can't go wrong.

So one wet evening in March I arrived at Tim Burton's office in Belsize Park and the door was opened by a legendary casting witch called Susie Figgis. We sat down on a leather couch in a big empty studio where our bottoms made embarrassing sounds against the cushions, and she informed me with shining eyes that Tim was looking for the 'real thing' for this role 'and that's why we want you!'

'Oh, great,' I replied. 'Super.' When someone refers to you as the 'real thing', look busy because they are usually being reductive. You can't necessarily act but you 'are' the part anyway. A little alarm bell tinkled and I wondered what about me was the real thing for Mr Barron. He was an alien – a 'peculiar'. I suppose I was, too? Or maybe Babinho was right after all. Maybe Tim Burton actually liked me. This hardly seemed possible. Meanwhile Susie and I chatted amiably about Catholicism. She had been at a convent in India; I at a monastery in Yorkshire. She always wanted to be a casting director. I wanted to be Saint Bernadette.

'Oh really?'

'Yes, completely.'

'Did you perform any miracles?'

'I'm here, aren't I?'

Tee-hee-hee and Tim arrived, a bundle of raw energy, and took me out to see some gravestones in the garden. The house once belonged to Arthur Rackham.

'Tim. Are you really offering me this part?' I asked, incredulous.

'Yes.' He laughed.

'I don't have to audition?'

'No, of course not.'

I was overwhelmed. I hadn't been offered a good part in at

least five years. Not a really good part. We went back into the house and the three of us sat there and I began to talk about Mr Barron. I was giddy with excitement. Tim seemed to love everything I said. 'That's so true,' he screamed, pointing at Susie victoriously.

'Wait!' screamed Susie back.

'I just felt reading the script that his character completely disappeared once they got to Blackpool,' I continued smoothly.

'Exactly,' gasped Tim.

'Stop!' shouted Susie, and we both looked round.

'You're not playing Mr Barron,' she cried, breathless. 'Your part is the Ornithologist.'

Silence. Freeze-frame. They both looked at me, smiling, eyes glittering. I couldn't even remember the Ornithologist.

'Samuel L. Jackson is playing Mr Barron,' said Tim apologetically after an appropriate pause.

Thank God for being a hooray. I slammed into dinner party overdrive.

'Oh well, of course, yes. How silly of me. He's absolutely marvellous. Golly. I'm sure the Ornithologist will be very exciting too.'

'Oh, yes,' agreed Tim. 'He's absolutely perfect. He does everything right. He's a typical English gentleman.'

'The real thing, you mean?'

'Exactly.' Talentless Toff. I was right.

'Great. Well, let me have a read again, because honestly I can't really remember him that well.' I artfully funnelled a sob into a burp and beat a hasty retreat.

My phone rang as soon as I hit the street. It was Sue. 'Susie just called me. She told me there was some confusion with the role.'

'Some confusion? Yes. You told me I was up for Mr Barron.'

'No. It was always the Ornithologist.'

'Well, I do get things wrong sometimes, but this is very peculiar.'

'Maybe someone at the studio told you the role was Mr Barron,' ventured Sue cautiously.

'No.'

'Well it certainly wasn't me.'

'No, of course not.'

Back in bed that night my previous suspicions were confirmed.

'You see, Babinho? It IS just one line after all. Well, ten actually.'

To add insult to injury the character was described as being in his thirties and very athletic.

In reality I was approaching fifty-six and had just developed walking pneumonia.

'Sue,' I wanted to say on the phone the next day, 'aside from the fact that IF anyone had ever said the actual word "ornithologist" I would have remembered it, in the script this Ornithologist is thirty years old. It seems strange that you have been working on getting me this job since Christmas and never once did you think of saying, Oh, by the way, Rupert, ignore the fact that there is only one line and he's thirty and athletic. That's all going to change.' I rambled on like this, seething with impotent fury, lying rigid in bed – this is what we actors did – but on the phone the next day I took the easy option. Sue and I had just started. It couldn't go wrong right out of the stable.

'There's not much there to get your teeth into,' I whined carefully.

'The role has been cut.' Sue was decisive, famously so.

'I mean, I would never do such a small part.'

'Really?' she chirruped. 'I don't want to force you.'

'Good. Because I'm not doing it.'

She knew I would and a month later there I was, dining on the crumbling cliff.

Actually I really enjoyed the job, and the role of the Ornithologist was a real character. I made my entrance from a tent in a trilby and plus fours and I loved Tim Burton. He was a one-off, extremely kind, sensitive to us actors. If he gave you a note he always took you aside, away from the others. He was the film and the film was him. He loved seeing it take shape at that snail's pace, moment by moment, dashing around the group when a take went well, beaming and waving, or wringing his hands when it went wrong.

I was engaged to wait for two weeks even though I was in no more than a couple of scenes, so I sat on the cliff waiting and wondering while more old upper-class couples arrived as if for some secret spring solstice of discreet good manners.

I left the hotel at dawn and walked home from the location every afternoon across the cliffs. I stopped halfway at a little pub called the Ship in another village where – slightly sheepish – I revelled in being treated like Hollywood royalty. I didn't have the heart to tell them I only had one line. A girl with a cough like mine served behind the bar and a good-looking boy made scampi in the kitchen while I sat in a bay window and watched the trees struggling towards spring, the naked branches sprayed finally with that strange mossy haze.

I was reading Mary Renault's trilogy about Alexander the Great and spent hours wondering about that curious lesbian (Mary, not Alexander). According to Philip Prowse she hated women. She seemed to revel in underage gay sex. If the books had been written now she would have been clapped in irons. It was all very Operation Yewtree. Musing about the shifting moral tone in the birdlife on our island occupied my solitary hours on the beach, or sitting in that pub window, when I was not being the Ornithologist.

The two actors on the tree stump were called Asa Butterfield and Chris O'Dowd. They were the stars of the show. Father and son. Chris O'Dowd played the father. Initially I had confused him with Chris O'Donnell – the star of one of my favourite films, *Blue Lagoon* – and I was very much looking forward to seeing how he had aged. Those stunning Californian blonds normally shrivel to prunes in their early thirties, and end up looking more like janitors than movie stars by the time they hit their fifties. What had he been doing since *Blue Lagoon 2*, I wondered excitedly on my first day. I was dying to find out.

Well, for one thing he had grown about two feet. That was when I realised I had got my wires crossed. Chris O'Dowd was the Irish giant from *The IT Crowd*. He stayed in character all day, talking like an American general. His voice boomed across the set. Was this even Chris O'Dowd? Just when I thought I was going mad, he reverted to his natural brogue and became himself as we got into a car at the end of the day and headed back to the base.

It is definitely much easier to stay in character on a film set, particularly if you are attempting a foreign accent, but much harder for anyone wishing to have a normal conversation with you. Who am I talking to? Can I say, 'We're all going out for a curry later on, do you want to come?' Not really, because he must answer in character and his character doesn't know you, only your character and your character probably wouldn't be going for a curry anyway. It's all very complex and gets the intended reaction, which is that people tend to leave you alone and so the general strode around in splendid isolation.

Our base was a vast camp of gigantic tents and trailers, mine being the biggest one I had ever had – bigger than the trailers of my heyday – and this made me feel even more unhinged, as if I was in some dream where nothing made sense. Trailers are one of the things that differentiate actors from each other, a yardstick with which to measure our importance/impotence on the set. Once we've seen our trailer we know who we are. Tim's had an AstroTurf garden with a white plastic table and two chairs surrounded by a mesh wall. Samuel L. Jackson's had a kind of second floor and went on forever. I had braced myself for a three-way – one of those little cages with a couch for the young and unimportant that I actually quite liked and had got used to – they were cosy and you could lie there with the door open and watch the world go by like a dog in a travelling cage. But I found myself in a prefab palace with a granite kitchen nook, an upholstered leather couch, a vast bedroom and an electric armchair that reclined and shot back up at the touch of a button, throwing one across the room and onto the set. Outside, jeeps and trucks zoomed by and a lovely French assistant balanced cappuccinos on a tray.

The whole thing was a convention, or an army manoeuvre, with General O'Dowd striding around with the volume on full blast and Tim peeking from the shadows of his tabernacle.

General O'Dowd's son in the film was Asa Butterfield, not to be confused with Ada Butterfield, the cleaning lady with the quivering chins from the 'Mrs Harris' books of the fifties. (I worshipped those books.) ASA had been a child actor and turned eighteen on the film. He was tall and terribly thin with large blue saucers for eyes that stared out solemnly under a thatch of black hair. He was the director's muse, a glamorised version of Tim Burton himself. He had a strange poise and must have grown late and fast. His legs were stilts. He was the latest in the new aesthetic craze for geeks. Asa's delivery was flat and detached, from the school of Andy Warhol, but it had a certain weird intensity that was all about good screen acting. He certainly knew what he was doing.

Watching Tim direct him was rather touching. Tim's shock of black hair had thinned and greyed and waved hopelessly at

Asa's sleek thatch; Tim's face was taut, drained of youth. Asa's was an alabaster vase, prettier perhaps – this was Hollywood, after all – but with the same strange other-worldliness, the locked-in syndrome, an extraordinary and timid creature hiding on the other side of round blue eyes. Tim should have played the father in a way because Chris and Asa looked as though they came from different planets, but maybe that was the point.

Standing there by the tree stump in the magic night light of movies with its horror film mist, the scene was enchanting. Asa was a Martian beauty and Chris a bewildered earthling. Tim dashed around them on tiptoe, adjusting and observing, directing in whispers and the whole scene was utterly brilliant before it even began. I watched from my new position – the shadows.

The script supervisor was a lady of a certain age with waffled hair under a baseball hat that whipped around her face in the sea breeze. She came up to me on the second day.

'You don't remember me, do you? You once saved me from being raped.'

'Really. How awful. I mean, how great.' It had completely slipped my mind.

'You probably do that sort of thing all the time.' She laughed.

'Yes. Every day. Where was it? When?'

'In Dubrovnik. On *Arthur the King*. This man was trying to force his way into my room and you came along the passage and saw what was going on and got rid of him. He was one of those drunks from that bar downstairs. Don't you remember?'

I looked at her closely. She had piercing eyes and pointed lips – jungle red. She was about my age. 'You must have been a very young script supervisor.'

'It was my first job.'

'Mine too.'

'Well. We're still here. I should have stopped years ago.'

'Me too.' We both laughed. Then someone called her.

'Nicky! Tim wants you.'

'Excuse me,' she said and went off towards the director.

Nicky.

I stood on my mark while they set up the shot and watched her as she worked, rummaging through my brain for any surviving images from *Arthur the King*. Out of the gloom flickered the director, tiny Clive Donner with his smiling face and jaunty little sailor cap. Certainly I would never forget Malcolm McDowell, who played King Arthur. His two bug eyes appeared sharp and sudden, blue and bloodshot. He fell asleep, after all, in the middle of my big speech over his dead body. One doesn't forget a slight like that.

'As long as men dream, your legend shall live on,' I had whispered as Lancelot, with all the Garbo-like intensity I could muster. Snore.

Now I could see that sleazy bar in the basement of the hotel with its big leather bar stools and Eastern bloc pop music where the local lotharios sat, handsome Bosnian giants with enormous hands and noses and all the trimmings. They cruised the tourists in the summer months and dealt us weed and coke in winter.

I could remember the scandal of the paper cups ... and suddenly there she was, peeping out from behind a bush. But the lips weren't so smiley or red in those days.

'Nicky, darling?' someone shouted across the gulf of time.

We were sitting in a garden on the fortified walls of a castle in Dubrovnik. It was September 1982, my first job. Four actors in a row. All dressed as Knights of the Round Table, taking part in a miniseries called *Arthur the King*. We were trussed up in tights, boots, tunics and swords. Our King was at one end wearing a lavishly jewelled crown. He was Malcolm McDowell. His sidekick on the film sat next to him. His name was Patrick

Ryecart. We queens nicknamed him the Duke of Darling. He had a booming voice, suspiciously blond curly hair and limpid eyes, pale blue in a ring of mist surrounded by clockwork orange eyelashes (dyed).

Next to him sat Philip Sayer – now dead – all in black with raven hair and a nose like a hawk. He was one of the villains and the funniest actor in the group. An ornate raft had just appeared in the sea to transfer Arthur to Avalon. One of the barge ladies (girls imported from the latest Bond film) had just looked at Philip's costume and asked, ''Ere. Are those theatrical boots?'

'Yes,' he replied without a flicker. 'They say "hello darling, are you working" when you open the box.'

I sat next to him. We were friends from before and – this being my first job – I clung to him, and he was the other half of 'we queens'. The rest were all straight and we queens were cautious not to reveal too much. Philip was the barrier behind which I hid in my dealings with Patrick and Malcolm, neither of whom I liked. And they didn't like me. Something chemical, an echo from schooldays.

'Hetero hell,' Philip had declared and I repeated everything he said. However we were united by an anarchic streak concerning the film, which was unutterably trashy and that day Patrick and Malcolm had just finished secreting paper cups in the bushes to sabotage the shot.

'Nicky, darling,' bawled Patrick as the young script girl walked past. Already wearing a baseball hat. And moon boots.

'Yes, Patrick, what is it?' She was used to them ragging her and gave as good as she got. She had a serious face, concentrated.

'Darling, do you notice anything amiss with that hedge? Continuity-wise?'

'No, Patrick, I don't.'

Screams from the group.

'Really. What's that over there?' He pointed to one of the paper cups.

The art department had spent the morning studiously placing garish plastic flowers in the hedge, to which Patrick and Malcolm had taken exception. 'Clive, darling, these flowers are ridiculous,' they had shrieked and Clive waved them away.

Now Nicky looked at the hedge and those sharp continuity girl's eyes (that's what they were called in those days) located the offending cup. She dashed over and removed it.

'Ha, ha,' she said.

Soon we were in our positions to start a take. Malcolm had to pace up and down while Patrick and I were to drag Philip in and throw him at Malcolm's feet. Then the army – fifty Bosnian extras on horses – had to charge in and Malcolm was to wave Excalibur and then we all rushed off to war. It was a big scene. The first assistant – a legend called Ray Corbett – bellowed into a megaphone like a sergeant major.

'This is a very important scene. Look interested. Turn over.'

These words of wisdom were repeated in Croatian through another megaphone – to no effect – and we were off. All went according to plan and the horses were about to be waved clattering into the yard when suddenly there was a scream.

'Cuuut!' It was Nicky. Everyone looked round in shock. It was unheard of for a continuity girl to call 'Cut'.

'Then I saw another three paper cups – right in the shot. I could have killed them.' Nicky and I are having coffee during the lunch break.

'How long ago was it?'

'Thirty-three years!' We whistled and laughed and looked out to sea, as if somewhere out there that faraway roster of stars still twinkled.

'Clive Donner was a sweetheart.'

'Ahhh.'

'Quite useless though, unfortunately.'

'Gone. Did you know?'

'Yes, I did. And Jocelyn.' (Rickards, his wife, a famous costume designer from the sixties.) 'She's dead, of course.'

'Do you remember? She stayed in bed all day reading like a beached whale. They rented President Tito's summer house.'

'And HE had only just died then.' The list went on.

'And Dennis Lewiston, the DP,' giggled Nicky guiltily.

'I saw it on one of those awful lists at the end of the BAFTAs.'

'Isn't that list awful? He wasn't very good either.'

'He always had a whisky and soda at five thirty. What was the name of the costume designer?'

Neither of us could remember.

'Edward Woodward played Merlin. He's dead, of course.' Noël Coward had said his name sounded like a fart in the bath. 'I hated him because he used to make me laugh during the scenes and then complain that I was unprofessional.'

'He had his comeuppance though, if you remember, doing that magic spell that went wrong and his hands caught fire.'

'Oh God, yes.' I had forgotten that too. 'And they sprayed him with the fire extinguisher.'

'Lucy Gutteridge.'

'She was going to be the new Audrey Hepburn.'

'Too highly strung, probably. I adored her.'

'And of course, darling Philip Sayer.'

'He was the first to go.'

It could have been a scene from *French and Saunders*.

'Do you remember how Dyan Cannon would scream for hours every morning in her trailer?'

'And then appear on the set wreathed in smiles.'

'It was called scream therapy. The latest thing in Hollywood that year.'

We laughed and were silent. It was a marvellous meeting and

made the whole experience feel terribly important.

Later in the day we were just about to start a scene in the sudden blistering heat. The crew crouched around the camera. Tim was under his awning and I suddenly remembered the name of the costume designer.

'Phyllis Dalton. Alive. And living in Devon!'

Everyone looked round. Nicky winked.

CHAPTER NINETEEN

Musketeers in May

Now, as if by magic, I am back in the Eastern bloc. From *Arthur the King* to *The Three Musketeers* has taken thirty-three years, a whole lifetime to get back to the same place. What a trip! What a life. Via Goodwood, Pinewood, Hollywood(lawn) and Bollywood I am back in panto. These are the grunts and groans that lead the air hostess to enquire if I need special assistance on arrival, as the plane sinks under the clouds towards Prague in a dramatic cross-fade – from lacy waves breaking on a Cornish beach to the emerald plains of Bohemia – rolling over into the haze.

The beauty does nothing to rally my sinking spirits. Soon the obligatory Soviet tower blocks in neat rows and colours, beige and white appear next to power stations and tall chimneys, dachas in suburban woods, blinking lights and touchdown. Gravity thickens as I stagger through the airport. Gloom does that. Crushes the bones back into the earth.

The series is called *The Musketeers*.

The driver is called Dave. He plays Phil Collins on the journey into town. 'I can feel it coming in the air tonight.'

I catch myself in the wing mirror of the people carrier, my drink-thickened jaw flapping in the wind. 'Oh Lord. Oh Lo-or-ord,' sings Phil, and I join in.

'You like Phil Collins?' asks Dave.

'Not really.' He looks crushed. A visiting lady celebrity mustn't shock the local folk with her views. 'Yes, actually. Quite a lot.' He turns the volume up.

I am back in the Eastern bloc.

Later, I sit on my bed at the Mandarin Oriental Hotel looking at the rain pattering on the leaves of a solitary tree in a large garden and the terrible gloom descends. A weird promotional film plays on a loop on the TV in which a Chinese ladyboy flies back and forth across the screen on a swing; a nasal soprano sings a woeful Asian ballad. 'Chin chin chin,' she warbles as various high-life images merge with her swinging legs.

I am squeezed through the grinder onto the set via Hayley, the bouncy costume designer from Australia, a pretty girl with straight sandy hair and skintight jeans and a strange tattoo. When I ask her if I will be wearing a hat, she tells me that Jess (the producer) isn't too crazy on 'hats', or the 'period' in general and that the costumes are 'fusion'.

'As in cooking?' I ask, trying to sound withering.

'Exactly. You got it.'

In other words one foot in the period, the other in Miami. At least that's what it looks like when I arrive on set for the first day and meet Louis XIII. His outfit is a ruched Adidas track-suit. Fusion.

Hayley provides me with several crushed velvet dressing gowns and a chain of office that looks decidedly gangsta.

'Am I wearing this robe to go and visit the king?' I ask, my voice quivering.

'Ah. Yes.'

'But shouldn't I be in a uniform of some sort? I am the head of the Red Guard, after all. Not the red garter belt. Shouldn't I go to court in uniform, and not a dressing gown?'

'Good point.'

I shouldn't have asked. A few days later the uniform arrives. Now I look like a time lord from *Doctor Who*. (In the eighties.)

I had asked for a wheelchair but it has not materialised. A pair of sticks do. They are as tall as me, the sticks of a town crier. 'Hear ye, hear ye.' They are cut in half and I set off to the set.

The director is called Andy, a tiny man in a pork-pie hat. I am just about to start loathing him when I notice that he is actually brilliant and doing an amazing job. Say what you like about the script and the fusion aesthetic, but this man and his DP are shooting the shit out of the scene. It's very fast and curiously exciting. Unfortunately, no one survives bad dialogue. It is like leukaemia. It attacks every cell. Added to which it possibly doesn't help to be dressed like Hugh Hefner. On the other hand, it may end up being a plus. In my wig I look quite like Ozzy Osbourne. Maybe I shall take fusion to new heights. I have asked if my character could be on morphine. That way I can at least gag out if the acting challenges become too intense.

The other actors seem delightful and go out every night to a bar called the James Joyce, where they stay until dawn, returning to work for another day's hanky-waving. I don't know how they manage but there is a technique, which I discover while chatting with a colleague as we are standing around between shots.

'What are you doing next?' I ask.

No reply. I turn towards him. He's fast asleep. Leaning slightly this way and that. I look round – slightly aghast – this has never actually happened to me before. I knew I was boring, but this is ridiculous. I catch the director's eye. He winks. Welcome to *Musketeers*. As some dream gathers momentum, this darling actor is on the verge of crashing and wakes. His eyes open to slits.

'I might do a play,' he says.

'You might indeed, dear, but you'll need to pick up your cues,' I think but do not say.

He is amazing. He can answer questions in his sleep. He is also a lovely man and an excellent actor. On top of all this he invents the best term I have ever heard for doing a line of coke.

'You look tired,' he says to me one day. 'Would you like an amuse-nez?'

The musketeers are great hosts, very funny and they have a great attitude towards the work. They don't take it too seriously but at the same time they do it very well. All us newcomers are invited everywhere and it makes me feel suddenly proud to be an actor, and I haven't felt this way for years.

On the first day I am doing a scene with the king, played by Ryan Gage. He sweeps onto the set – he arrived this morning from London. 'They call me Elaine Paige,' he announces. (He is straight, by the way – a straight queen, that hysterical breed, like the male lesbian, the fey cis. FC. LGBTQ+FC.) He is dressed in white with long black hair and drop earrings. Large suede buckles adorn his thigh-high boots. It is a radical interpretation of the Sun Queen, and I am terribly excited and get my line wrong. I am supposed to say 'Your Majesty. He is nothing but a money lender who operates in Denmark and the Low Countries', but I quickly become confused and say

'He is a money lender who operates in Denmark and the low cunties.'

Elaine has hysterics. To such a point that after a while she can no longer look at me, and Andy begins to get edgy. Time is money, after all. We start a take. Everyone strides in. (It's all terribly butch, which is funny enough already.) Elaine and I try hard not to look at each other but at a certain point we must.

'Your Majesty,' I say, trying to think of horrible things like cancer and murder, but Elaine takes one look at my face and her lips begin to quiver. Soon she is in floods of ecstatic tears and so am I. It is impossible to explain to a civilian the mixture of agony and ecstasy when one gets the giggles on a film set. First of all the whole machine grinds to a halt. Nothing can happen if the actors can't perform and normally the crew can't see the joke, or if they can they don't find it half as funny as the poor players, for whom the hilarity gathers a sickening momentum.

Elaine and I try to pull ourselves together but the joke has taken on an hysterical dimension. I can hardly breathe. One look at Elaine makes me shake with terrified glee.

'Cuuut,' snaps Andy for the third time.

This is a disaster. Matthew the producer arrives on the set. Now there is an uncomfortable silence between takes, but it only makes things worse.

'Action,' says the director. We strain every nerve. We can't laugh again.

But of course we do. Finally Andy starts to swear and throws his script on the floor. He suggests a break and we stand around like chastised schoolboys. It doesn't help, and right at the beginning of the next take Elaine is on the floor. We never finish the scene. I feel terrible.

Our principal location is in the countryside an hour outside Prague and I travel to it in a people carrier navigated by Dave, Phil Collins blaring, in the pink-splashed dawn. The world rolls over before us, oceans of corn, Bohemia stretching for ever, the odd solitary mountain rising above it, incongruous and flat-topped, the kind of weird hump a spaceship might be seen hovering above. The corn is emerald green, thrashing around in the cool spring breeze. It turns to peroxide blonde before our very eyes as the summer comes in waves of white heat and Dave and I drive along on its crest. It's not very chic being in a people carrier, but on the other hand the windscreen is huge. I watch the view with tons of queeny gasps while Dave, chunky and misunderstood, watches the road doggedly through hooded blue eyes. He is quite moody. The seasons change but the song doesn't.

'I can feel it coming in the air tonight . . . oh yeah.' It will soon drive me insane, but for the time being (April) I sing along at the top of my voice in order to discourage any further instalments of Dave's life story. He wants to be an actor. His girlfriend has left him. He has written a script.

'Oh, no. Oh really? How awful. Good for you,' I squeak, inwardly recoiling.

Soon I have managed to add 'Native New Yorker' to our repertoire, and by June the car is throbbing with disco – 'I Love America'. 'On The Radio'. 10cc. 'You're no tramp, but you're no lady,' I scream to Dave. I want him to think I'm mad. 'Up in Harlem, down on Broadway . . . Talkin' that street talk.'

Or further down in Doksany.

Doksany is an abandoned monastery on the edge of a small village folded into the rolling cornfields. (It reminds me of family holidays in France, one of those places one beetled through on a rented mobilette aged thirteen.) A long tree-lined street, a little garage with a solitary petrol pump, pebble-dash bungalows festooned with net curtains and suddenly the monastery entrance bricked up with sandbags, a collapsing triumphal arch with saints reaching (armless) for the sky, the whole thing sagging against makeshift wooden buttresses.

Its church is a large white rococo galleon – several sizes too big for the village – its two onion towers surrounded by fluttering poplars. It is a still-functioning place of worship, but the monastery itself has been abandoned for years. It's full of dusty rooms, unopened, wallpaper peeling, windows broken, long halls and sweeping staircases, all collapsing. Half the place was appropriated, dismantled and drowned in vomit-green paint by the communists into a hospital or an asylum and then that too was abandoned. In the faded church the putti still hang on by their fingernails to the crumbling lightning bolts of plaster above an altar, but it's only a matter of time. More special needs saints support another, lopsided altar. Under the church vast underworlds of vaulted cellars are full of silent screams and perfect for the late-night tavern and brawling sequences in which the musketeers specialise.

In short, Doksany is a film-maker's dream. I could make my whole film here. The production has built its own back lot, a weird wonky medieval Paris that leans cleverly onto the sinking building in streets and courtyards, a barracks and even a river. It's very impressive. Around it swarm troops of local extras in ill-fitting jerkins, looking grumpy.

In July we move to a town called Osek on the Bavarian border, a dilapidated spa, fashionable in 1914. Wide tree-lined avenues, crumbling villas, a theatre and a beautiful park filled with Muslims at dusk, at least two thousand people sitting in circles, men cross-legged on the ground in shalwar trousers and waistcoats, black-sheathed women nearby on chairs stoically knitting, only their hands and faces visible in the gloaming. Children scream around waving sparklers. Old men on sticks are escorted in slow motion by veiled women along paths laced with pretty lamps, which – as if on cue – light up as we enter the park. We are suddenly very visible, but there's nothing for it. We are on our way to a restaurant in the fairy-lit pagoda by the lake and gingerly make our way past circle after circle, the girls suddenly aware, like Eve, of their bare arms and low-cut T-shirts.

In the pagoda we get the giggles. It is an aquarium and the whole park is looking down on us. Through the windows the scene looks biblical, more like the feeding of the five thousand than afternoon tea in a pleasure garden. We are literally marooned. At a certain point the young boys seem to be running round and round waving their sparklers.

I meet my death in Episode Six – the best written of the series so far – at the hands of my own protégé, Grimaud. He is played by a brilliant actor called Matthew McNulty. He kills me in the small orchard of another derelict monastery before the whole of my Red Guard – twenty Czech extras standing around looking bored.

'Would they just stand there and let me be killed?' I ask Nick Not Normal, the director. He too is a genius, very eccentric. I have loved working with him. 'One is, after all, their chief.'

'Darling, it's too late to stage a revolt. And anyway, they might save you. And then what?'

'Good point.'

I am almost totally crippled by now from osteoporosis and hobble about with the help of two sticks, but I still manage an assassination attempt on my half-brother the king, shortly before my own execution. Elaine is in some sort of travelling cape for the scene and looks rather like the singing nun or Bilbo Baggins, but we are past the laughing stage by now. We are in the royal crypt on the anniversary of our father's death and Elaine shows me a special tomb that she has had knocked up for me. I am suitably thrilled. As a bastard I never expected to be buried en famille. It is quite a weird scene. I decide NOT to kill him, thereby signing my own death warrant.

Gallantly I hobble out into the noon blaze and death, observed drearily by my merry men. 'This is my time,' I tell Grimaud, and I throw myself onto his sword. Ozzy Osbourne goes down. I wriggle to a tree, sit against the trunk, fire a warning shot from a tiny lady's pistol I seem to have about my person and slump forward, a position in which I have to spend the rest of the afternoon as first the musketeers gallop up, then the king, and then my other sidekick Matt Stokoe, who plays my second in command, Georges. He is another brilliant actor and is very upset by my death. He places his red leather cloak over me as if I am a parrot being put to bed, and that is the end of Feron.

I lie there feeling foolishly proud of our gang of baddies, me, Grimaud and Georges, and even if my death wasn't the swash-buckling scene played from a bath chair that I had proposed to the producers I feel strangely fulfilled sitting there under the cloak, listening to them all talking about me.

'He wasn't all bad,' one Musky says.

'Thanks, Tom,' I whisper.

'A state funeral,' chimes the king.

Gasps all round. All's well that ends well and I settle down for a small snooze while the scene plays out for the rest of the afternoon.

I have loved doing *Musketeers*.

PART THREE

CHAPTER TWENTY

A Year Later, June 2016

L ights. Camera. Action. The film is finally set to go.
I just have to tour *The Judas Kiss* to Toronto and New
York, and then I fly to Munich to start pre-production – straight
from the stage to the airport to the café next to our hotel in
Munich to meet my TEAM.

I am waiting with David, numb with jet lag, staring into the
middle distance when suddenly I realise that the café is actually
a gay bar.

'So it is,' laughs David, unconcerned. Neither of us is wearing
our glasses and it's quite dark. I quickly put mine on. Gasp. An
older crowd swims through the shadows in beards and plaid
shirts and leather braces. A covey of off-duty drag queens are
playing up at the bar.

'Not a very serious place to conduct our first meeting. Maybe
we should go somewhere else?' I whine.

'Too late,' says David, pointing to the door.

John Conroy has arrived. He is my director of photography,
a huge Irish rugby player with a shaggy beard, thick black hair

and menacing blue eyes. He might have stepped off a medieval tombstone. His jersey looks like chain mail. He lumbers into the room and everyone turns. We wave sheepishly from the corner but he makes for the bar instead. The noisy drag queens are like parrots on their stools, suddenly taut, heads cocked, silent and staring as John approaches, then suddenly screeching into action as he orders a drink.

'Ich denke ein fick kompt nicht in frage, schatzi?' one trills, while the other offers simultaneous translation. 'Is one schtooping out of the question, dearest?'

John's droopy eyes give nothing away. He may be about to headbutt them. It's hard to say. 'I'm sorry, I don't speak German,' he replies, and now his gaffer, a compact cockney with a ponytail called Charley Cox appears. I fold into myself.

'Ees your boyfriend,' a parrot shrieks, pencilled eyebrows darting.

'We work together.' Squawks of laughter and flapping of wings. I break into a cold sweat.

'Oooh. Éducation anglaise!'

'Irlandaise, actually.' And now John is laughing too.

I hardly know John at this point. Does he have a sense of humour? Is he a homophobe? Probably not, because now he's buying the drag queens a drink and with a gigantic sigh of relief I have one of those strange out-of-body feelings – a kind of short circuit where the scene freezes and the sound cuts out. Just a strange ringing and I'm floating above it all, this moment and the whole adventure – it's already happened and I suddenly know it's going to work out. For a second I can feel the hand of God (hashtag He too).

John and I are polar opposites. He is patient and kind until he rears up, which he can do quite suddenly, while I come in screaming and then collapse like Uriah Heep. He loves football and rugby. He's a man's man surrounded by a coven of plotting queens. The droopy eyes are hard to read but so far he seems to be amused by our antics, unshockable, easy-going in that way the Irish are and the English often are not. He is the father of five children – separated from their mother – with a beautiful girlfriend called Yvonne and they're all coming over. He has a Herculean tenacity and will carry our film like the ball in a rugby game, barging through all obstacles towards the touchline, dragging me along with him. He only gets angry with me once. But this is all for the future. For the time being I say 'John, I hope you don't mind. This seems to be a gay bar. I had no idea.' I am gabbling like a vicar's wife passing round the nibbles.

'Jaysus,' he replies, regarding me evenly with the headbutting eyes. 'If you don't know ... then we're up shit creek without a paddle.'

'Oh, really?' I titter nervously.

Now Brian Morris our curious production designer sidles in, like a crab, scuttling across the bar. He peeps out from behind a cluster of men, sees us waving (more waving) and laughs. He designed the first film I was ever in and here he is, neat and pristine, still going at seventy-eight. He has arrived in his own light aircraft, the Biggles of the design world, not wearing goggles but his rimless glasses glint weirdly in the light. Invisible behind them lurk two large blue saucers of disbelief with leaky ducts that occasionally release a gigantic tear.

'Only you could have a production meeting in a leather bar, dear.'

'Don't! I think John is a little shocked.'

'Well, she'd better get used to it.'

'How was the flight?'

'A little bumpy. We ran out of gas and had to touch down in Cologne.'

'God. How terrible. What a business.'

'It was a gayday mayday.'

Brian is wry and funny and essentially Northern, a legendary figure from a bygone cinematic age with a background in rationing and advertising, a few of my favourite things. He designed all the

Daz commercials and also my first film, *Another Country*. He was at Salford Art College in the late fifties, arriving in London at the same time as Ossie Clark and Celia Birtwell, his billing at that point being one name on a cluster of buzzers at the front door of the damp and peeling Notting Hill villa where they all lived. He was an integral part of the whole look of British films in the eighties. Call it Hovis if you're being reductive like Philip Prowse, who knew Brian from those early days in Ladbroke Grove, but it's a look that I love.

I introduce everyone and we all settle down. Spirits are high and I have to pinch myself to make sure I'm not dreaming. Watching us all (outside again – it's probably the jet lag) I suddenly realise that's me in the middle. They are all looking at ME. Waiting for some direction.

Brian loves humming. In awkward moments and tense silences he resorts to music. Dum dum doo doo di dah dah. Watching now, I notice he has another strange habit. In the middle of a sentence he stops dead in his tracks and mimes the rest with his hands, followed by a wide-eyed 'hey presto' expression on his face. 'You see?' he exclaims afterwards, and of course nobody does. Maybe that's the point. He is a genius and can run rings round us all. One of the Germans mispronounces his name one day, calling him Brains. It's the perfect name.

Maurizio Millenotti and Gianni Casalnuovo are the Italians of the group. They are designing the costumes and are both quite highly strung. Maurizio is nearly seventy, always wears a skullcap and has beautiful black eyes with clockwork orange lashes. Gianni – younger – was his assistant but now they are designing the costumes together. His nickname is Gianni Vagina.

I have worked with them both many times over the years and we have only had one big falling-out – over a tiny thing, or so I thought at the time – during a scene in *The Importance of Being Earnest*. I wanted to look like Cary Grant and wear my shirt collar over the lapel of my jacket. Big mistake. Maurizio didn't

talk to me for two years, and things have never been the same –
the proof being that he has tried to wriggle out of this movie on
several occasions. I have had great difficulty wrangling him back
into the herd. But he is one of my oldest friends, so eventually I
manage. His proviso: that Gianni co-design the film.

Maurizio is a Gemini like me so you never know what new
resentment he could be harbouring. In character he switches from
Auntie Mame (very extravagant, always paying, no money) to *Sunset
Boulevard* (plotting diva, the movies got smaller). To make matters
worse Gianni's poodle Nero is at death's door, staggering around
the fitting room at Tirelli's costume house in Rome so that his
mistress is a little bit absent-minded. He stuck a pin in me just last
week, narrowly missing my jugular vein. In my new role as project
manager I must try to soothe their nerves and make them happy.

We move to another bar where the producers are congregated
and David's boyfriend Willy, the unpaid (everyone's unpaid)
unit photographer takes the first picture. In it we are happy and
jangly around a table under a blurred string of lights hanging
between two trees. Inside football blares on a TV, throwing its
weird green light over a crush of upturned faces that suddenly
explode with cheers and screams. The English are being mas-
sacred by the German team in the European Cup. Not a very
promising start. Next stop, Brexit.

These matches are the soundtrack of our summer as we congregate outside other bars in other towns and our film slowly
begins to take shape – like a time-release photograph – all the
sketches and photographs unfolding into empty rooms and
streets filled with cars, while the rest is conjured up in feverish
conversations and waving arms in bar after bar, as the football
plays on and goal after goal is scored by any team but ours. The
crowds go mad and I have another fabulous idea!

I say conversations, because the first thing that strikes me tonight
under the coloured lights is that nobody understands a word anyone

else is saying. Toby the first assistant is explaining something to the Belgians, but phrases like 'What we're hoping to achieve here' always flummox the practitioners of the romance tongues, particularly if they are being delivered in a Bugs Bunny voice.

Toby is marvellous and reminds me a bit of Marty Feldman in *Young Frankenstein* (without the hump). He should be in music hall, but unfortunately for him he is stuck in the role of first assistant. At the drop of a hat he turns into a cartoon character. Suddenly his eyes are on stalks, his jaw rotates and he goes into a kind of yubba-dubba-doo delivery which I adore, but I can see the faces of our European friends begin to look slightly desperate through their encouraging smiles as they try to follow the thread of his conversation. We catch each other's eye across the table and both giggle.

'Am I being naughty?' he asks.

'Not at all, darling. They just can't understand a word you're saying.'

He looks horrified. 'What do you mean?'

'No one French understands when you say "This may sound bonkers". They don't do that kind of phraseology. You need to be more clear. "Stand over there, please". Things like that. And maybe not in a Bugs Bunny voice. That could confuse them as well.'

Toby thinks I'm joking. I am. I adore him.

Meanwhile Brian is describing something to Jörg in sign language. Jörg watches like an excited child at a magic trick. 'Know what I mean?' says Brains with the trademark eureka smile.

'Totally,' nods Jörg sagely.

'Dum dum digarry doo doo.'

Maurizio and Gianni sit on a bench like two monks who have taken the vow of silence. They are being cross-examined by Stefaan Schieder the chain-smoking line producer, who doesn't like them and is horrified by their ideas. He wanted a German costume designer.

'Absolutely NOT,' I breezed – way back, drunk and showing off at an early dinner. 'On the whole, Germans just don't DO costumes. And don't talk to me about *Das Boot*.' It always comes back to *Das Boot*. 'Some people are good at some things. Others at others.'

Stefaan doesn't like me either.

Tonight Maurizio speaks exclusively in Italian – pretending he doesn't understand a word of English – very fast with huffs of exasperation and only addresses Gianni who, also wearing a skullcap, translates in a strange sing-song voice through pursed lips, staring into the middle distance – a clairvoyant relaying messages from the other side. Stefaan smokes a whole cigarette in one puff and his eyes are smashed plates of sheer horror boring into the poor Italians through the tendrils of smoke.

He leaves them and goes over to complain about what he has just learnt to Bettina our new producer from Cologne (North West Australia). She is a beautiful buxom blonde with blue eyes, a wonderful nose and a tongue stud. She has been provided to us by Sébastien the Belgian producer, who seems to have more or less disappeared. He is making a rare apparition tonight, however, crouched over his cell phone tap-tap-tapping to his parallel universe. Apparently he is doing another film and also owns a hotel in Spain. Who knew? Then he is going on a road trip across America with his family that has been booked – according to him – for ages.

'Like my film,' I remind him tersely.

'Yes, but more sure,' he replies.

This European union only has me as its interpreter. Only I know what everyone means – Brains' half-sentences and aeronautical instructions are crystal clear to me. No one understands the Italians' concerns except for me. (No one wants to.) Everybody speaks flawless English and yet they are flummoxed by Toby. I will have to explain everything to everyone. What a thought. Tomorrow we go to Franconia.

CHAPTER TWENTY-ONE

Wagner Country

A fter a terrible struggle I have managed to convince
the producers to shoot the German part of the film in
Franconia. It's a three-hour drive from Munich, which means
that either we have to find a crew out there – which is impossible – or import everyone from Munich at great expense.
However there is not a house or a wall or a cornice or a
window or a floor that is remotely usable in or around Munich.
We don't have the money to build sets and we must shoot
half the film in Bavaria. It's part of the deal with the Bavarian
fund who are bankrolling our film.

Everyone seems to have forgotten that three months ago we
had all agreed the only way was Franconia where, thanks to
Bap – a wonderful man from the tourist board – I have found
three incredible old castles, unrestored, with some decent
furniture and very good rooms in which we can create almost
everything – from our Neapolitan interiors to our Paris cafés, our
streets and slums and even the Old Bailey, as well as endless
other brothels and bedrooms, offices, workshops and dressing

rooms for the actors. It's a miracle, in fact. Not to sound like Trump, but I've done an amazing job.

'Try telling them that,' says Brains gloomily.

Working in Franconia also gives us a chance to be based in one place for the first five weeks of the shoot. IF there is a way in which I can succeed in making this film with its insane schedule, its directing and acting challenges, this is surely it. I have seen film after film fail because some poor director has been pecked to death and – totally disorientated – agrees to shoot Versailles in Vancouver. I refuse to budge. But I can see that Stefaan our line producer is already incensed by this type of insubordination from a first-time director. He wants to stay in Munich and travel to various unsuitable locations outside the city, ideally with a German hairdresser called Kurt. Every day – moving our whole operation with us like a travelling circus, costumes, props, generators and the obligatory potted palms to disguise the disabled parking space or the speed bump – everything crammed into the backs of trucks, three days here, two days there in my opinion is a recipe for disaster. In the opinion of Maurizio and Gianni – they will walk off the film.

'You cannot work from the back of a truck,' says Gianni.

'Unless you're a prostitute,' adds Maurizio.

Franconia is a north-eastern province of Bavaria best known for Bayreuth, the birthplace of Wagner. It is Wagner country, and there is a slightly lunatic landlocked feeling as we crawl down the autobahn from Munich – David is driving at his signature snail's pace and all the flash German cars fly past at two hundred miles an hour – further and further from the sea, ploughing through the waves of forest into the haze of Central Europe, next stop Bohemia. Thick brown rivers ooze through valleys past medieval towns carved into the rocks and crowned by vast fortified castles, Coburg, Bamberg, Kronach and Kulmbach. It is

also Pinocchio country and there is a wonderful puppety feeling
to things, foaming beers on tables, bearded men in lederhosen
flapping their arms, steeply gabled houses, half-timbered, on
cobbled streets winding towards some evil king's tower. Coburg
is where our royal family flapped in from, so a lot of people look
like Prince William.

From the forest comes a thick menu of boar and venison, with
berries and cabbage. The Italians waste away. (At one point
Maurizio orders a calf's foot by mistake and nearly has a stroke.)
We move to a hotel in Bayreuth called The Golden Boar where
apparently Hitler stayed. IN MY ROOM! They are winding me
up, of course. It's too tiny for Hitler, but it IS at the end of the
corridor as described online in one of those creepy fact websites.
The hotel has been in the same family for five hundred years
but the owners pretend to know nothing.

'Which corridor? Hitler who?'

In the following week the whole crew assemble – the camera
department, the props and the set decorators. Bettina and
Stefaan open offices and the planning begins in earnest. Bettina
talks about sitting down and making some 'difficult decisions',
so I try to avoid her as much as possible. Something more in the
script is going to have to be cut. She wants to lose the exterior
of the Old Bailey where Lord Queensberry gives a speech
about family values to a rowdy crowd and a group of London
prostitutes dance a victory gig. We have planned a shot worthy
of James Wong Howe and Brian has found a great place to shoot
it – not easy in Coburg – but it's too far away and anyway we
can't afford it.

It's a big wrench, being one of two scenes where the real force
of nineteenth-century homophobia can be seen in the swarming
crowds that celebrate Oscar's sentence. The prostitutes danced
with joy that night because they thought the inverts were taking
away their trade. (Fag-haggery hadn't been pioneered by then.)

It could have been a marvellous *Day of the Locust* moment, with the crowd rocking the paddy wagon as it clattered out from the Old Bailey, Oscar looking terrified through the bars. Anyway, it's cut.

The Schloss Thurnau stands on the floor of a valley around a large cobbled yard with a fountain, and the town, built into the hill, rises like a pantomime backdrop behind it. One flank – early nineteenth century – in honey-coloured stone has been turned into a hotel. Another – slightly older, more whimsical – is a music school. Together they are the two arms that hold the derelict face of the medieval castle from caving in. Its keep, its gatehouse, its crumbling turrets all sag visibly, propped up by metal plates and wooden buttresses.

A cheap roof has been nailed on like a bad wig but underneath it's a treasure trove about to be ruined by an oatmeal renovation rising like cancer from the dungeons. But for the time being – mercifully – an old piano nobile, three floors up, has been closed and forgotten since the family moved out in the seventies. Old wallpaper hangs off the walls and pigeons nest in the gigantic fireplaces that are held up by tottering putti bearing arms but not heads. The ceilings buckle and bulge and the floors are rotten. There are sweeping spiral staircases, poky back staircases, long thin passages, secret doors to old loos replete with stone seats and chutes for shit that must have slid down the walls. There are gigantic vaulted cellars, a dried-up ditch or moat – a narrow gorge between two of the old buildings – which is going to be perfect as the set for my Parisian favela. There's always a mood in old rooms that can't be bought or painted on. The camera steals the soul and this particular house pulses with a forlorn energy. As we strip it gently away it feels as if it is giving itself to us with little sighs of falling plaster.

Meanwhile an Aladdin's cave is being assembled in another part of the village – a whole warehouse full of props – china, glass, cutlery, tablecloths, pens, watches, money and wallets, sticks and photographs, all the paraphernalia of 1900 laid out on long tables by the amazing German props team. I am thrilled.

The old border between East and West runs through Thurnau and the wardrobe department is on the other side of town in the old Eastern bloc. Once a grim gym, it is now a full-blown Italian *sartoria*, full of costumes, rail upon rail, boxes piled up to the ceilings of hats and gloves and veils, rows of shoes and boots. Six Roman seamstresses have magically appeared and sit at sewing machines all day long. They cook pasta on spirit burners for lunch.

Bettina produces the Grizzlies. They are the standby carpenters. There are about eight of them and they live in a caravan by the props warehouse. They are quite exotic, like gypsies, in cargo pants and work boots. David and I fantasise that one of them is gay but of course he's not. They have already built an enormous favela in the moat.

'Isn't it amazing,' says Brian, showing it to me on the first morning. 'These guys can do anything. They found all this old wood. They said how much do you want, so I said as much as possible.'

Stefaan Schieder doesn't see the new favela in quite the same light. He is furious. It's triple the projected size.

'But the wood just arrived from Romania. And the boys were there . . . so,' reasons Brian. 'Dum dum de doo do.'

It's all one and the same to the Grizzlies, and now they are building a treadmill for the prison sequence. Then they're going to convert the gym in the next village into a café-concert, the Old Bailey AND a gentlemen's toilet. Their leader is an Englishman called Christian who came to Germany with the army and never went back. Now he has a German accent. They are funny and sexy and generally amazing and they embody the German spirit of our film.

The Mayor and a couple of other burghers from the village are the castle's custodians – responsible for the oatmeal renovations – and appear most days as we potter about the ruins plotting our film. They watch me screaming at Brian one morning in the courtyard. As my voice bounces across the walls, Brian nudges me in the ribs.

'Bandits at two o'clock.'

'What?'

'Behind you.'

I look round and grind into reverse. These people can close us down at any moment. 'Schoon sie zu sehen mein Schatz Bürgermeister!' I say, repeating a Sally Bowles line I remember from *Goodbye to Berlin.*

They all laugh politely. They have round country faces with bright amused eyes. Apparently they need to make holes all over the castle's interior to check for termites.

'Now?' I screech. It was scheduled long ago, like Sébastien's holiday. Another expense for our haemorrhaging budget. 'You mean we must close up the holes for the shoot and open them up again afterwards?'

'Ja, ja!' They are laughing, patting me on the back.

There is a charming old-world boarding house by the church. It reminds me of the hotel in *The Lady Vanishes.* I move in when the film starts shooting and David asks the Mayor to turn off the church bells that clang every quarter of an hour through the night. More bemused smiles. The bells have rung consistently since 1640. But David pulls it off. This is enormously empowering and I feel like Elizabeth Taylor.

After work we all go to the Greek restaurant next to the castle. It has a terrace that looks over a lake with tables, benches, geraniums and a nutty waiter straight from *Trainspotting.* The weather is beautiful, a summer from childhood. As the dusk closes in on the bulrushes, the old castle and the town beyond fade prettily along with the day's problems into jagged silhouettes. Ripples on the murky lake catch the final glimmers of sun and the nutty waiter carries trays of beer, gold and foaming while the odd carp plops lazily about in the black expanse.

But there is very little 'me time' for a director. Along with the mosquitoes swarm the human bloodsuckers and they attach their feeding pumps and drain me of all remaining energy. The tree where people were hanged is now black and terribly seductive in the gloaming. Pigeons rustle in the high branches. Bettina hoots with laughter and an owl hoots back from the other side of the lake and finally everyone heads back to Bayreuth leaving me, David and Willy for one last drink before making our way to our respective boarding houses in the silent village. Theirs is by the lake. Mine is up the hill.

Walking back past all our trucks parked in rows by the castle, up the deserted cobbled streets, the tight nut of my brain suddenly expands. The moon rises and the smell of the countryside falls like a mist onto the town. Little lights glow high up in the castle and someone snores inside an open window. The shoot gets one day nearer.

I buzz around Europe like a moth on meth – London to finish the casting with Celestia Fox, then Rome for fittings with Maurizio and Gianni. On to Naples to make sure the garden at the villa is being cleared and planted. (It isn't.) Brussels to meet the strange freaks from the special effects company. Back to Munich, drive to Franconia. Turn straight around and rush back to London because suddenly there is a problem with Colin Firth's dates and maybe he can't do the movie.

CRASH. Life freezes over and the sound cuts out. Again.

Talking to Duncan Heath our mutual agent on the phone (Sue and I have parted company), my heart flutters like a trapped bird banging against my ribcage and capillaries bulge dangerously near my brain. Our whole financial plan relies on poor Frothy. I frantically get one of my in-laws to do some macumba. It's worked before and it works now.

Almost immediately I am summoned to Chiswick for breakfast. My desperate B plan is to offer Colin the smaller role of the priest and I'm ready to beg and weep but straight out he says, 'I think I can work things out. The only thing is I can't do more than two weeks.'

Two weeks? I was thinking of two days. I say nothing, of course. I just thank my in-laws and all the gods and then the tears come anyway. It's terribly humiliating and I think Frothy is rather shocked so I pull myself together, but I've never been saved or helped so much by one person before and it's overwhelming. Viva Frothy.

However I don't have time to reflect beyond wondering if I should borrow a biro and quickly scribble a contract and get him to sign it because I must rush, snuffling, back to the airport and get on another plane to meet Colin Morgan at Tirelli's costume house for a fitting. The caravan is back on track, wobbling and lurching on down the yellow brick road towards the haemorrhoid city.

I am already a nervous wreck and we haven't even started shooting. Me, who never travels anywhere for less than two weeks is rattling around Europe and I don't even have air miles. Plus it's the holidays and we are definitely in the economy section so the check-in desks are seething with angry travellers and the waiting lines snake round the block.

I stand with my wheelies while the business class passengers skim past. That used to be me, I think one day at Munich airport as I lug my two large suitcases full of winter clothes from the theatre tour onto the inspection table. The rest of our party has disappeared, leaving me to negotiate my excess baggage and now I'm getting a good frisking as a potential terrorist.

I haul open the cases under the beady eye of the security guard, a white rat with tiny red eyes and green teeth, suddenly alert as I pull out my two precious fat suits. He scrutinises, prods and squeezes their cocks. Obviously he thinks they might contain something explosive. Only my performance, I say – very Oscar – but he is not on my wavelength. He takes a swab. It's like being in the VD clinic. The other passengers are fascinated as the poor lifeless suits are put onto the conveyor belt. Officials crowd round the TV screen as they tumble obscenely through the hatch, all arms and legs. He examines my false teeth with rubber gloves and gingerly frisks my wigs as if they might be sprayed with polonium rather than Elnette. Lord, what fools these mortals be. Where is my team? My producer? They're all having a coffee in the lounge.

CHAPTER TWENTY-TWO

Tirelli's Costume House

Tirelli's costume house is on the ground floor of a faded stucco villa in the Prati district of Rome. It could be the house in *Psycho* or a mountain retreat in colonial India. The garden is slightly overgrown and one urn has fallen off the once-imposing gates. Marcello Mastroianni used to live on the first floor. His daughter Barbara lives there now.

The Bates motel theme is continued in the interior where mad costume designers with pinking shears can sometimes be seen chasing their assistants from room to room. Tirelli himself is dead, but his widow Dino Trappetti still reigns – if not with a rod of iron then with a magic wand.

He appears from the office, a shuttered mausoleum with a large polished desk and walls covered with posters and sketches, the lonely witnesses to a thousand forgotten first nights. From La Scala to Grauman's Chinese Theatre, Tirelli's costumes have travelled the world and now hang in the Tirelli warehouse, strange stained corpses waiting for reincarnation. All the dry-cleaning in the world cannot remove the sweat and tears of the tortured souls who have inhabited them. Callas. Taylor. Nureyev. Magnani. Among others.

Tirelli is the house of Tosi, the greatest costumier in the world. His rival, Danilo Donati – now dead – had his camp in the other great house – Farenni – on the other side of town. There lie the costumes of Fellini and Pasolini, while at Tirelli can be found the shrouds of such legendary films as *The Leopard, Death in Venice, Matrimonio all'italiana* and *Mamma Roma*.

Piero Tosi is eighty-nine, but when I arrive he is sitting in the atelier before a rail of clothes that has been bequeathed to the costume house by a dead contessa. Her dresses hang limp on wire hangers, straight from the cleaner's – flat and sad – but for Piero they are very much alive. Each pleat has a message, and every dart is examined with care by hands that are not long and tapering as one might imagine but with palms like slabs and the thick fingers of a *contadino*, all the more tender as – shaking slightly now – they stroke the dresses, lift the fabric, dropping it to see how it falls.

Holding a psychedelic Pucci dress from the sixties against his body, he is still wonderful-looking with sandy hair and kind blue eyes. He is quietly spoken, reserved. 'Guarda,' he gasps, discovering a rigid old ballgown, 'questa è Roberto Capucci.'

In the golden era of my dreams, Piero worked for Visconti and De Sica and shared a flat with Franco Zeffirelli – overlooking a bakery. As they partied through the night – 'non abbiamo mai dormito' – they could see reflected in the windows the glow of the baker's ovens, like lava flowing through the darkness of the street. Pasolini, Visconti, Gore Vidal, Tennessee Williams, per-haps – momentarily distracted – their faces pressed against the panes as some shirtless, much-discussed beauty shovels bread into the furnace over the road. Dawn approaches and they leave for Cinecittà, where perhaps *La Dolce Vita* is being shot, perhaps *Cleopatra* or even *The Roman Spring of Mrs Stone*. This was the world I searched for but never found. Right place. Wrong time. Story of my life. Maybe it's happening now, but as Jean Rhys remarked on being rediscovered aged sixty – it's a bit late!

Today Maurizio and Gianni are waiting for me in the fitting room. Gianni's dog Nero has gone insane and growls in the corner. His opaque eyes stare madly at all the imagined enemies and he bares his teeth at anyone who dares to approach his master.

'He's very ill,' explains Gianni.

'Hopefully it's not rabies,' I reply as we kiss and Nero sinks a rotten tooth into my ankle.

Hair and make-up are family affairs in Italy and Luigi Rocchetti and Francesco Pegoretti are royalty. Luigi owns the celebrated wigmakers Rocchetti, and Francesco is the heir apparent to the great Maria Teresa Corridoni – the undisputed global queen of hair.

They arrive with all the tricks of their trade – the curling tongs and colour charts – to turn Colin Morgan into Lord Alfred Douglas. Bosie was blond, and today we are to bleach and dye Colin's thick jet-black hair and I am breezing along in this fantasy made flesh – chatting with Piero Tosi, making lofty pronouncements about the costumes, amazed and dazzled to be conducting my own fittings at Tirelli's where over the years I have sat in the hall (waiting for Maurizio) watching the famous directors sweep by, in loden coats and flowing scarves, flanked by assistants loaded with reference books and scripts, being greeted by Gabriella Pascucci or Milena Canonero, the other two starlets of the Tirelli stable, Trappetti appearing from the office, beaming, bouffant, arms outstretched, coffee appearing by magic on a silver tray as they all settle down to laugh and reminisce about former glories in the fitting room and wait for the movie stars to stagger in from the airport.

This time that director is ME, but when Colin Morgan arrives

I discover to my horror that he has had all his hair cut off – not only cut off, but cut off in clumps – for the TV series he is currently working on. (*Humans*.) It is meant to be – and was when I saw him last – shoulder-length. I nearly faint and the bubble abruptly bursts.

Today in the huge three-way mirror Colin looks like a wonderful street urchin who has just returned from the Easter Uprising. Gorgeous as usual, size zero but definitely NOT Bosie. I stare at him aghast as he apologises about his hair. He is soft-spoken, with a wonderful accent, Belfast born, the perfect romantic actor in the Irish tradition, charming and courteous – wonderfully detached – but right now I want to kill him.

Out of the corner of my eye I can see Maurizio and Gianni go into an elaborate commedia dell'arte, making eyes at one another, shrugging their shoulders and looking at me with disgust. How can this wiry waif play Lord Alfred Douglas? I am about to break out in hives when Luigi and Francesco – who have just finished laying out, with the precision of surgeons preparing for an operation, all the instruments of blondery: the brushes, the bleach, the tinfoil, the capes and bath hats, hairdryers and scissors, all on a linen cloth – look round and, unruffled by this latest turn of events, produce from their seemingly bottomless bag of tricks an amazing wig on a stand which they have rustled up just in case.

'Don't worry,' says Luigi. More accents. 'We gonna fix everything.'

'But I don't want him to wear a wig,' I whine. 'They take so much time to get right. We won't have the time if it goes wrong.' I might cry at any moment.

'Just let's look.'

Well. The wig is amazing, and Colin is completely transformed by it. I have never seen anything like it. His whole face takes on a new dimension. His lips are pinker, fuller, decadently sensual. His face is suddenly pampered and patrician. His nose looks completely new. The hair – in three or four different shades – falls in snakes around his neck. Now Luigi applies the make-up while Francesco sticks pins in Colin's head. Maurizio and Gianni watch carefully.

'Leave the eyebrows.' I'm shouting now. They are dark and look marvellous with the wig, which Maurizio wants to cut short.

'She looks like a gypsy. Una zingara,' he hisses under his breath to Gianni – but I adore it.

Colin stands in the middle of the room watching himself in the mirrors as straw hats, top hats and felt hats appear and disappear on his head, jackets and trousers are fitted and exchanged for others and a sweet little tailor creeps in through a secret door with pins in his mouth and a tape measure round his neck. The actor is studied and prodded and discussed – always in Italian. Maurizio is quite violent, throwing a scarf around Colin's neck before ripping it off in disgust, or tugging at the bottom of a jacket so that he nearly loses his balance and collapses to the ground.

'Calmati,' says Gianni.

'CalmaTI,' replies his boss.

Bosie finally appears, like a magic trick, held together by pins and clips. It's an amazing metamorphosis, and as soon as the vision is complete it is undone, dismantled and folded away. Colin must return to the airport and in fifteen minutes he is back in the real world of clumpy black hair, in jeans and a T-shirt.

The rest of us adjourn for lunch at the restaurant round the corner. It is called Villini. Owned by the same family since 1937, three generations of them sit by the till, depending on the time of day. The grandmother and great-aunts have lunch each noon, observing grimly as their daughters run the restaurant. In the evening when the matriarchs have gone to bed the third generation arrives, and young men with floppy hair and their spotty friends are all fed by mothers who have worked from eight o'clock in the morning and will not finish until after midnight.

Around our table only Francesco is young. His father was a famous hairdresser who was killed tragically in a park a few years ago.

Maurizio tells us all how beautiful Luigi was in the old days. Luigi laughs and says, 'Grazie. Anche te eri bellissimo.'

'Bugiardo,' is all the maestro will say. (Liar.) Then he launches into a song by the famous Italian siren Mina and we all join in – 'Bugiardo e incosciente'. He sings well, His eyelashes shudder and flap like two old butterflies. Gianni sits with Nero on his knee. Both of them are staring at a parallel universe, bored stiff. The old ladies wave from the corner. I am in heaven. This could be it. Things may not get any better.

CHAPTER TWENTY-THREE

Silk Interiors

Back in London a couple of days later, there is a meeting in Little Italy on Frith Street to finalise the budget. Sébastien and Bettina have come over. Brian and I must find a way of squeezing some more out of the budget and we go through every scene, slashing prices, extras, sets, anything we can.

'Oh yeah,' says Brian nonchalantly. 'That should be easy. We can do a little bit of . . . ' a few twirls with his hands and then 'doo de doo dah day.'

I am not terribly convinced but decide to keep quiet for the moment.

We cut and compromise and by the end of the day the film and the budget seem to be in place. This has been the third attempt, but each time new costs have been unearthed. This has got to be the definitive version.

'Are we all agreed?' I ask.

'Yes. This is it,' replies Sébastien.

'Great,' agrees Bettina.

The producers rush back to the airport.

'Bri,' I say carefully as we walk down Frith Street arm in arm. 'I don't want to be tricked into starting the film and then find out we have to reduce the whole thing by another half.'

'I'll say,' replies Brian. We walk in silence for a moment.

'So you really think we can do all those cuts?'

'Absolutely.' Another pause. 'Remember we said we were going to have fun?' says Bri.

'Easier said than done if the whole thing falls apart.'

'Well, let's just plough on then. It's too late to turn back now.'

I leave him on the corner of Oxford Street and watch him beetle off into the crowds.

Brian can snap. Now we are all sitting in another bar – in Brussels this time – a tiny coffin-shaped place with an open door on to the street. More football. Molenbeek is a hot and dusty mirage outside. Everyone in the street is *en djellaba*. Things are not going terribly well at this point and I am hoping to be kidnapped.

'Wait till the movie comes out,' suggests David sensibly.

We are nearing the end of the technical recce. Poor Sébastien has still not been able to close the completion bond. The bond is a sword of Damocles over our production, the insurance policy that takes over if we fuck up. The problem is that we still need more money. The budget must all add up for the producer to be able to sign the bond – otherwise it's perjury – and normally speaking all this must be done before the film actually starts to shoot.

Bonds are expensive, and Sébastien never wanted to have one in the first place. I agreed. It's a lot of money for a lot of pain. In France and Belgium films are not generally bonded. However ours is, and Sébastien and Stefaan have accused Brian of going crazily over budget before we have even started. Brian is furious and denies it. He says they are using his budget as an excuse to cover their tracks. It's possible. I can get nothing out

of Brian's assistants Renate and Nane – they are brainwashed
moonies. They surround him hissing like cats at the rest of us
and I am stuck in the middle. Luggage of all shapes and sizes in
powder-blue leather has just arrived for Oscar. Made in London.
No expense spared. The cases all have silk interiors.

'Silk interiors, Bri?' I gasp, lips quivering. 'Is that really necessary?' I look at him beseechingly.

'Oh yeah,' he answers, eyes overflowing with tears. 'Otherwise
you won't be able to . . . ' Swinging into charade mode he mimes
the opening of a trunk, followed by a horrified gasp as he discov-
ers it's not lined. He's a good actor and of course I laugh.

'You see?'

'I see.'

He has also had Oscar's coffin made in Paris. 'In Paris, Bri?
Was that really necessary? Can't they make them in Germany?'

'I don't think so,' says Brian vaguely.

'You know it's meant to be a pauper's coffin. No adornment?'

'Mmm.'

I force him and Sébastien into a confrontation in a miniature
bar with the football blaring – just us and a skeleton in a skullcap
and trackies on a fruit machine. He's having a good run. His
efforts are punctuated by loud fairground music as coins pour
from the machine.

Since we are having money issues the tension is too much
for Sébastien and he gets up to leave. I grab his wrist and force
him to sit down. It's a big mistake. The beginning of violence.
There's no point in confronting Brian. And there's no point in
grabbing Sébastien. They both know all the tricks.

'That's it,' says Brian apropos. 'I've had enough.' And he
makes for the door, lingers there backlit for a dramatic moment
before dashing into the swarming souk followed by his moaning
assistants.

Sébastien makes a run for it too, and I walk up the road with

David to look for Brian. We find him holding onto a pillar box –
as if for dear life – surrounded by his wailing girls.

Everything depends on who blinks first. I decide to charge
on. Nothing and nobody is going to stop me. (Scarlett O'Hara.)

CHAPTER TWENTY-FOUR

The Normandy Landing

John's German camera crew get a shock on the first day of filming – it's 23 August 2016. We are still in pre-production and perhaps they have been confused by the tempo of our technical recce – a ramble across Europe, deceptively jolly in the nice weather and painfully slow. We have been in Germany, Italy, Belgium and here we are in France.

The recce is the last thing that happens before the actual shoot begins. The whole team visit the locations and are talked through the plan for each scene by the first assistant, observed haughtily by the director. Twenty people crowd round with pens and puzzled expressions as Toby sets the scene with one of his signature phrases. 'What we're trying to do is . . . ' or 'I know this sounds completely nutty . . . '

('What eez ziz nuttee?')

Occasionally I have had to channel Miss Fritton and swoop in with a few words of one syllable, but on the whole I hold back. This is a hierarchical operation and now is the time for the first assistant to assert his authority – he is the sergeant major. I am merely the fey officer striding around being encouraging. 'All right, men? It won't be long now.'

Finally here we are in Deauville and the moment of reckoning arrives. We are shooting for one isolated day before going back to Bavaria where we will start the film properly in a couple of weeks. It's a great opportunity for me to find my way and regroup after. The French holiday season has kicked in and it's unusually hot. Hopefully the weather will hold and my dream of an enchanted Normandy summer as the romantic painted backdrop for the first section of my film will be achieved.

Because. Picture this.

On a May dawn in 1895 Oscar Wilde arrives in Dieppe. The Newhaven packet boat emerges from the mist. The smoke from its funnel is a smear across the horizon (*Death in Venice*) and the wail of its horn bounces across the port (*Death on the Nile*). Robbie Ross is waiting on the dock. Oscar lumbers down the gangplank. In one of the great scenes from literature he divests himself of the great letter 'De Profundis', written in blood and tears in prison.

'Make three copies. Send one to Bosie Douglas, one to me and keep the original under lock and key,' says Oscar. Then a carriage ride through the sleepy town to the Hotel Sandwich where Oscar attempts to rebuild his life. It's the most optimistic part of the story and it's got to be sunny.

Almost immediately things go wrong. A group of degenerate poets show up to welcome Oscar into exile and a rowdy dinner at the Café des Tribunaux lurches out of control. Shortly after, some English students chase him through the town for a lark. At least they do in my version of the story. A letter arrives from the chief of police warning him about his rowdy behaviour with the French poets. His true identity revealed, Oscar retreats from Dieppe to Berneval, a sleepy village further along the plain. Alone now, he swims in the sea and walks on the cliffs and sets about writing his last poem 'The Ballad of Reading Gaol'. In a dramatic scene on the beach he reveals to Robbie Ross – who is visiting – that he intends to return to his ex, Lord Alfred Douglas. Robbie is furious. I can't remember if this is true or I made it up.

This is the first act of my film. There must be haystacks and hedgerows and pink misty dusks and God knows where we will find a steamship. Our first day of filming is very ambitious. Nobody thinks I will pull it off and the producers are hovering like vultures ready to swoop in and replace me with a pet puppet.

On the evening before the shoot Sébastien is murmuring to a small Scottish man in the foyer of our hotel. It's a secret conversation, huddled.

'That crane was an extravagance,' whispers the Scottish man. 'They'll never get to it. A lot of money for that.'

'I know,' sighs Sébastien.

I surge into the room. 'Sébastien?' I shriek. 'On a Belgian film does the director always get the smallest, loudest room on the whole crew? Or is it just me? We may as well pull the plug now if I am never going to be allowed to sleep.'

I instantly feel better but the colour drains from Sébastien's face.

'Rupert, I don't think you've met Neil.'

'No, I haven't. Hi.' I spin to leave.

'Neil is from the bond,' says Sébastien in a strangled voice.

Gasp. I spin right round, wreathed in sudden smiles. 'Neil, hi. Welcome. Sorry about that. I'm just teasing. My room appears to be next to the laundry. That's all. How great that you came.' Everyone breaks into peals of canned laughter.

Neil thinks my entrance is a deliberate joke. 'I feel as if I'm on candid camera. You nearly had me fooled.'

Outside in the courtyard of the hotel we inspect his silver Aston Martin. It's a boy's moment. 'What a car,' is all I can muster, hoping to sound like one of the lads. Small pause.

'I see you ordered a crane,' says Neil.

'Did you drive all the way here?' I ask at the same time.

We both sing 'yes' in unison, then laugh.

At 5 a.m. I am pondering all this in the room next to the washing machines at the back of the hotel. They have been on fast spin all night and I have hardly slept. But I can tell that Gloria is looking down in a good mood because the dawn comes with the kind of haze that promises to burn off into a scorching summer day. I wonder how I will be able to cope running up and down the cliffs as Gianni zips me into my fifteen pounds of fat suit and laces me into my corset. Collars, studs, false teeth and wig follow and with each step there is a strange sweaty squelch from deep inside me.

'Queaves,' says Gianni.

I must be careful. I had no idea his English was so sophisticated.

We found the beach one May four years ago. Through a locked gate in some fields, down a long muddy lane through woods of bluebells, past a herd of retired donkeys to a solitary caravan where a couple (straight from Catherine Tate) sell sandwiches, God knows to who because Panini Beach – our name for it – is one of Normandy's best-kept secrets and hardly anyone can find it. From the caravan armed with a panini down a steep gulley, and suddenly all the country noises – the faraway tractor, the chattering birds, the breeze – are lost in the sudden roar of the ocean as we tumble and slide onto a huge pebble beach.

It's very dramatic. The chalk cliffs tower majestically on either side, rising and falling towards Calais in one direction and Le Havre in the other. Seagulls wheel and shriek high above. The sea cracks and hisses against the pebbles and the cliffs themselves are like slices of white cake with delicious green icing – France's ramparts disappearing into the haze. From the cliff edge you resist the urge to hurl yourself off, and you can really feel how our two countries split at some geological Brexit moment because these cliffs are identical to the South Coast of Merrie England except that Newhaven – all Nissen huts and pebble-dash – is not a patch on Dieppe, decimated though it was during the war.

The big day flies by like a scene from Benny Hill. The crew swarm from the cliff edge down to the beach and back again, a colony of ants in bright tank tops and shorts, waving and shouting, their long dawn shadows shrinking and expanding as the sun rises behind Calais, flies over the beach and splashes into the sea.

At daybreak they are perched romantically on the cliffs. Far below on the beach itself Brian and his girls, in long shirts and chiffon scarves, are trying to stop a flapping tent from flying away in the wind. On the other hill – to the right of the beach – the advance crew are building a tower on the cliff edge so that they can get the best, scariest angle on my suicide scene. My head – shot from above – with the ocean crashing against the rocks below.

The first disaster happens at about 6.30 a.m. The walkie-talkies don't seem to work and are not going to work. Our receptor is not bleeping, or whatever it's meant to do. On inspection these walkie-talkies – yellow and red with big knobs – look suspiciously like children's toys but their Belgian masters huff and puff with indignation when I suggest this.

'And where exactly IS this receptor?' I ask, but no one seems to hear. Back in Brussels, probably. At any rate, now it is impossible for anyone to know what anyone else is doing. Cell phone reception is zero. The actors (me and Edwin Thomas, who is playing Robbie Ross) are getting ready at the hotel in Fécamp – two miles away.

It's a car crash waiting to happen. To reach the cliffs we must drive from the main road along an overgrown track across some fields and then walk. From the base it takes about half an hour.

It should be a manoeuvre operated with military precision. But now we are all cantering over the field – late – a strange caravan in the scorching heat: Maurizio, all in white like a poltergeist in a straw hat, me and Edwin dressed as Oscar and Robbie, Luigi and Francesco laden with all their boxes of hairspray, glue, pancake and powder. Two terrified assistants bob along with umbrellas trying to keep up. We arrive panting and sweating at the cliff edge to find the Belgian line producer in an orange flying jacket with a thousand insignias sewn onto it. He is a dayglo cockerel, crowing into a megaphone. Neil from the bond observes from the cliff edge.

The second bad thing to happen is that Rudi, the head of the German camera crew, decides that the Belgian truck drivers are too useless and moody and has fired them or threatened to fire them, it's not clear which. Either way they have gone off in a huff and now there is no one to carry the equipment from the cliff to the beach, but we don't know this yet.

For the time being we are all up on the hill. Brian has made a beautiful display of all my props – they are laid out on a rug in a hole he has dug specially and he runs up from the beach (aged eighty) to show them to me. There are fabulous rings and sticks and cigarette cases and watch chains. He is an old campaigner back in the saddle and his face is a sweet inspiration, hair blowing, glasses glinting, breathless, my very own nutty professor.

'Remember, dear,' he warns. 'We said we were going to have fun.'

Unfortunately I don't really have time to go through his amazing booty with a toothcomb and I notice the fun level drain slightly from his face as I apologise and run back to John, who is ready to shoot me clambering up the hill.

And ACTION.

We are off. I zoom up the hill a few times. We change lenses. I climb some more. We move the camera. We do it again. And again. I am so anxious for the scene to be finished – for us to be able to move on to the next location – that I charge up that steep slope like Usain Bolt, and just as we are packing up and moving on to the other side of the cliff, I suddenly realise. 'FUCK. Stop!' I screech. 'We need to go again.'

'Why? It was great,' protests John.

'No it wasn't. I was going much too fast! I'm meant to be half-dead.'

Nobody noticed.

In a letter written at Berneval, from the Hôtel de la Plage, Oscar wittily describes his daily walk as a pilgrimage. His destination is a chapel on the cliffs called Notre Dame de Liesse. 'I go there every day. It takes all of three minutes to get to it and just as many to get back,' he writes.

'The priest,' I add, possibly gilding the lily, 'who is charming and terribly attractive has become a great friend. Yesterday he showed me all his vestments. He looked particularly captivating in his martyr's garb. Rose dorée streaked with blood.'

A few years ago, during one of those dead periods of collapse that punctuate this story, desperate to stay engaged, I took the ferry from Newhaven, booked into a hotel at Dieppe and the next day I drove to Berneval.

Oscar and Robbie made the same journey in a horse and cart, rented for the day – probably on the same lane – across the flat green fields above the cliffs. They had planned on getting out of the town for a drive in the country – the place was swarming with English tourists – but the horse had other ideas. It came from Berneval and was hell-bent on returning. When they tried to turn back it cantered on, clattering finally into the yard of the Hôtel de la Plage. I had to cut this scene in the end – or right at the beginning actually – which was sad because the road from Berneval down to the beach is still there (walking down it is almost unbearably exciting for a Wilde moony), but also lucky because a horse

and cart galloping out of control with two nervy actors on board
down a steep hill and into a hotel yard – all to be achieved in a
couple of tense hours – would probably have been a time bomb
waiting to explode. Nevertheless, seeing Berneval that first time
was a pivotal moment for me. My focus on everything changed.

CHAPTER TWENTY-FIVE

Our Lady of Happiness

It was a beautiful day. I parked in the village and walked down a road through a steep wooded valley towards the beach. Houses and villas perched in the trees, locked up and shuttered. Not a soul in sight. No sound. Only the branches sighing in the breeze. At the bottom there was a path down to the beach. It was called Allée Oscar Wilde. There was an incongruous street lamp at one end that made me think of Narnia more than Worthing. That's all there was.

Slightly deflated, I sat down on a wall and waited for something to happen. Maybe Mr Tumnus would trot past. It was a strange submerged sort of place and I wondered why I had bothered to come. There was no message – except for the general failure of my endeavour, about which the birds chirped mournfully and the leaves whispered. The wall I was sitting on curved up the hill towards a run-down gate. It was swamped in ivy. My gaze distractedly froze on it.

After a minute or an hour – God knows how long I sat there – I became aware of a squirly letter peeping out through the leaves.

It was an H. And an O. HO. I tore away some of the ivy and the words Hôtel des Plages appeared in crumbling concrete relief. I had found the hotel.

Time stood still. The house behind, a strange red-brick building in gloomy shadows, was now a block of run-down flats. A squeaky swing door banged shut in the breeze, and then opened again, slowly, as if ghosts were coming in and out.

I couldn't resist going inside, and found myself in a corridor leading to a dirty staircase. At the top were two locked doors and a long cramped corridor. The place was completely deserted, just the wind in the trees outside and the pigeons moaning in the branches. Through a dirty window for a moment I could almost see him. Sauntering down Allée Oscar Wilde, that elephant gait, all alone, looking at the trees and listening to the birds, the man who held the Café Royal in thrall reduced to a bedsit in a country boarding house.

I walked up the cliff he described in the letter but there was no chapel at the top, just a statue of the Virgin Mary of Liesse looking gloomily out to sea.

'Did you know that Liesse is the medieval word for happiness?'

It was a strange feeling to be walking in the footsteps of one's subject – trudging up the same hill towards the same saint, nearer and nearer, panting and sweating, the sea and England on one side, France and the future on the other – and it struck me suddenly that the letter describing it was particularly touching. Reading between the lines I think that Oscar was telling his friends that he was trying to keep going. The message was camouflaged in the usual flippancy but now I could see him very vividly, sitting in that room with the trees waving through the window, nothing to do and another long day ahead, just the lonely coo, the murmur of his sinking heart and the sound of a pen scratching on paper. That room was another kind of prison.

With this daily walk he was trying to keep it together – stay healthy – to be engaged. 'I go there every day.' Walking up the hill and then back down again. 'It takes all of three minutes to get to it and just as many to get back.'

It took me nearly half an hour!

It's taking the crew a lot longer.

In the next scene I must walk from the hotel to the beach, where hopefully Brian has secured the bathing tents. At any rate the wind has now dropped completely and the heat is suddenly intense. Looking at the world from inside the construction of Oscar, not really able to move without breaking into a muck sweat, is a strange locked-in experience. I have a different costume, so I must squelch across the field and drive back to the village and change my clothes.

I get into a terrible state on this long journey. I have no contact with anyone. No walkie-talkie. I am the director. I must be there. It's like being in a terrible dream. 'I could have walked down and changed on the beach,' I scream at anyone who will listen back at base.

'Don't blame me,' huffs Gianni as he helps me to dress.

Nearly an hour later I get back to the set – quite nervous by now – but no one seems to have noticed that I wasn't there. They still haven't got all the equipment down the hill. (No drivers.)

But now I'm Oscar walking down to the sea, and going into my little bathing tent. Waiting inside is Klaus – David's fix-it friend from Berlin – who has agreed for some reason better known to himself to be my body double. He has been glued into a terrifying wig and looks utterly insane when I slip inside the tent. He is having a flash of first-night nerves, so I have to shove him out in his all-in-one bathing suit and he stumbles over the agonising pebbles into the freezing water and swims off towards England.

By now it is over 40 degrees. Everyone is swooning. We have lunch.

We have made it through the first morning. But trouble is brewing.

After lunch we set off back up the cliff for the suicide moment. I am busy trying to summon up some suicidal feelings but it's not easy because the Belgian art director – who we were all rather suspicious of – has cordoned off the cliff edge. According to Brian he is one of those holier-than-thou floppy-haired show business bores and is meant to be finding us fabulous churches and houses. Instead he has found a pothole near the cliff edge which he thinks is going to bring the whole cliff down. He has built a little fence around it and is now waving hysterically at the whole crew.

'The cliff may collapse. People could be killed.'

'Jaysus,' fumes John. 'Let's shoot the scene at the end of the day then.'

'Zis is not funny,' fumes the art director.

We shoot it anyway. Luckily the camera doesn't see my face because I am looking murderous rather than suicidal. You could tell, and the scene hit the cutting-room floor.

It is four o'clock by the time we start work on the day's main action, in which Robbie and I are walking and talking – always a challenge for actors at the best of times – along the beach. I am a bit worried about Edwin. He is inexperienced and innocent. He's the only actor I might need to help. But will I know how?

I have developed a new training technique which is to rehearse while jogging. To this end Edwin and I have jogged endlessly around London, and yesterday evening we jogged up and down the beach at Deauville where I nearly had a heart attack in the heat. My aim is to exhaust the actor so much that he can't do anything but say the line. It seems to be working, but I'm scared that Edwin will freeze on the day – today – and there won't be time to defrost him.

Edwin is quite like me as an actor. He wants to learn the tune of a phrase and then stick to it. It's quite sweet to see him sitting on a chair between takes, saying his lines over and over again, the same notes, like a parrot, head cocked, listening to the music but not always thinking of the words. He is wonderful-looking, with beautiful red hair and pale blue eyes. He has a coiled intensity, while at other times he appears quite vacant, which I think is an essential quality for film acting. The best piece of direction ever was given by Rouben Mamoulian to Greta Garbo at the end of *Queen Christina*. Garbo was straining every nerve to act going tragically into exile, and it wasn't working. 'Just think of nothing,' said Mamoulian, finally. 'Let the audience have the emotions.' (Easier said than done for some of us busy bees in the business.)

The long and short of it is, Edwin has got to be good. My take on the Wilde legend is not focused on the gilded passion of Oscar and Bosie.

For me, Robbie was the one. Oscar didn't realise it – until it was too late. If we are to believe both their stories, it was Robbie who deflowered the great Irish Elephant in a public loo one afternoon, and introduced him to the world of 'Uranian' love. It was Robbie who loved Oscar unconditionally, who met him in exile when Oscar was so toxic that just to know him meant social ruin. When Robbie left the Hotel Alsace to accompany his mother to Menton during the final illness, Oscar broke down completely and held on to him for dear life. 'Find me a little cup in the hills outside Nice where I can go to recover and be near you.' He sobbed as Robbie prised the poet's arms from around his neck. (We shot this scene but it hit the cutting-room floor. As Roger Michell sagely noted after an early screening – once you get to the death bed, die. Don't hang around. He was right.)

Tensions are mounting in the heat. John's crane and tracks are laid down but Neil is right – we never get to use them because at this point communication completely breaks down and the camera crew go into open revolt. They have never been worked so hard and in such heat. One of them says he can't go on. He's going to faint.

'Faint later, please,' is all John says. 'I don't want to talk about this now.'

He himself is dripping with sweat, looking as though he may suddenly take a swing at someone. It's quite dramatic. One of the grips spits on the ground and says that they all want to leave at the end of the day.

'Fine,' John replies. 'Leave.'

He is like the Incredible Hulk and standing there in front of him – me and Edwin whispering our lines and jogging up and down rather pathetically on the spot, trying not to let the explosive atmosphere drag us in – I do wonder for a moment what kind of monster I have unleashed. But actually I don't care if John is a psychopath – I will be his Lady Macbeth. Now his forehead throbs and his eyes have sunk, glittering with madness. I haven't seen this look since working with that orangutan in *Dunston Checks In*. One false move and he will probably leap over and throttle me.

Now we are waiting for a lens. I decide to look busy – jog jog jog – hoping that Edwin won't suddenly collapse screaming.

'Where is the fucking lens?' snaps John, finally.

'It's coming,' says the focus puller, looking vaguely towards the end of the beach. Tick-tock. Minutes drag by. Actually it is not coming, and this is when we discover that the camera crew have fired the drivers – and all hell breaks loose.

From inside the fat suit, nearly boiling, everything seems far away. Voices echo and cut out. I think I am going to faint. All the equipment is at the other end of the beach.

'Who's gonna bring it over? Jaysus Christ,' shouts John.

The crew drift in and out of focus, shifting and sweating while John storms off down the beach followed by Charley Cox. And

Neil from the bond. It takes about ten minutes and soon they are wobbling mirages enveloped in the scorching air.

'What's happening?' asks Edwin, suddenly close. I look slowly round. He's still jogging.

Before I need to answer, John reappears – backlit through the surf, etc., carrying two lamp stands on one shoulder, the camera over another – swearing blue murder, dripping with sweat, burnt to a cinder, followed by Neil from the bond laden down like a mule.

John barks orders. 'The legs. Where's the fockin' legs?'

I adore him. He is SO my type of guy.

Meanwhile Toby has caught sunstroke and is weaving across the beach towards us. He has lost his voice. The sun has beaten down on his bare head all day and he has continued to march around getting everyone's attention, no walkie-talkie, giving orders, and now he is quizzing the sound guy about the radio mics which we have been waiting for all day. They haven't appeared.

The sound guy – a Belgian legend – is seventy years old and he really IS about to have a stroke. His face has turned grey. He looks into Toby's sun-blasted face. It's like a war film. 'I didn't think they would be necessary.'

'Not necessary? But there's a long scene of dialogue and it is played on the move. How were you thinking of covering the wide shot?'

The old man stares at Toby for a long moment. 'We use the boom,' he whispers finally.

'Oh, great,' snaps Toby, and now the two sound guys – father and son – go into a routine that would be funny if the clock wasn't ticking and the sun wasn't about to disappear into the sea, and the crane wasn't sitting there unused with Neil from the bond watching. They are trying to untangle their cables so that they have enough length to walk with the boom the two hundred yards of the scene. A good technician has his cables in neat coils, but these two are looking at a plate of spaghetti.

With comic timing borrowed from Jacques Tati, they stand back, scratch their heads, take a cable each and begin the laborious chore of winding it around their arms, before crashing into one another and starting the whole laborious routine again. Half an hour later they still haven't managed.

'We can't wait any longer,' somebody screams. It's me.

We are shooting without sound. It's unheard of. Not even in a student film does something like this happen. I fire them at the end of the day.

Anyway, we finish the scene. Edwin is excellent. He doesn't buckle under the strain although we are moving at a breakneck pace to get all the coverage we need. We have wasted so much time on the sound issue that of course we have to sacrifice the crane shot. I catch Neil's eye when the decision is made.

'Pity, that.' He smiles. 'If it hadn't been for all the sound issues you would have got it.'

The final scene is of me swimming. By the time I jump into the water I think I am going to have a heart attack – the change in temperature is so intense that my arm goes stiff. Oh well, if I go now, so be it. Neil from the bond will have to give me mouth-to-mouth.

The scene is beautiful. We have about fifteen minutes of light. The sun melts into the sea. The pale sky is shredded with thin pink clouds and the evening star twinkles suddenly. John is in the water with the camera and I swim back and forth in front of him like a mad fan or a porpoise in a wig. Shades of my mother's swimming technique, chin stuck out, trying to keep her bouffant out of the water. The waves crash gently against the pebbles and the crew observe listlessly. Toby can hardly stand up. Behind them the cliffs are luminous as the day fades quickly.

There is something biblical about our exodus from the beach

that night. The retired donkeys line our route, smugly watching. Everyone – cast and crew alike – trudges up the hill, dragging the equipment, dead with fatigue, while the producers report back to Germany on their cell phones.

Ironically it is Neil who carries the weights that held the crane in place. He has worked tirelessly all day. I am very touched.

'I think it's going to be good,' he says before jumping back into the Aston Martin and heading for home.

The whole *Carry On* team. The only picture I have of Jörg, fourth from the right.

Fawlty Towers.

The infamous pauper's coffin, imported from France.

John Conroy in the $20,000 grave.

Me (bald), directing the judge, Ronald Pickup (wigless).

David judging the directing.

The brilliant Patrick Hannaway brings Clapham Junction to life.

Philip Noel, Julian Wadham and Anna Chancellor, entranced by Oscar's
first-night speech.

Enjoying a break.

Toby, the first assistant, sets the scene and explains that I am the tennis ball.

And now Toby in the role of prison warden, handcuffed to his director.

The Neapolitans listen to Toby's instructions. Unfortunately, they don't speak English.

The Normandy landings.

Maurizio Millenotti – in virginal white – performs final checks on me.

John Conroy carrying the camera in the blistering heat.

Our friend Klaus standing in as my body double. Before, during and after. He had to be hauled from the sea by divers.

Emily Watson, exquisite as Constance Wilde.

Me, John Conroy, Tom Colley and Colin Firth in another scene where the sound didn't work.

Our pop-up restaurant in the hills above Naples.

My two lovers.

Colin Morgan as a beautiful, unblinking Bosie.

Edwin Thomas, coiled and slightly masochistic as Robbie Ross.

Maurizio plotting.

Nic Gaster, our editor, observed by his Belgian assistant in the Eastern bloc.

The magic of cinema. Before . . .

After.

John Standing as Dr Tucker from the Embassy.

Silk interiors.

Johanna Kirby as the nurse.

Strip musical chairs at Villa Giudice.

Me at the piano.

Antonio Spagnuolo as Felice the fisherman.

Back on the stage at the Citizens Theatre.

Little Pluto at six months.

CHAPTER TWENTY-SIX

The Shoot

The first six weeks in Franconia are the best part of the whole adventure in many respects, like the summer holidays or a school trip. We set off each morning from the hotel in Bayreuth after breakfast in its quaint dining room – me, John, Brian and David and Willy, sometimes together, sometimes at separate tables.

The Goldener Anker hotel (aka the Golden Bore) is locked in a Wagnerian time warp. Two sweet girls in old-fashioned maids' outfits rustle and giggle around the dining room. There is no menu. You just ask for what you want and get what you deserve.

A bearded lady with wild hair monitors the front desk. Gloomy portraits swamped in varnish hang from the walls on the long corridors upstairs and photographs of men in uniform from the thirties tell us what we already know. Everyone came here from Adolf Hitler to Angela Merkel and members of the Wagner family still seem to have a finger in every pie.

As usual I am in the smallest room of the hotel, although my bathroom is rather grand for some reason. Each night I lie in the enormous green tub, surrounded by green tiles, and pretend I'm John Huston. If my room was Hitler's then all I can say is – as usual – no message.

David says that because he was raised on a tiny island he has little sense of direction and that his new role as driver to the director could be a metaphor for our rudderless ship. The poor thing also has panic attacks. All I have to do is look at his knuckles on the steering wheel. If they have gone white – unfasten your seat belts – we're going to proceed very slowly in the wrong direction.

We lose our way to the location on a daily basis so we normally arrive in a jangled state. The producers and their assistants observe us grimly through the window of the production office as we crawl to a halt and tumble from the car fighting.

'I told you to turn left.'

'We're here, aren't we?'

'We're late.'

'Only a few minutes. Chill.'

'This isn't Barbados, David! This is a film set.'

Luckily for me the production offices are housed far away – their lair is in the Eastern bloc and they only appear at mealtimes along with the editor Nic Gaster – a strange man dressed as a French peasant in a beret. Poor Nic leads a completely isolated existence away from us all and we more or less forget about him in the rush to finish our work each day.

The Neapolitans arrive. At great and unnecessary expense, according to Stefaan Schieder. He says we could just as easily make do with fifteen local Italians – if indeed there are any in these farthest reaches of Franconia. He says that there are thousands of Italians in Munich. He also thinks we don't need our Italian costume designers. Apparently Germany has a long tradition of costume drama. I suppose he's talking about *Triumph of the Will*.

I have tried to explain that Neapolitans are a different race to Italians, but I can tell that he thinks me spoilt and flighty. The point is they have to work in Italy as well, where the Italian exteriors will be shot.

'So either the real ones come here or the fake ones go there. What's the difference?'

Stefaan thinks nobody will notice if we have two different sets. I have learnt how to put my foot down (and keep it there) and they all arrive – fifteen boys – one goes to prison just before the shoot begins and we have to hastily recast, but soon they are ensconced at Thurnau along with two wonderful old ladies who are playing the housekeepers of Villa Giudice where Oscar and Bosie lived. These ladies have never left Naples before, never been on a plane and it takes them both twenty minutes to walk up the three floors of spiral stairs to the set. We put chairs on the landings and they sit there talking – shouting, actually – in the impenetrable dialect of Naples.

The group is accompanied by their coach and tour manager Max – my wonderful Neapolitan casting director. Max is a tiny bird with bird bones and miniature hands. He has wonderful manners as he hops gently between me and the group, translating my desires into action.

We have conducted extensive tests in Naples to find our Felice – the main fisherman/lover in the story. Taking turns shooting on our iPhones, we have both been nearly knocked senseless – standing in for Bosie – by some of the enthusiastic acting. I had written and imagined a purely verbal confrontation but all the boys – weaned on the Mafia series *Gomorrah* – have other ideas and I find myself being thrown against the wall, held in an agonising deadlock, spat on and kicked in the stomach on a daily basis. 'Cuuut' is the 'safe' word I gurgle when things go too far.

It is thrilling to see the scenes being ripped from the page by these tornadoes. Neapolitans are built for acting – they are a race apart – and what Stefaan can't understand is that they are vital to the success of the movie. With their languid machismo, the rough and tumble of their extraordinary language, their wild Arab faces and their natural ambiguity, they will be able to show us exactly how homosexual relations might have developed between a local heterosexual fisherman and a flighty queen from abroad at the end of the nineteenth century.

Of course most of them are chunkier than their period selves and all of them pluck their eyebrows, but apart from that they are worth their weight in gold. (We send a letter before shooting. No bikini-waxing, eyebrow-trimming or manicures, please, boys!) They are completely overqualified for the job but they give themselves to the film completely.

In their first scene they must play strip musical chairs with Bosie in the Villa Giudice on Christmas Eve 1897. I am playing the piano. We are all wearing paper hats and little else. The set is the long thin room on the third floor of Thurnau with its crumbling stucco walls, its sagging ceilings and the warped parquet floor. Brian has built a stained banquette in the bay window, produced an upright piano and some moth-eaten rugs. A few chairs, some candles, paraffin lamps, and the room suddenly jumps to flickering life.

'It looks wonderful.'

'I'll say,' agrees Brains.

John's lights shimmer over the sweating, half-dressed boys. Their shadows leap around the room. Candles gutter prettily on the Christmas tree – decorated with spoons and seashells – and the old walls soak it all up. It's a dream come true. We have created something quite lovely. All the years of preparation, all the trials, the trips and the tantrums have been distilled down to this single point, this crafted moment, and it's thrilling.

Even Maurizio is briefly excited. He escorts the (un)dressed boys onto the set. 'Non è male,' he sighs, eyes on stalks. 'Hai fatto un bel casting.'

'Hai fatto i belli costumi,' I say as a nude Neapolitan passes by.

CHAPTER TWENTY-SEVEN

Saint Colin

Colin Firth arrives on a hot Sunday morning at the end of September. Our knight in shining armour is delivered to the Golden Bore. He checks into the rather chic room I picked out myself on the first floor. The rest of us are working at the castle preparing for the week ahead, but his movements are constantly monitored and snatches of his progress can be heard in those peculiar, truncated conversations – back and forth – between assistants on their walkie-talkies (working now, this is Germany), recounted in grave Germanic detail and punctuated by explosions of static.

'Go for Katja. Over.'

'Colin loves the room.'

'Copy that.'

'Colin's going for a wonk.'

'A wonk?'

'A walk.'

'Copy that.'

'Go for Colin.'

'Go for Katja.'

Champagne and chocs are on the bedside table. Call sheets and scripts have been discreetly slipped under the door. The transportation of our prize pet is being achieved with much ado if not military precision because we all wait nervously for him to arrive for lunch at the Greek restaurant under the castle and he doesn't show up.

'Goodness, he's late,' I say at about two o'clock. 'Who's collecting him?'

Nobody, as it happens. In the frenzy of micromanagement we forgot to have him picked up. David thought that one of the drivers was going. The driver thought that David had gone. Both are sitting at different tables in the restaurant calmly eating their lunch. Copy that. Panic attacks all round. Where is he? Apparently pacing up and down outside the hotel.

'Colin is waiting. Over. What should I tell him, Rupert?'

'Maybe he should go for another wonk.'

'Copy that.'

David grabs the car keys and sets off to collect him.

'We could be here all day,' remarks John Conroy. David's driving is famous now.

'All year,' corrects Brian. 'Yesterday she took me halfway back to Munich.'

'Who's she?'

'David.'

'Jaysus.'

By the time Colin arrives I am reduced to a fawning over-spanked dog.

'Colin, darling. Thank you thank you thank you,' I yap, waving my bottom in the air.

'Don't worry,' he says evenly. 'I wouldn't miss this train crash for anything.'

'Oh. Well you will if no one picks you up.'

We both laugh weakly.

'So. Shall we do a spot of rehearsal?' I am Mrs Everett the vicar's wife again, and we all move off towards the castle.

Colin is with us for a week. It's the most important week of the shoot. We are working in the room at the Hôtel d'Alsace where Oscar dies, wrapped in the famous wallpaper, surrounded by the faithful friends.

'My whole career's on the line with this fucking wallpaper,' groans Brian one day after a sleepless night.

So is mine. The room is one of the most important characters in the film. It has to look perfect. Brian designs a wonderful dark green wallpaper. Nana and I nearly come to blows over her choice of fireplace.

'I only take orders from Brian,' she announces, but 'It can all be fixed,' smooths Brian.

'But we're shooting tomorrow.'

'You're screaming,' whispers David.

I am nervous. All my stars are here. On Thursday Tom Wilkinson will join us. He plays the Irish priest, Father Cuthbert Dunne, and will administer me the last rites and hopefully bring a bit of much-needed comedy to the last act of the film. John Standing has already arrived to be Dr Tucker from the British Embassy and has been practising with his stethoscope all morning, strangely tap-dancing from room to room. My darling Johanna Kirby is playing the nurse and she has been rehearsing with a syringe, and Colin Firth's brother-in-law is being fitted with a crown of thorns because he is Jesus. In short there is going to be a lot of acting.

Oscar's room is almost impossible to find in the vast castle – up a hidden spiral staircase and at the end of a long, thin corridor. Shooting in a small space for any length of time tends to drive everyone to the edge and over. The crew is jammed into one corner, the performers in another. Tiptoeing between the two groups, hair and make-up execute their last-minute tweaks, the dressers obsessively remove non-existent flecks of dirt from the clothes of their charges and the continuity girl, motionless on one leg like a bird of prey, beadily scours the terrain for something that is in the wrong place. With a splosh she suddenly pounces.

I lie on the bed lurching from a death rattle to screaming at whoever is talking in the corridor outside. From Oscar Wilde to Orson Welles and back again. According to Stefaan Schieder it's gone to my head. Possibly. I have finally managed to make myself the complete centre of attention. After trying and failing all my life, here I am, tucked up on the deathbed, an expiring general and a regiment of strange mercenaries waging war on the tiny battlefield of Oscar's bedroom.

It's my own mad world and it's electrifying. Lamps like vast robotic sunflowers on metal stands droop their wan moonlight over the tricky terrain. The room is so cramped it makes you want to scream but the battle rages on five days a week from 8 a.m. until 6 p.m. It's us against the elements – us against time, Germans against Belgians, the continuity girl against the director of photography. She already looks (and acts) like Edith Cavell and John Conroy reminds me of that holy terror of the Indian Mutiny, John Nicholson – God to some, demon to others. Tempers fray. (Unfortunately to little effect, because they normally fray in a language incomprehensible to the frayee.)

'I think Heinz is trying to tell me something,' I hear someone say.

'Yes, he's telling you you're a cunt,' mutters someone else passing by.

Only I notice – I am the still eye of the storm. One thing is certain. I watch John at work and thank my lucky stars. He is amazing. His energy is unstoppable. I adore him. His sergeant major, Charley Cox, never buckles under the strain. They have a strange violent relationship with comfy phrases like 'Get the fuck out of my way' abbreviated to save time (GTF), and between them they pull the room into the light in record time. Shouting fades to talking fades to whispering as the sacred moment of a take approaches and suddenly it feels as if we are actually there. For a weird 3D moment I wonder – maybe I am Wilde dying in the bed. The crew huddle round the camera, merging into one person – a many-faced monster surrounding the blank black eye of the lens. Booms stick out like strange antennae. Smoke belches from plastic arteries slithering across the floor. A bony arm with the clapper board reaches out. The big black eye briefly inspects it.

'Fifty-two, take one.' Clap.

A moment of silence, peace. A car grinds up the hill.

'Cuuut,' shouts Toby. 'What's with the traffic, people? Let's go again. Aaand . . . action.'

I lie in my bed wheezing softly. The door opens. Colin Firth enters. Backlit. He closes the door quietly and leans against it. He is dressed almost identically to Tommy Judd – the character he played in our first film together thirty years ago. Then I was the up-and-coming star perched on a windowsill wielding a pair of binoculars. Now he is in the ascendancy and I am the beached whale on the deathbed. Colin watches me for a long moment before striding into the room.

'Oscar, you old fraud. You look perfectly well.'

'I know. Can you believe it?' I whisper. 'One poisonous *moule* three months ago . . . '

It's one of my favourite scenes.

Sadly though, on the week after this – the third week – our ship hits a rock. There is a new hole in our budget and we're sinking. All hands on deck.

The first I hear of it is from David at breakfast.

'Now. Don't freak. Keep your hair on – but Sébastien is arriving today and he needs to speak to you urgently.'

'Oh God. Why? I thought I told you to keep them off my back. I'm working.'

David and Willy exchange a concerned glance.

'It's nothing,' says Willy, waving dismissively.

'Willy, it's NOT nothing,' snaps David. 'It's really serious. Sébastien says they have been working on the budget for the Belgian side of the shoot and there is still an eight-hundred-thousand-euro hole.'

'Whaaat?' I start to feel faint.

I have been expecting something. Sébastien has been bombarding me with apocalyptic texts for the last three days, making it almost impossible to concentrate on making the movie. We sit in silence for a moment as the full implication of the situation becomes clear. We could be closed down. Or worse. The bond could send in a new director. Time stands still. A depressed clock ticks over the fireplace. The swing door to the kitchen creaks. A German couple giggle and whisper at a table across the room.

'I think they knew about this all along.' I am thinking aloud. 'They just assumed I would run aground after a couple of days and in the ensuing chaos they could slip in the eight-hundred-thousand shortfall without anyone noticing.'

'Exactly,' agrees David, always ready to join in on a conspiracy theory.

'Bettina said at the beginning that we'd never make the schedule.'

'But we did. Not only that, but we're doing well. Not that anybody seems to have noticed. Anyway, I can't think of this now. I've got to have a stroke this morning. At this rate it won't be acting.'

After a tense morning, we break for lunch. As part of my stroke I have just puked all over Colin, but my heart's not in it. No matter. It's amazing what one can do with a bottle of

Guinness. It's quite lonely being the director because you can't tell the others what's really going on.

'Are you OK?' asks Colin. 'You look a bit done in.'

'I'm acting!' I snap. You have to act (more acting) like everything is running smoothly.

At lunch all the producers are squeezed around a table. They remind me of the Krypton elders from the first Superman film. Even Jörg and Philipp are here because on top of everything else, today is the day they have invited the German press to join us for interviews and a group photo. Emily Watson has arrived for a dream sequence. I am dressed like Scrooge in a nightdress and a bandage around my head. Or Basil Fawlty. Colin plays along out of good manners, and luckily Edwin adores being photographed.

We all line up looking like the characters from a Carry On film, but the German producers have been adamant. 'It's really important for the fund. We have to announce.' Whatever. Our travails are reduced to postage stamps scattered across the world's press but at least we have a four-page spread in *What's On in Franconia*.

After the photo is lunch. From the frying pan onto the pyre.

Stefaan inhales his cigarette and his face is sucked away. Bettina is silent beside him. Her blue eyes are no longer laughing. It's 'difficult decision' day, finally. Only Jörg and Philipp beam and bellow. Otherwise there is no foreplay.

'We are eight hundred thousand short,' says Sébastien bleakly.

'But how is that possible?' I can hear my voice trying to locate its reasonable pitch. 'We signed off on the budget in London at the end of June. How can it have increased so substantially?'

'There are things we didn't calculate,' he says evenly.

We are sitting in the courtyard of the castle. One hundred people are having their lunch, enjoying themselves, their voices bouncing off the walls. The actors all have Kleenexes tucked into their collars like little children. They are sitting at a table dissecting some droll moment from the morning's shoot and I watch them jealously. Their carefree bursts of laughter come now from another world. I will never complain about being an actor again. My vision blurs slightly. Blink, bitch. This is no time for tears.

'So what do you suggest?'

'We need to make some serious cuts.'

'We need to lose the boat and the trains,' says Bettina. She has said this before. It's her mantra.

'But it's a road movie,' I whine. 'It's about someone who is being constantly moved on. Oscar's arrival must be epic. The packet boat is vital. He can't just BE everywhere.'

'About the boat.' Sébastien pulls out a paper napkin with a sketch he's made with a black felt pen. He bangs his finger on an X. 'That's you and Bosie.'

'Robbie.'

'Robbie. You hand him the Reading Gaol poem. A ship's horn blows off-screen and you both climb into a carriage. Voilà. We can do it in a car park. We don't NEED a boat.'

The tears are back. My hands have turned to fists. 'It's "De Profundis", Sébastien. It's a famous moment in literature. Have you read the script?'

'Sure. The letter,' he concedes, like water off a duck's back, and he ploughs on with his plans to turn my film into an episode of a daytime soap. 'As for the chase scene, we don't really need a church. The cricket team could just trap you in an alley.'

'It's not a cricket team,' I sob. 'They're undergraduates.'

'Better. They don't need to play cricket.'

Now Bettina picks up the slack with her pet subject. 'The trains cost twenty thousand for each carriage. We could just do interiors.'

'But then what do we have at the station?'

'We shoot around it. Use a bit of smoke.'

'But this is precisely what we talked about in Soho in June. I said we should halt the production if we didn't have enough money to make the film and you all assured me that we did. It's not fair. That's why I agreed to sign the bond.'

'Yes, but then you insisted that we came here to Thurnau,' exhales Stefaan, his face briefly reappearing through the smoke. 'Another insane expense.'

'Wait, Stefaan. I said – a year ago, by the way – that I couldn't make the film if we DIDN'T go to Thurnau. It's completely different. Thurnau was a part of the deal and everyone signed off on it. Including the Bavarian fund by the way, whose suggestion it was to come here in the first place. You're just trying to find a way of blaming me for the fact that we have a shortfall. I know it's standard behaviour to headfuck a first-time director into submission. But not this old hag! You all gave me your word that we had the funds to make the film, and I am going to continue making it. Now if you'll forgive me. Some of us have to work!'

In the ensuing silence I flounce off to the dessert trolley. By the time I get back to the table only Sébastien remains.

'Listen. I will put in five hundred and you put in three. What about that?' he suggests. 'But also we have to try and get some of the actors' fees back.'

'Christ. But Colin Firth has already deferred half his payment. We can't take the rest.'

Sébastien regards me solemnly. 'Or can we?'

I look over at the actors' table again. This time my vision is not blurred. Colin Firth throws back his head laughing. He may not think things are quite so funny after lunch. 'This is really taking the piss, isn't it?'

'Look, Rupert. I'm doing what I can. You know? I always said I would NEVER put money into a film, and here I go.'

I wave him away. 'Yes, but everyone always says that. It's a golden rule and all that. But I think it's bullshit. If you want to make a film, make it – come what may. If you don't . . . don't.'

I get up and leave the table. I am about to weep. Sébastien never forgives me for this cavalier attitude towards his contribution and of course in a way he's right. It IS generous of him to pledge his own money. The film is not HIS dream. It's mine. But at the same time I feel tricked. He is the producer. He got us into this mess. We should never have started the film if we didn't have the money.

The actors all amaze me. Colin Morgan agrees to give back a part of his fee. It's agonising to be asking and his agent has a conniption but he is very good-natured about it. 'The important thing is to make the film. I have total faith in you and let's go for it,' is all he says.

And Firth, too. I text him at one minute before midnight, 'Don't do it.' But he agrees to all the producer's suggestions and eventually does the film for nothing.

The next day Stefaan sends an email to everyone suggesting that we fire Brian and that I am nothing more than a 'self-centred egotistical director' who 'changes his mind every day'. According to him we are heading towards a 'minor-league *Heaven's Gate*' and Neil from the bond should be called in 'to put an end to my attitude'. A minor-league *Heaven's Gate* sounds rather chic to me.

After a flurry of emails from several of the injured parties he offers his resignation which – at least on my behalf – is eagerly accepted. He has neatly turned the tables on me and branded me as the amateur villain of the piece. He has suggested that the crew are very unhappy – which may be true – and that essentially nobody can do their job because of me.

It is extremely unjust. Of course I am self-centred and egotistical. I wouldn't be trying to make a film if I wasn't. But Stefaan seems even more self-centred and egotistical. If you love him, maybe he can make the numbers work. If not, he seems to go on the attack. On top of that, it looks to me as if his primary motivation is to prove that the German crew is competent, while the rest of us, Italians, Belgians and Brits, are inept. He refuses to see that I am making the film well and that I have defended its aesthetic values, such as they are, and have never gone into overtime (one hour over five weeks) on a schedule that is agreed by everyone to be virtually unachievable. I found the money. I wrangled the actors, and suddenly I am the film's enemy. As for changing my mind – I rarely have. I simply haven't liked or accepted some of the dotty ideas the German set decorator ambushed me with.

A film crew crash into town like the circus. One day the trucks roll in, observed in the flicker of net curtains with equal measures of hostility and excitement by the local population. Strange things begin to happen. The local telephone box is disguised as a tree stump. The roads are covered in sand and the local supermarket is suddenly swamped in foliage, its blinking sign removed for a week. Then suddenly the village is invaded by aliens, men with walkie-talkies telling local people where they can walk. Unfamiliar faces in the local bars make jokes about snaggle-toothed monstrosities limping past. The further into the hinterland, the more reserved the reaction and Franconia is the beginning of Central Europe. Franconians are brisk with strangers, already pushed to their limits by the Wagner festival each summer where opera luvvies overflowing from Bayreuth flood and congeal in the outlying villages and market towns.

If there is a recognisable star in the troupe, he or she may break the ice and draw the people out of themselves – sometimes too far. Over the hills and far away for some when the film crew leave town. (The most poignant example of this happened in Colombia. A little boy had been helping the electricians shooting in Mompox, a small village on the Magdalena River. He was an orphan, living with unsympathetic relations. We left town for ever to continue the shoot in Cartagena – one day away downriver on the coast – and the boy appeared there. He bought a one-way ticket with some of the money the crew had left him and with all his worldly belongings showed up for work the next day. I think everyone cried when we sent him back.)

Unlucky local beauties are left with new life inside them and no forwarding address because one evening the trucks roll out of town and all trace of our presence is gone. No more incongruous folk in medieval garb flicking cigarette butts into gardens. No more Colin Firth marching across the village green with tissues tucked into his collar talking on his cell phone.

Thurnau is not sorry for our departure. Hardly anyone has ever ventured outdoors while we have been in town and even the sweet couple who own the guest house look exhausted, firstly because the Neapolitans have smoked like chimneys and talked all night, then because I screamed at them about the church bells and finally because Brian tore through the house one day ripping pictures off the walls – old watercolours and lithographs – to put up on the set without even asking.

On the day we leave the church bells are switched back on and clang non-stop. It feels like the liberation. The only people who seem to be sad at our departure are the mad boys in the Greek restaurant. And of course the village elders, those men who facilitated our work at Thurnau – the Mayor, the castle's custodian and the secretary. They wave sadly as we drive very slowly away through the portcullis. They show up at the German premiere in Munich eighteen months later and apparently there is a permanent exhibition of the film in the castle featuring some worn-out examples of Brian's sets, and you can even be locked into the prison cell at Reading Gaol for the total Oscar Wilde experience.

Now we move – like a virus – twenty miles down the valley to a little village called Schmölz where there is a tiny schloss by the side of the road owned by a pint-sized noblewoman called Gaby and her American husband Jerry. Jerry – also petite – is a rough diamond who arrived with the US army in the seventies and never left.

No wonder. Gaby is a German Barbara Windsor, tiny, giggly, *pulpeuse*, in leggings and tight tops. She is gorgeous and generous – makes coffee for everyone – and we immediately christen her GI Jane. She speaks good English but Jerry has learnt little German after forty-five years.

They are an incongruous yet well-tuned double act. He mumbles and smokes and she bubbles merrily with surprised blue eyes. They are adorable. They dream of moving away from landlocked Franconia but the house is unsold and so they remain. Shades of Chekhov. They own Segways and can be seen skimming across the horizon at dusk, like aliens looking for a place to land.

During the long nights at the local hotel we start to invent the usual stories – all war-related, of course – of Jerry bursting in with the liberating army, dressing up in his old uniform and discovering Gaby in her underwear hiding in an attic cupboard, dragging her by her hair kicking and screaming to the kitchen for interrogation. The evenings are high-spirited, made blurry by tall glasses of opaque beer and strange stews cooked in great pots by the suspicious ladies who run the Wasserschloss Hotel where we are now billeted.

Gaby and Jerry's house converts neatly into the Hôtel de la Plage at Berneval. A front desk magically appears in the hall, replete with pigeonholes and keys, and – unable at this point to afford a real actor – we cast Jerry as the hotel manager. We put him through a crash course in French and dress him up in an apron and waistcoat. He is adorable and starts making plans for a career in show business. On the big day Gaby asks her girlfriends from the village to come and watch. Jerry is very nervous and keeps repeating his line. 'Venez, Monsieur. Venez, Monsieur.' Finally we are ready to shoot. 'Aaand action,' commands Toby, but Jerry opens his mouth and nothing comes out.

'I forgot the line.'

Gaby and the girls squeal with laughter.

I remind him. 'Venez, Monsieur. And remember to give us the key to the room at the same time.'

And the next time he gets the line right but forgets to give us the key. On the third attempt he says something like 'Baday manoo' but gives us the key. By this time he is in quite a state.

'Just relax,' I whisper.

He looks at me with terrified child's eyes while the whole crew watch.

'It's not so easy,' he says.

I agree.

'Breathe.'

'I am breathing.' And this time he gets it all right except that now he is rooted to the spot.

I whisper, 'Now lead the way upstairs.'

He almost jumps into the first step but up we go and the whole crew applaud. The shot ends on a close-up of my expensive blue luggage. Funnily enough, during the post-production rush – and in the shadow of our third bankruptcy – we overlook dubbing Jerry's voice with a real French actor so he can still be heard. Dear GI Jerry from Schmölz. Long may you Segway.

CHAPTER TWENTY-EIGHT

Emily and Constance

Emily Watson is my ideal actress. Everything about her is perfect. I was working with her and Tom Wilkinson on a film called *Separate Lies* in the early days of the century while I was still dreaming up *The Happy Prince*, and I knew that she would be the perfect Constance Wilde.

Emily was unusual for an actress of her age and calibre. There were no games, no lofty ideas, no covert shaping and peddling of her own image. Rather she was warm, acutely sensitive and extremely intelligent. Her beauty was saintly rather than sensual and she looked at you with grave forget-me-not eyes. She was serious but not a bore and the tragic eyes turned merry at the drop of a good joke into the conversation.

Tom was a different kettle of fish – a great tragic actor in the Russian tradition. A black cloud hovered over his head. He put up with people in the same way that a tranquillised bear acquiesces to its captors. Occasionally he roared. More often he simply looked blunt daggers at you through hooded eyes. People were afraid of him and kept their distance. I adored him. He played a lawyer. Emily was his wife and I was the local landowner, a Byronic type, mad, bad and dangerous to know. As Tom was in the City all week Emily was lonely and we started an affair. After a boozy lunch in a pub one day she ran over the local gardener in my car. We didn't stop.

I wanted my character to be one of those hippy aristocrats who took heroin and knew the Rolling Stones, but perhaps the production wasn't really made for that type of interpretation. After my first take at a village cricket match – sprawled on a rug in white flannels and punky hair – Julian Fellowes, who wrote and directed the film, walked over from the monitor with a troubled expression. 'That was a bit Darth Vader, dear.'

'Oh. Do you want more Princess Leia?'

'A little.'

I enjoyed this type of directing. Julian was a bear too. One who could walk on tiptoe and talk like Noël Coward. It was fun to watch him negotiate with Tom. Julian danced around with his tambourine while Tom stood there growling. But Julian was also very intelligent. There was no point in directing a bear like Tom, so he trilled back to the monitor and watched.

Us three actors, each radically different from the other, got along very well and I was thrilled to be invited to Tom's trailer after work for a chat. Under the wild side was an awkward warmth and a gallows humour and the three of us would workshop the usual litany of complaints until the assistants poked their heads round the door to ask if we were staying the night.

Emily was much less complicated than Tom. After make-up in the mornings we would go for walks in the woods and talk about everything under the sun. She wore a pale blue anorak over her costume and in the waving light she was like a little girl who had parked her bike at the edge of the woods. A film set is a wonderful no man's land. Secrets can be shared and hearts laid bare, and we talked quite frankly about our lives. Emily was one of those women who inspired trust. She was soothing and funny, brilliant at her job and always encouraging.

'That was a masterclass,' she once whispered to me after a take.

When I confessed that I was writing a part for her in my film, she rolled her eyes.

'I'm not promising anything. I have to earn my living. You have to realise that. We (her husband and her) have been trying to get our film off the ground for five years. It's really tough.'

I didn't believe her. I still thought everything came easily in those days. On the other hand I did manage to extract from her and Tom two of those meaningless letters of commitment that agents write on behalf of their clients. I extracted one from Colin Firth, too, in a dull moment on *St Trinian's 2* and I waved these letters up and down Europe trying and failing to raise money over the next few years, spouting the usual symphony of bullshit.

'I was on the phone to Emily this morning and SHE said, "Come on, Rupert! When are we getting started?" '

Never, of course! Five years later we worked together again. This time I was George VI and she was the Queen Mother.

'I'm still making that film,' I told her. 'You'd better be ready.'

'I advise you to let it go,' she said rather sternly one night at Chatsworth. 'It's going to eat you up.'

'Does that mean you won't be in it?' I gasped.

'No. It's just that you could waste the whole of your life and it might never happen.'

Our last scene together was on the balcony of Buckingham Palace. Waving to the ecstatic crowds on D-Day. We shot the scene in a car park – at 2 a.m. – on a small podium, behind us a green screen. The ecstatic crowd below was comprised of twenty exhausted crew members wrapped in woolly scarves and parkas, looking bored.

Emily and I waved for what seemed like an eternity. Her

line was 'I could murder a g and t', while I waved relentlessly, wondering if we would ever be reunited as Oscar and Constance. The bleak reality of show business froze through to the bones along with the cold.

Soon it was over and we were wound up in scarves and blankets like antiques and after hurried goodbyes – they are always rushed, for some reason – we were bundled into cars and driven up to London through the night.

'See you in the next reel,' Bob Altman used to say. We wouldn't meet for another five years.

Actually, though I say it myself, we were the best bit of that film, but it ended up being a little disappointing. It was a shame because *A Royal Night Out* was a brilliant idea, about the legendary evening at the end of the war when Princess Elizabeth went out into the crowds in front of Buckingham Palace incognito. But someone had the foolish idea to turn it into a screwball comedy. Most of the people who know how to make that kind of film are dead or American, and certainly our director – the very talented Julian Jarrold – was not one of them. It should have been a romantic drama – *Roman Holiday* – well-observed and bittersweet and Julian would have made it exquisitely. Instead it tried to be *The Pink Panther* and failed.

Emily's domain in our film is also our last stop in Franconia, the end of the German leg of the tour. The Wasserschloss is a fortified castle with a moat in a place called Mitwitz. Its dower house is an incongruous French villa tucked into the hill above the village with a gloomy interior and a wonderful time-warped kitchen.

When we visited on the technical recce a rather grand family – relatives of the owner – were camping in the upstairs rooms on a hunting trip. More shades of Chekhov. The ladies spoke wonderful English and sat around elegantly bored at the kitchen table while the men hunted all day and we came and went with tape measures and potted plants, gasping and screeching at the wonderful old range and the beautiful sink.

'Is everyone in the movie business so enthusiastic?' one lady asked.

'No!' chimed me and Brian together.

In the sitting room there were no curtains, just dark panels, grim cupboards and a heavy gothic table. It was like a prep school or a presbytery, perfect for Constance's house in Heidelberg.

I have persuaded Emily's son Dylan to play Vyvyan – our son. He is seven years old, angelic-looking and has promising instincts. He watches with Emily's grave eyes and listens carefully as his mother directs him gently through the scenes. He is shy and deep. His screen brother is a real child actor – extremely nice but already a pro. He knows the ropes. He arrives with his own stage mother and together they form a nursery group, huddled away from the ladders, lamps and coiled cables. The ladies whisper and encourage their boys, who half-heartedly do their homework.

Emily is everything I had dreamt she would be.

Constance Wilde could be the title of a great romantic novel from the nineteenth century – a tragic heroine whose life is swept up and torn apart in the wake of a husband's ruin. Life had probably not been easy with Oscar during the good times. What did she know of his sexuality? It's one of the elements of the story that fascinates.

From our perspective – post-Freud, post-suffrage, in the wake of the sexual revolution and gay liberation – it is more or less impossible to imagine how women thought about male-on-male sexuality in the nineteenth century. Would they have considered it at all? The idea that men might stick their dicks up each other's arses is rather mundane today but unimaginable to a woman like Constance. She must have known she had lost him as the years thickened around them – but that was a normal part of the marital landscape. Sometimes it was even a relief. Soon after the birth of their second son Vyvyan, the lover's odes to her coils of hair seemed to curdle into quips about the odour of her breath as Oscar, a chubby Alice, fell down the hungry hole into the Wonderland underworld.

From the dreary perspective of today's new puritanism, how intoxicating that rough-and-tumble orgy must have seemed. Against nature, against God, in sealed rooms scented with incense, naked stable lads and randy dukes, bossy bank clerks and submissive priests were up for anything – a secret society, each member recognisable at a glance in the crowds and no boring post-Freudian quibbles to spoil the fun.

One look into Oscar's eyes must have told a sensitive woman like Constance that he had gone. But where? If you had said to her, dutifully sewing the long evenings away in Tite Street, that her husband was on all fours being pleasured by a guardsman she would have simply thought you mad.

People coyly surmise that Oscar was nothing more than a voyeur in those years of his sexual spring. But why would he have been? I think he got right in there, and if he didn't write the novel *Teleny* (that gay classic in which a soldier gets penetrated by a bottle that breaks inside him and goes home to shoot himself rather than face the humiliation of hospital) – then he certainly knew the world where that writhing partouze took place.

And so he came home less and less. There is a poignant moment when Constance delivers letters to the Savoy Hotel where Oscar is staying with Bosie. (Another scene that never made the final cut.)

'Come home soon,' she pleads.

'If only I could remember the address,' jokes Oscar as Bosie appears from the bedroom. I fucked up the scene by putting Bosie into a hopeless djellaba. He should have been properly dressed.

Two weeks after Oscar went to prison Constance fled

England and under an assumed name made her way across Europe, finally settling in Italy. Apart from social ruin she had to cope with two sons who didn't get along. One can only imagine the sleepless nights she must have spent worrying how they would navigate the rapids of scandal without being shipwrecked themselves, both of them far away at boarding schools with new names, separated for safety.

She must have felt herself waning. Something was very wrong. By the time Oscar came out of prison she was more or less crippled. She had fallen down the stairs at Tite Street some years before, injuring her back – and things had gone from bad to worse. Eventually she agreed to a fatal operation from a rogue gynaecologist in Genoa and died under the anaesthetic. (He was later shot by the angry husband of another fatality in his care.) In fact, according to Merlin in *The Lancet* (2015), she probably had multiple sclerosis, but of course that disease was relatively unknown in those days.

In four or five short scenes Emily manages to convey all this and more. It's uncanny. With no visible effort, no acting, she owns the character from the first moment she comes onto the set as a ghost. It is the night of Constance's death and Oscar has a vision of her in his dream. He wakes suddenly. In the Villa Giudice. (It didn't actually happen there but remember, it's a movie.) The house is bathed in a strange orange glow. Vesuvius has erupted. Constance/Emily appears from the shadows. She walks across the salotto as lava streams down the volcano. It's spine-chilling. Gabriel Yared's music is like pins and needles going up and down your spine. At the end of the scene she says, 'I loved you so much. Always. Odd, isn't it?' and then disappears into a wall.

On her last day she sits round the Christmas tree with her son on her knee and they all sing 'Good King Wenceslas'. They pull crackers and wear paper hats. Her red hair glows against the dreary panels of Mitwitz. The wonderful dresses Maurizio and Gianni make for her draw out her pale skin and sad blue eyes. Everything works.

It's a masterclass.

CHAPTER TWENTY-NINE

Taxi to the Métropole

The pocket history of Belgium can be gleaned at a glance entering the Hôtel Métropole in Brussels. Built in the reign of King Leopold II as the Congolese genocide raged, the Métropole is a fin-de-siècle mausoleum on the verge of collapse. (Belgium's present king and queen confront one in an official photo in the foyer, her dress badly hemmed, his suit crumpled, amateurs compared to our own pressed and polished Lilliput Lilibet.)

The halls of the Métropole are lined with marble the colour of rotting flesh, brightly lit by clusters of old lamps like dirty teeth hanging from the ceilings on long chains. Nothing has changed; not even the staff.

Upstairs the corridors and rooms have been refurbished in the eighties with false ceilings, weird flameproof curtains, juddering air conditioning units and small biscuit-coloured bathrooms.

And yet, there is something enchanting about the Métropole, living and dying in its own shadow. I adore it and have stayed there through every one of my Belgian incarnations, and because of the tax incentive – the one that is no longer available in the

UK – most of us British actors have flapped through at one time or another. In the Café Métropole, where some of the moodiest waiters on the planet rehearse their next withering glance in the tall mirrors behind the bar, one is almost certain to meet some cohort from a long-ago show. The staff has shrunk as the hotel careers towards bankruptcy and now only two men seem to work in room service. They are charming and make the breakfast themselves – boiled eggs and biscotti – served on a Formica tray covered with doilies.

The chambermaids on my floor are quite morose, and doggedly hoover around the same book left on the floor for a week. To all prospective travellers, it is essential to have the air conditioning switched off at source – down in the hotel lobby – otherwise a night's sleep is virtually impossible.

Nowadays Brussels is on high alert, and the Métropole has been requisitioned by the military to protect the city centre from a terrorist plot. It's quite exciting, like living in the occupation. The soldiers congregate in the hall in twos and threes, in their caps and crew cuts and khakis, leaning lazily against the marble walls, their hands stroking the heads of their machine guns.

Once, David and I get into the shuddery old elevator with six of them and it gets stuck. In the ensuing silence both of us strain every nerve to look butch and unconcerned, but after a few minutes I get the giggles because somebody's weapon is pressing against the small of my back. I try the Mae West line. 'Is that a gun in your pocket, or are you just pleased to see me?' It seems to break the ice and we get talking. One of them thought of becoming an actor before joining up. He asks what the best way is to get into the business.

'The casting couch,' suggests David.

'Is that a magazine?'

It should be.

The lift gets going again. Unfortunately.

In the afternoons they sit in groups at the windows smoking and cruising the girls who teeter across the no man's land in front of the hotel. In the evenings, they patrol the streets, zipped into their combat gear, their arms leaning lazily on their machine guns. When they see us, they give us a thumbs up and we wave back with girlish abandon.

Adding to the Métropole's woes, a new railway is being built under the square in front of the hotel. It's been going on for about four years now – as long as we have been coming and going – and one more or less tumbles headlong into a huge hole on coming out of the front door. The tables in front of the famous Café Métropole – once seven rows deep – now teeter on its edge in one ropy chorus line of broken chairs and chippy tables. The hole is the hotel's grave, the last nail in its coffin, and the building leans into it – forlorn and empty – while the flow of fashion coils away in a new direction towards the boutique hotel with its space pod bedrooms decorated with driftwood where at least you can find a taxi. At the Métropole even that simple amenity is denied one, which in a way is a relief. Belgian taxi drivers are slightly more poisonous than their Parisian counterparts, if such a thing is humanly possible. Of course, one can't generalise, but then again why not? Driving you from the station they will invariably take you all the way round Brussels, under two tunnels and back via the cathedral, whereas in fact you can walk to the Métropole in ten minutes.

That wide boulevard which leads from the Métropole to the station is lined with cafés on both sides of the street. Trade is lazy during the day. But as dusk falls the tide turns and every bar is crammed to bursting. Exclusively male, exclusively Muslim, all manner of sects, some in the pristine white djellaba of the Safadist, some – chicest of all – in djellaba, jeans and pinstriped jacket, some in tracksuits with religious headgear. They sit in rows watching the world go by. There is not a woman in sight and no hint of ethnic diversity.

The odd gaggle of queens is observed warily as they dart across the road, flaring up under the scrutiny. Like comets hitting the earth's atmosphere, they dive screeching into the labyrinth of streets where the gay bars are – and also our favourite restaurant, Aux Armes de Bruxelles. We go there every night. Partly because with the EU in town every good restaurant is fully booked – months in advance – by glossy lobbyists and radiant MEPs from all the far-flung provinces of our great Union, fluttering and flirting, toasting each course with a new wine, bursting with bonhomie and a little bit of business on the side and why not? None of them is paying taxes or picking up the bill.

Aux Armes de Bruxelles is in the gut of the old town on a cobbled alley of restaurants that leads into the wonderful nineteenth-century shopping arcade, the Galerie du Roi. It is brightly lit with pretty banquettes, starched tablecloths and aproned waiters, and our reception in the restaurant is initially quite hostile – David, me and Willy look a bit like Scarecrow, Lion and Tin Man (don't ask me which witch is which) – but we keep coming back and finally make friends with one of the waiters and then new vistas open up. Tables available in every cosy corner. Thank God.

Each night we sit there, David, Willy, John Conroy and me and whichever of the actors has flown in for the day, drinking Leffe, that bloating Belgian beer that will soon make my fat suit superfluous. Through the windows we drunkenly wave at Dani, Pascal and Florent – our new soldier friends – as they patrol the street outside.

Making Paris out of Brussels is a challenge. Like the dear old Métropole, the city feels unloved and bedraggled. Viciously modernised in the years after the war, a lot of the French architecture in the centre was torn down and replaced by squat towers of black glass.

The most important thing to find is a place where we can shoot the first scene of the film in which we are introduced to Oscar Wilde, sitting drunk on the terrace of a café. But it's not going to be easy. In the scene he must pay his bill and wander out into the night, colliding with a group of English tourists, one of whom – Anna Chancellor – recognises him and gives chase through the streets, finally catching up with him in a misty backstreet.

Writing this scene merrily at home ten years ago, it never crossed my mind how difficult it might be to create a busy Parisian boulevard – traffic, trees and lamps, etc. Its brasseries and bars. Even if we were shooting in Paris it would be difficult. But here in Brussels it's virtually impossible, and over the years of recces and meetings we never manage to resolve the problem. The story of Oscar Wilde in exile is also the story of Paris. If we can't conjure it up – dynamically, evocatively, so that you can smell the drains – then the film will just be another wrecked starship, beached on its own failed aspirations.

Then one day, leafing through a book of photographs by Brassaï I see some wonderful pictures of Paris under a 'pea souper', that lethal smog created by coal smoke that used to sit on a city for whole winters, and that's when I have a brainwave. (Finally, one!)

I will shroud Brussels in weather. Fog, rain and snow.

By pumping smoke into the pointed Flemish streets, we manage to erase all trace of the city and suddenly it's Jean Rhys's Paris, a film noir. By swamping the Place des Martyrs in a CGI snowstorm we miraculously turn it into the Place des Vauges.

Everything falls into place with the weather. Suddenly the underwhelming exterior of the Café Cirio – the last period bar standing, its exterior overgrown with air vents and escalators (another underworld parking system) – is thoroughly disguised by Brian's canny awnings and a backlit summer downpour, so that all you can see is the glittering rain, the tables and chairs, the ladies and gentlemen, Oscar and a few well-placed vegetable stores.

The only snag is that our smoke and rain man is one of the most eccentric characters in the whole troupe. His name is Serge and he dresses like an Impressionist painter in a large smock with long frizzy hair under a beret. He could be Peter Sellers in disguise. He walks with a limp and has a tiny dog with him at all times.

Under the dog in the chain of command is his own long-suffering wife and a platoon of shocked students from the local film school. He and the little dog give orders from a chair on the sidelines, she waves her arms and the students look horrified. Pretty soon he and John are at loggerheads. The students are without experience and take forever to get the streets smoked up and then they can't stop, and suddenly we are away in the clouds.

'Too much smoke!' I yell, and the dog yaps in agreement.

I have three fabulous actors for this first scene. Julian Wadham and Philip Noel were my two best friends at school. Together we acted in all the school plays. Me and Wadham normally played the girls' parts while Noel, for some reason – perhaps because he had quite a big chin – got the character roles. Wadham and I went on to drama school but Noel was sensibly forbidden by his family from going on the boards and embarked on a career in Lloyds.

Now for the first time since our smash hit production of Schiller's *Mary Stuart* in 1974 we are reunited. Forty-two years later they are both in my film as English tourists along with Anna Chancellor in this first all-important scene. Life has come full circle and there's an invisible magic. (I have known Noel since I was seven.)

And so everything finally comes together, the actors, the bar, the wonderful Galerie du Roi filled with beautifully dressed extras and an enchanting alleyway that poor Peter Sellers never quite manages to fill with smoke. Anna catches up with me, dressed to the nines by Maurizio and Gianni, sparkling with jewels in the shadows, wafts of smoke coming in behind like a Hammer horror film, but who cares – the scene is played so brilliantly by Anna nobody will notice. I ask her to lend me five pounds and she starts to cry as Julian storms up. He has finally realised who I am and has come running after his wife to save her from social ruin – contamination with the unspeakable. He commands her 'to go back to Geoffrey' while I secretly pocket the money she has given me. 'If you ever speak to my wife again, I'll kill you. Do you hear?'

Noel arrives at the end of the alley. It's a thrilling moment. Like drowning. My whole life passes before me. Julian signing my death warrant as Queen Elizabeth I. Julian as Ruth in *Blithe Spirit*, wagging his finger at me as Elvira, flitting around in my mother's nightdress, and finally this. 'If you ever speak to my wife again, I'll kill you. Do you hear?'

If only I knew that this day was coming as we took our curtain calls at school I might have been able to relax a bit in the interim.

CHAPTER THIRTY

Caught on a Train

I had scribed a laborious and interminable sequence about Oscar and Bosie's fabled reunion in Rouen. After a bombardment of letters – sometimes two a day – Oscar made his last fatal mistake. He had left prison a born-again Christian vowing never to speak to Bosie again, but within two months – bored stiff of exile in a country village – he was on the train to Rouen. As it chuffed across Normandy, could he hear all the doors slamming behind him? Probably.

'I know what I am doing is fatal,' he wrote later from Naples. 'I love him as I always did. With a sense of tragedy and ruin.' There was no going back. Oscar's fate was sealed in Rouen. He would never see his children or his wife again.

In the script I had them talking in restaurants, walking around the cathedral, shots of its summer silhouette against the hazy Norman dusk accompanied by lots of flighty conversation. In the park, in a carriage, in bed, my lack of imagination knew no bounds. Philip Prowse surged into my flat one morning for one of the writing sessions I came to dread, and I showed it to him. I watched tensely as he twiddled the mole on his neck. (Always a bad sign.) He read and sighed and read again. At one moment he was about to speak, six fingers fluttering over a furrowed brow, thought better of it and plunged into the text again.

'Oh Christ, darling,' he said finally. 'This is interminable. I've had a much better idea. You should set the whole thing in the station.'

'What? The whole weekend?'

'If necessary. They are both such fucking bores, dear. I know you love them but honestly, it's sheer agony to have to watch them banging on all over Rouen. Trust me. I'm your average audience.' The idea of Philip being anyone's average audience member always made me smile.

'Just sitting on the platform then?'

'They can go to the buffet.'

'And stay the night at the station hotel.'

'Exactly. And then Oscar gets back on the train and off he goes, chuff chuff chuff in a cloud of smoke to bore everyone shitless in Dieppe again.'

He was making fun of me but actually it was a wonderful idea. A no man's land, in between destinations. It was the perfect overture for the second act of the film.

I love trains. Like Paris, like the hotel room, like the packet ship, they are central to the story. Some of my favourite moments in films are on trains or at stations. Liza Minnelli waving goodbye at the end of *Cabaret*. Peggy Ashcroft and Judy Davis in *A Passage to India*, tucked up in bed as the train crawls across the plains at night. *Madame X* with Lana Turner. Lana – in top form – is forced to roam the world by the wealthy family she has married into and disgraced. Tragic, restless, running away from herself, she always ends up on a train – drunk – staring at the view. It's epic. She slides from first class to third into an absinthe haze before meeting Burgess Meredith (biggest cock in Hollywood) and going to her death.

Like Lana, Oscar is all about trains and absinthe. He arrives out of the mist on a boat and ricochets from one poky hotel to another – by train.

But unfortunately the trains are on the line.

On the other hand, early on in the recce we find a wonderful station in Wallonia called Binche, and God must be on my side because there is also a small railway museum twenty miles away with engines and carriages and a ravishing blond with a thick sinewy neck called Henk who drives the trains and speaks perfect yet incomprehensible English. He explains that unfortunately the railway company won't allow the trains to come to the station on the tracks.

'No?' gasps David, eyes on stalks.

'Oh yes, man,' beams the driver, slinging a thick marble arm over David's shoulder. 'They must to be weenched and dileever to the station.'

'Weenched? No!' we screech. 'God, how awful.'

(We are both wondering if we will be able to stand between his legs when he drives the train.)

The station dominates a large sloped square, gothic and run-down with steep slate gables and chunky stone walls liberally sprayed with graffiti. Like most provincial stations in Europe, it has taken a seedy turn and odd sorts hang around the square. (The weirdest station of all is Assisi. St Francis would have loved it. You can get anything there from a passport to meth-amphetamine. Body of Crystal.) Inside the station the waiting rooms are deserted. Their damp peeling walls produce a strange sinking feeling.

The town below might have been built by Tim Burton, streets stacked up with black and brown houses, tall and thin, winding round the hill up to the station. The ticket office got a

Nazi makeover – for a film – at some point years ago and there are still directions written in German all over the main hall.

The journey from the Métropole to Binche can take forever in the morning traffic, so we leave at four and arrive early at six. The café next to the station is already open, its lights spilling onto the dark square, its proprietor a comic silhouette sweeping the pavement. David and I huddle over coffee on the terrace as the moon fades and the crew begin to limp across the square towards the station, like the undead. We are all exhausted and there is a general feeling of collapse, but the end is nigh – if I can make it through this week – then three more days in France and I can die. I feel like death this morning. Bloated, frenzied and foul-breathed. At any second some tiny vein behind my brain might burst. My eyes are about to explode from their sockets and I am drinking and smoking to keep going.

Goods trains tear through the station as we wait, horns wailing, mechanical ghosts. It's strange; the trains have represented the whole struggle of the film. How many stations have we had to rattle through to get here, how many meetings, back and forth, before huffing and squealing into the station at Binche?

Just two years ago we were lunching in this same café during an early recce – we all thought the movie was about to happen – when Maurizio called from Rome to say that he had thought about it for a long time and he couldn't do the film. Apparently his leg was giving him trouble. His back was playing up. There were all sorts of problems and dilemmas. No budget. No assistants. No deal.

I walked back and forth that day, listening and wondering who might be available to replace him at such short notice, wanting just to sit down and sob. The whole group were inside having lunch – so instead I acted nonchalantly because you never knew whose beady eye was fixed on you. You must act like the queen on a stamp and reveal nothing until the right moment.

I needn't have worried. The film never happened. Not then, anyway. By the time the wind had changed and we were off to the races again, Maurizio had staged a change of heart.

Now I see him walking across the square all in black like a defrocked priest. I wave and shout. 'This is where I was sitting when you abandoned me, caro.'

'Vero?' he says vaguely, pretending not to remember.

Everything goes well at the station. Our carriages come and go without a hitch. Henk – in costume – is pretending to drive but actually we are being pushed by a locomotive. Startled civilians disembark from real trains on the other side of the platform and are herded through our flimsy nineteenth-century world like ghosts of the future. A commuter recognises one of the extras and makes a big fuss. The extra looks embarrassed and his colleagues eye him disdainfully. The fourth wall has been torn apart.

After the fast train to Antwerp has left, Colin Morgan makes his fabulous entrance into the film appearing through the smoke. It's like a scene from *Brief Encounter*. As dusk falls he and I are sitting on the deserted platform waiting for the stationmaster to light the lamps.

Unfortunately the actor playing the stationmaster has been sent home, so we hastily recast, somebody, anybody who fits the costume and we just manage to squeeze the scene in with a bewildered but rather brilliant electrician in the role before night falls on Binche and we are back on the motorway, tumbling into Aux Armes de Bruxelles seconds before ten o'clock and last orders.

The next day we move to platform two and miraculously we are at Clapham Junction. Oscar is being transported from Wandsworth to Reading Gaol manacled to a prison warder who for some reason – another economy drive, probably – is being played by Toby, who as I mentioned before harbours secret longings for the stage and so studiously prepares for his role while I try to get the scene off the ground. He looks wonderful in the costume – like Jacques Tati. He has a moustache and a hat and reads his newspaper while the crowd stands around looking glazed. Unfortunately somebody has lost the key to our handcuffs, so each time I wave my arms in an attempt to direct the scene he is yanked out of his Stanislavskian reverie like a ventriloquist's dummy.

Today's extras are about as responsive as a herd of cows. I explain (in French) that this is a real scene from history and that they must all start to shout and spit at Wilde. Instead during the first take they gather round and regard me solemnly. Moo. In desperation I leap up from my seat dragging Toby along the platform as I try to shoo them into action.

'Come on, everyone. Shout at me. Spit. Spit. On my face,' I scream.

The camera crew observe grimly from the other side of the tracks. I have finally gone mad.

As for the spittle, the props boys have cooked up an evil syrup in their van which they shoot from syringes over my face from beside the camera during my close-up.

'Jaysus,' shouts John Conroy from behind the camera. 'This looks like a happy ending. Someone's shot a load over your face.'

Finally there is a reaction from the extras and they all laugh. A lot. 'Happy ending' is part of the international language.

It seems unfair in a book about making movies not to shine a little fairy light on that strange substratum, that poisoned wail of wannabes always waiting in the wings with the newspaper and never really getting on stage, that herd who are shunted to another tent for lunch – the extras.

In the old days the most lethal ones were the dress extras – the dancing crowd. In my first-ever job at the BBC – a thriller called *The Manhood of Edward Robinson* – I was a bright young thing and had to dance in the Café Royal with a hundred flappers and failed Bing Crosbys in white tie and tails. In those days one was filmed by huge lumbering cameras that looked like daleks or iron lungs. They slithered across the floor on a trail of cable. Little red lights shone on their heads when it was their turn to film the action. I was to charleston over to one with the exquisite Cherie Lunghi, flip her backwards and then do a little bit of dialogue when the red light blinked. I was about to open my mouth when a wave of waltzing, grinning, spinning monsters crashed through us – the dress extras heading towards the light. Unfortunately I was in the middle of an extravagant back kick and was knocked over in the rush and fractured my collarbone.

Extras are as important as the stars in a way because they sell the scene and give the decoration its authenticity. I have had some marvellous luck on the film. Early on at Thurnau we had an open call for anyone in the neighbourhood who was interested in taking part. It was big news, page one in *Franconia Today* and after work one afternoon people arrived from all over the state. It was a cross between a studio cattle call from the thirties and a market scene from a Thomas Hardy film. Three or four hundred countryfolk gathered in the courtyard of the castle and I passed among them flanked by assistants with clipboards (David with a biro), eyes peeled for new talent to sign up. Young girls in spandex dazzled me with their wacky smiles. Old men who weren't sure what they were doing looked on furiously as I wafted by.

'Ask him if he speaks any English,' I breezed. 'I love that hair. Sign him.'

In this way we found Queen Victoria, whose husband had a stroke on the day of the shoot, which probably accounts for her steely glare in the scene. I asked her if she wanted to go home but she said she'd rather keep busy. Such is the allure of the silver screen.

The man I chose to play the priest in the Miranda Richardson/ Lady Queensberry scene promised he understood English perfectly only to look insane on the day, winking or looking aghast in all the wrong places. He was one of the reasons the scene hit the cutting-room floor. When Lady Q acidly recounted how her 'flesh crawled when Oscar Wilde came into a room', the priest snickered and winked. When she asked him if he wanted more tea, he looked horrified.

There was a group of about forty extras for the theatre scenes, and we filmed them in different positions against a green screen to replicate the thousand spectators of a glittering first night. They were inexplicably fabulous, full of energy and laughed and clapped late into the night. I explained that they were watching a play by Oscar Wilde and that when I raised my arm it meant that the actors were being very funny. With each cue one particular woman cracked up into infectious peals of laughter, holding her sides it was so funny. She looked as though she could dislocate her jaw at any moment. She was so good that I had her in a box, in the stalls and up in the dress circle so that when the scene was cut together she popped up everywhere.

On the station at Binche in the gloomy weather, the crowd take a lot of fluffing to get into the mood. But this is Wallonia – the county in the EU that always manages to hold everything up. Luckily I have a secret weapon – Patrick Hannaway. I did my first-ever job with him in 1979. He was one of the improbable stars from the golden days of the Glasgow Citizens Theatre, a tiny bulldog of an actor, and he is electrifying as the traveller who recognises Wilde on the station. In a bowler hat and a briefcase, he elbows the extras into a frenzy like a music hall hoofer.

Philip – for whom Patrick worked for thirty years – has written him some wonderful dialogue, and his performance reminds me of Arthur Lowe in *Dad's Army*. A nightmare version.

For me it's another of the wonderful moments. Patrick saying

the lines that Philip wrote – all these years later – being so brilliant, bringing one of the most challenging and epic scenes in
the whole Wilde cycle so terrifyingly to life. His performance
renews my belief in myself, in the film, in life – because come
what may, however it all turns out, he has shown us, in every
frame of the footage – he doesn't make one false move – exactly
how one person can whip up a crowd of cows into a stamped-
ing, spitting herd. Everything works perfectly. Oscar is isolated
on the bench. The crowd closes in. Patrick wheels and points.
'Backs to the wall, boys. We don't want any of that love which
dare not speak its moniker here,' he screams.

And then the spitting begins. It's a scene as horrific and
heartbreaking as Jesus being delivered by Pontius Pilate to the
mob, and has a resonance right through to the killing of Stephen
Lawrence at a bus stop by a group of village idiots.

'I shall see it on my deathbed,' says Oscar to Robbie and
Reggie in the film.

CHAPTER THIRTY-ONE

The Last Day

It is the last day. A huge sigh of relief hangs over the troupe with the low grey weather on the port of Deauville, shooting – last but not least – the arrival of the packet boat, that ship of dreams that has been the nub of so much contention between myself and the powers that were.

We finally found a working boat – the *Waverley* – on the Clyde in Scotland. John Conroy shot it over a weekend during its final sortie of the year on the Firth of Forth, and here on the port we are going to replicate it later in CGI.

For the time being all we have – as per Sébastien's sketch on the back of that napkin – is a gangplank against a green screen with the two blinking green and red lights of the Deauville harbour in the background. We have some horses and carriages, a crowd getting off the boat and our faithful street lamp, which has been with us for the whole shoot and which today falls over as Willy is standing under it. We all watch in horror – unable to speak as the sharp edge of its lantern bears down on his head – but Willy is the cat-of-nine-lives, and nothing like a falling street lamp is going to get him. As if by magic he leans about three inches to his left to take a photograph and the lamp crashes to the ground beside him.

Released from our frozen horror, we all rush towards him and he beats us off indignantly. David nearly faints.

'Oh, pull yourselves together,' snaps Willy. 'You've all gone mad.'

The news spreads around the troupe like a number in a musical.

'What happened?'

'Willy nearly got killed.' It is the perfect vignette, the final twist.

And so we fade out on a blustery Deauville dusk, a street lamp falling in slow motion on a man in a mackintosh. The picture freezes, the victim steps neatly out of the frame. He walks into a nearby bar and orders a drink. The End. The film nearly killed us all. It crashed, but we survived.

PART FOUR

CHAPTER THIRTY-TWO

Post

The next station of the cross is the cutting room. In the eaves of the Warner building in Dean Street, it seems at first glance to promise the most lugubrious tableau of the film's memories. A quiet room with an editor and a mountain of magisterial material, punctuated by long Soho lunches with one's dazzling acquaintances while the petals of one's oeuvre slowly unfurl upstairs, like a time-release photograph, quivering towards the sunlight in an orgy of self-congratulation.

It's not going to be like that at all. First of all, Sébastien is an invisible poltergeist quivering with indignation from the other side (Brussels), and is determined to make this experience, the cheapest part of the whole process – it is after all just a room, an editor, his assistant and me – a living torture chamber. To this end he has employed the only real twat that ever came on the film. Our post-production point person. His name shall remain unwritten, like those of certain macumba gods of whom one dare not speak – but suffice to say that he looked harmless enough to start with, like a young Professor Calculus from *Tintin*. I remarked on this during our first meeting – I thought I was breaking the ice – but he took terrible umbrage. He seemed to think I was making a xenophobic slur. I got down on all fours and begged forgiveness, but my subservient attitude didn't last very long.

'Could we have some petty cash?' asked Nic-the-editor politely.

'No,' said the Professor curtly.

'But how should we pay for coffee and tea?'

'I've no idea.'

He had a habit of appearing without warning. We would come back in from lunch to find him standing in the corner of the room like an apparition, with another list of dos and don'ts, our messages from the other side. He had obviously been instructed to make things as hard as possible. Or rather he had been informed that I was so difficult and devious that I must be thwarted at all costs. It was December and he expected us to work over Christmas. The eleven weeks that we had been given to edit the film apparently included the two weeks of Christmas. Who knew? When we both refused, he simply walked out. The long and short of it all was that we would have nine weeks to edit the entire film, and that was that. Any reservations Nic and I may have had about each other evaporated in our mutual loathing of the Professor.

Editors are strange, awkward birds, or bats, actually – happiest in the dark, making odd noises while hanging upside down. They slink around the film set squinting at the lights. Nobody is quite sure who they are. They aren't sure themselves. Cinema is full of exploding personalities, and the careful, burrowing editor sometimes doesn't quite know where to fit in. Occasionally they become assertive, charging from the editing room to the set waving a list of shots without which they are unable to edit the scenes. But mostly their aggression is on the more passive end of the spectrum.

Poor Nic was forced to be very self-contained during our shoot. Isolated and lonely in the Eastern bloc with nothing but a Belgian spy for an assistant, he knew we had no time to do anything but shoot the movie and only occasionally would he venture forth with a suggestion for an extra shot. In the rush of the funeral sequence we forgot to shoot the coffin – the money – in the grave. Reluctantly, after a surprisingly vivid outburst from Nic, Stefaan Schieder ordered a new hole to be dug – at considerable expense according to him; I think its price went up to twenty thousand euros at one point – and Nic stood over the grave, a surly parish priest in a beret getting soaked to the skin in the fake rain.

The first thing I discover in the intimacy of that darkened room is that Nic is much older than I had imagined. I thought he was fifty, or maybe sixty at the most. In fact, he is well into his seventies. After he admits this awful truth – which according to him is death to an editor – I inspect him closely and am amazed. He still has the bottom of a thirty-year-old. It is pert and muscular and there is no extra weight around his waist. He is still good-looking. He began his career in the days of real film and real editing. One spliced the soundtrack and the film by hand. Editing, like directing, was an act of creative imagination married to an incredible technical capacity. One had to have an idea of the rhythm and punctuation of a scene before shooting it, before seeing it.

Today it is a completely different job. Happily Nic is unfazed by the technology and types away like a demented secretary at his keyboard. Only occasionally does he raise his hands in anguish when the computer says no, or it freezes completely.

I watch all this from a sleazy leather couch upon which one can never get a grip, always sliding slowly down.

The only thing that could possibly give me a clue to his advanced age is that he is a curmudgeonly lefty from the old school – lights, camera, industrial action – and I certainly won't bother waving at him from the tumbril as I am being trundled to my execution. He will not come to work before the stroke of 10 a.m. and he doesn't much care to stay behind after six.

So much for my fantasy of long nights on coke editing the film. He has a wonderful wife from Barbados and they are endlessly going away on holidays, and weekends are out. He uses her to great effect as an excuse so I christen her the Swamp Bitch and they both adore the name. They are married but live separately and spend every January in Barbados visiting her family. One day he hears from David's accent that he also is from Barbados, and it transpires that the SB knew David's mother and that David's mother had an affair with the SB's brother-in-law. Small world. Too small.

There is some initial tension between us. An editor and a director must tune themselves to each other's key but we are thrown together and radicalised by Professor Calculus. We are shell-shocked after our first encounter with him and have to check with each other that we weren't dreaming. After a brief discussion we decide to ignore him and just get on with the job as best we can. If we haven't finished the edit in nine weeks, then we haven't finished. From that moment on we are bonded friends and Nic is a great source of strength for me, very encouraging and we also manage to laugh in that pressure cooker atmosphere of the editing room.

And so we only have one real run at the entire film and that's that. There will be no time for fine-tuning. No time for experimentation beyond the very basics, and within a few weeks we are screening the movie to the executives, Thorsten, his flat-footed partner from the sales company, Philipp Kreuzer from the production company, various people from the BBC, Lionsgate and of course Sébastien.

Each member of this group has a vote about the final cut of the film.

In these initial screenings nobody seems particularly enthusiastic. Our only fans are Alan Yentob and Robert Fox. Alan has been making a documentary about me-making-my-film for the last five years and we have become friends. He is very supportive, always enthusiastic, always ready with constructive ideas for the edit. Everyone else seems measured and reserved when the lights come up, their faces drained of expression. There is going to be a new head at the BBC – always a dangerous time for someone still hanging on from the days of the ancien régime. My champion was Christine Langham. Now we are waiting to see who takes over, but meanwhile various hopefuls come over from Broadcasting House and none of them seems to be particularly enthralled. One looks through one's own viewfinder as much as anything else when one sits in front of a film, and a young lady from the Beeb is convinced that the moans she hears from the next-door room in the brothel sequence (clearly a woman's voice, by the way) are actually coming from our young ten-year-old actor who is being raped while Oscar has sex with his elder brother.

Such an elaborate imagination is clearly what keeps our great British Broadcaster on the cutting edge.

Luckily for me this query is greeted with derision from the rest of the group during one of those agonising note sessions in the screening room when the lights come up, but of course as we are sitting in that darkened room under the eaves – it's January 2017 – puritan winds are already howling across Soho. By the time the movie comes out the whole landscape of our culture has been blown away and is unrecognisable to anyone born before the beginning of this cursed century.

But meanwhile we screen and screen. Zygi and Nick from Lionsgate are supportive and very constructive and despite all our wrangles behind the scenes, Sébastien always takes my side. Thorsten takes me aside and tells me he is worried that Oscar is dislikeable.

'You know, Rupert,' he murmurs in his perfectly measured English, 'the guy who is writing the press kit said to me the other day, "The problem is, Thorsten, that I just don't like him".' He is almost whispering. It reminds me of confession when I was small.

'How do you think I should make him more likeable?' I whisper back, genuinely curious.

'I don't know. But we have to try.'

One of the problems could be – I think to myself during a sleepless night – that there are two fairly identical scenes of vitriol between Bosie and Oscar once the two of them have established themselves in Naples. Both scenes say the same thing and by the time you get to the second, you possibly begin to lose patience. I decide on a radical cut – which sadly includes losing the scene with Miranda Richardson as Lady Queensberry – and it makes a real difference to the film and yes, Oscar is somehow more likeable.

We are closed down rather unceremoniously in February by Professor Calculus on behalf of a frenzied Sébastien in Brussels. Calculus also announces his retirement at the same time. Like a military figure from *Chitty Chitty Bang Bang* he clicks his heels in an insolent farewell and his replacement appears out of nowhere, a rather gentle Frenchman named Thomas Averland who reminds me of Geraldine Chaplin (I keep that thought to myself), and who will now be my point person for the next step as I trot on to Belgium and the sound edit.

I hate to say goodbye to Nic, his lovely assistant and her tranquillised dog. They have defended and supported me through Sébastien's austerity measures. I feel quite low handing in my pass at the Warner building and that establishment zips up behind me. I go back the next day to collect some things and I can't get in. It's just a building on a street again. From now on I will be on my own.

CHAPTER THIRTY-THREE

Sound

Pretty soon I am back on the Eurostar – destination Brussels.
It is a cold, wet March at the Métropole, where by now I am
almost the only guest – guarded by a whole regiment of soldiers.
David joins me for moral support and we soon slip back into the
old routine. Each morning we negotiate the sludge in front of
the hotel and spend hours trying to find a taxi to take us to the
post-production house, an underground bunker on three levels
in the suburb of Schaerbeek, a largely Muslim neighbourhood of
shrouded ladies, magnificent and medieval, their robes billowing
in the cold wind on the high street.

Agent is owned by Alek, our good-looking, no-nonsense
sound engineer. He is the adored scoutmaster to a brilliant team
of young cubs, and a kind of pop idol to the two lovely women
who work in the office. At lunch around the large kitchen table
they all chatter in French, English and Flemish when they want
to make sure we don't understand. Alek is fifty going on forty,
with long hair and a motorbike, calm and funny and tough as old
boots. On the other hand he is also a great friend of Sébastien,

our producer, so initially he is quite reserved. Our reputations always seem to precede us – larger than life, more angular, painted in cruel shapes but in the end a bad one is better than none at all and a kind of liberation to boot. Now the floor is yours to shock and awe.

Meanwhile all semblance of cash has disappeared from the kitty. Impotently we wave our invoices for taxis at Thomas Averland when he swoops in from Paris. He snaps them into his briefcase with a friendly smile and we never hear any more. More importantly we have next to no time to create the soundscape of the film. Hardly any of the sound recorded on the shoot is usable and we must revoice most of the performances. The actors troop over on the Eurostar for the final reunion of the film, watching themselves on the big screen, headphones pressed to one ear, talking into the mic, one eye cocked towards their own lips saying the same phrase from all those months ago. We've all changed since then, and it's a romantic moment of farewell. No sooner have they arrived than they leave again.

Sitting in the darkened dubbing theatre each one is subjected to a post-mortem from the team. Some actors are wonderful at revoicing, others less good. Colin Morgan is in control of every syllable. Ronnie Pickup, who plays the judge, is indignant that so much of his performance has been cut. After an awkward session in London, I escort him downstairs to his car. At the door he turns and says in a wounded voice, 'I'm sorry Rupert couldn't be here.' There doesn't seem much point in clearing up the misunderstanding.

'Yes. I'm afraid he couldn't make it. But he sends his best.'

The great actor grunts and waves me away.

Alek and his team do not buckle under the strain and do an excellent and detailed job. One of his brilliant boys threads birdsong through the film, wood pigeons to conjure up spring nights in London, swallows everywhere, of course, and a wonderful cock crowing three times in Posillipo as Bosie prepares to betray Oscar. It's magic. The distant sound of a barge on the Thames and a storm in the Bay of Naples evoke so much nostalgic emotion in me that I have to go to the loo and cry.

Yes. I am verging on collapse at this point. My brain has overheated. On the way back from one of these snivels another of the young cubs beckons me into his studio to listen to the breath track he has created for Oscar. He has used sound from a documentary he made about cystic fibrosis and has superimposed some of its rasping, chesty breath on my performance. My every hollow cough has been artfully filled with a rich phlegmy rattle. Each intake of breath is tinged with a wonderful wheeze like an old harmonium; each sigh is now a poem of collapse.

I am dumbstruck. Oscar has become almost too real, he's oozing through the screen into the room – a tubercular ghost. The breath changes my performance into something quite chilling and we have to tone it down a bit, but it's a wonderful moment of communion – a deranged old queen with a dream, a young stranger on a computer and a wonderful duet for voice and breath flung onto the screen to dazzling effect.

The time frame, the tiredness, the travel, the trying to juggle with everyone's point of view is fraying my nerves and a breakdown, such as it is, finally blooms – or bursts actually, like a spot or a dam – on a day in May when I must take the 6 a.m. train from London to Brussels for a screening and note session with the Germans in a studio outside the city, after which I must drive back to the station for another train – this time to Paris – to meet Gabriel Yared, the composer, in the afternoon and return to Brussels in the evening.

I miss the screening with the Germans because the taxi from the station takes me to the right address in the wrong suburb. The driver screeches off before I have a chance to ask him to wait. Like Madeline Kahn in *What's Up, Doc?* I peek through the squeaking door of a derelict warehouse but there is nobody there. Panic reflux gurgles up my throat. It's not a very savoury neighbourhood. Now I walk for miles, trundling my little wheelie past unfriendly staring faces – needless to say, no cabs – and suddenly I find myself in a huge square. I sit in the middle by a fountain and burst into tears.

I call Thomas Averland in Paris. He tells me to stop shouting but to stay where I am and he will send a taxi. It never comes. I finally get to the screening just as they are all coming out. I feel utterly deranged. I hate being late. Everyone is swinging in and out of focus. There is a fine line between a queeny fit and a nervous breakdown and I'm crossing it. Nevertheless I sit obediently – eyes popping out, dripping with sweat – and listen to more whispers from Thorsten. I can't really concentrate but it's the same old thing. Oscar is not this. He should be more that. Philipp agrees with Thorsten who disagrees with Sébastien who comes to my rescue, not through any kind of empathy but because he doesn't want any more discussion that could delay the end of post-production – the Germans don't pay for anything on the Belgian side – and Thorsten is advocating reopening the edit, so soon I am thrown into a cab and am on my way back to the station.

I get to Paris and my meeting with Gabriel. He is recording the music with a string quartet at a studio in Saint-Germain – and for a moment I am becalmed. I watch them through the thick glass of the control booth. In a large sealed room they sit in a semicircle around the conductor – Gabriel himself – with head-phones clamped over their ears as if they are animals involved in a strange experiment, obedient dogs watching their master with moist adoring eyes.

It's a picture of cleanliness and order – silent – until a pair of headphones is given to me and suddenly the plaintive theme, played over and over again, moves me to more secret tears in the loo. But there is no peace for the wicked, and soon I wave goodbye through the window – they all wave back and I return to the station to catch my train to Brussels.

All my tickets and reservations are stored on my phone, which runs out of juice as I hit the Gare du Nord. Howling, arms out-stretched, minutes to go before my train, I scream around the station looking for a plug and eventually find one on the floor of the ticket office. I sit down next to it sobbing – my cable is not very long – and fall asleep waiting for it to charge.

I am roughly woken by armed police several hours later. They think I'm on drugs. If only. They tell me to move on. Looking up from the floor at their crew cut pinheads peeping from bulletproof vests, they have a mechanical effect, navy-blue tin men with machine guns in their pockets. I can't help smiling as I remember my other brushes with the law – the time I was arrested with Antony Price outside Heaven, or when Catherine Ansel and I were held at gunpoint at the Bastille in Paris. On each of these occasions, on release I was recognised. 'Mr Everett. You have a wonderful career. Don't get in trouble again,' said the London duty officer. I was thrilled. To be recognised in the slammer felt chic. On the Île Saint-Louis the young night *flic* was less ceremonial. 'C'est toi, l'acteur? Pauvre con. Casse-toi.'

Tonight they just think I'm another washed-up immigrant waiting for a train to somewhere and they are about right. They poke at me with their machine guns and I stumble into the warm May night.

CHAPTER THIRTY-FOUR

Lockdown

A nd so the film is locked into place, like a body in its
tomb, never to be revisited, each frame in its sequence
for eternity. The shadows and lights have been graded and
fixed in Berlin by Natalie, a tiny Russian doll (KGB, according
to David) in another darkened room. Each music cue, so hotly
debated – should it come here, should it go there, too loud, not
loud enough – is engraved on the track, each noise – the owl,
the cockerel, the sea, the boulevard – will never be louder or
quieter again.

There will be no more witching hour texts or heated lunchtime debates, or sleepless nights worrying about the things that
can never be done – it's over.

I have to rent the dubbing theatre myself for the last couple
of days in order to finish the edit – Sébastien refuses to spend
another penny – but so what, and finally it's done and I leave
Brussels for the last time. Goodbye Alek. Goodbye Aux Armes
de Bruxelles.

The film is invited to the Sundance Film Festival and also

to the Berlinale. At Sundance we achieve a lukewarm reception and a killer review from *Variety* which sets a low tone for our American release. Nevertheless we manage to score a distribution deal from Sony Classics. Tom and Michael are old hands and they launched my first film *Another Country* when they were at Orion Classics in the early eighties.

At Berlin the film is pretty popular and even the Pet Shop Boys show up for a nine o'clock screening, which sends shivers down my spine. They are my household gods, and their appreciation trumps any tepid review from *The Hollyweird Reporter*. Jörg and Philipp give a stylish party in a collapsed dance hall on the night of the screening, but I finally fall out irrevocably with them two days later in a brief screamed telephone conversation which seals the fate of the film.

It's a shame and I regret it at once, mostly because the spiritualist daughter of Kiki (remember her – the present custodian of Villa Giudice at Posillipo) told me that under no circumstances was I to fall out with them otherwise the bright future scheduled for the film by the higher powers would be marred. I did, and it was.

CHAPTER THIRTY-FIVE

The Release

Now it is 2018. I am working in Rome shooting *The Name of the Rose*. It's made by Palomar, our Italian producers, and that's how I manage to score the job of Bernard Gui, inquisitor. It's a wonderful role. Half my team is on the series – John Conroy, Maurizio and Gianni, Luigi Rocchetti – and I begin to feel like Orson Welles. Shooting at Cinecittà, dining at Villini, lying sleepless in my blood-red damask bedroom at the Hotel Locarno – sleepless because the film is being released across Italy and there is no sign of a poster, a trailer, nothing online or in the paper. Whenever I ask for some details, the same reply: 'Ees all comin'.'

(Sumer is icumen in
Lhude sing cuccu)

So is Christmas. It's our first outing, before the UK even, and on every free day I set off up and down the country on the bullet train to promote the film. Italy tumbles by in a blur. It feels like another goodbye, impossibly beautiful, a mirage like the mountains that hang over Torino as I disembark for the gay and lesbian film festival in that city, or a misty Vesuvius, there but not there, as we coil around rainy Naples for our premiere.

At another festival, this time in the walled city of Lucca, I bump into Stephen Frears in the piazza. 'Where's my shirt?' he asks as usual. (We were once in the same hotel at a festival in Marrakesh and he left some things in his bathroom. I collected them for him – sponge bag, toothbrush and stripy socks – all the nécessaires of England's most prolific director – but somehow I couldn't face returning a rather matronly shift which he calls a shirt. It was just too embarrassing, like bringing soiled stays to a great actress.)

Entranced by the travel, my train hisses to a halt in the amazing station at Milano, once, twice, three times a week for chat shows and interviews followed by solitary drunken dinners at the Four Seasons Hotel in Via Gesù. It's off-season, and only the head waiter is in residence. How we all fancied him in the old days. He is still very sweet, still good-looking, married now. To a man. (So I was right.)

In my heyday the Four Seasons was one of the great stages, next door to the Versace mansion, for spring collections and cruise lines and general travels with my arse. But sitting drunk with Willum, we agree that it was all too long ago now for regrets and recriminations. Thank God. When he was just a busboy I used to order room service and be sprawled in Speedos across the bed when he arrived with it. Hashtag, he too.

Twenty years have zipped by, like Italy on the train. No more Donatella, no more Kate and Naomi, no more Michael Roberts and Suzy Menkes, just me and Willum drinking grappa in a pool of light in the deserted restaurant.

A nice lady from the Hollywood Foreign Press asks me to go to some Italian film festivals that she is the president of.

Desperate to ingratiate myself with that loopy crew (they control the Golden Globe Awards), I show up at the Taormina film festival and two more in the south of Italy. (Once you get onto the festival circuit you can keep going for 365 days a year, just showing up. There is one every day, somewhere. Present your dirty laundry at the hotel lobby on arrival and pick it up as you leave for the next festival. If you forget something, like Stephen Frears, you can always ask one of the other sluts to bring it along to the next gig.)

At one festival on a football pitch, the electricity shuts down in the middle of the film. But so what? I explain the rest. It's all a part of the mad game, and even if one has to sit through endless dinners with local dignitaries it's a game of dice and you never know what can happen. Once in Sorrento, for example, I got to stay for a whole extra week in the hotel.

Of course you rarely see an A-lister swooping in to any of these events – the goody bag is too vaudevillian, for starters – but the B-crowd are often much more interesting and can at least let their extensions down. This year's group of down-and-outs include Richard Dreyfuss and his adorable Russian wife Svetlana, Matthew Modine and his wife Caridad.

Richard – one of the most brilliant actors of his generation – talks non-stop but mercifully is incredibly funny. For example he once held workshops for young actors in Hollywood to tell them how to get on in the business. His methods were unusual. His advice was apparently never to send headshots or CVs to casting directors – a breed he considered bottom feeders in the cinematic pond life.

'Think about it,' he said. 'It's a total waste of time. They never look at your headshot. They just file it away if you're lucky. I went to see this one casting director and she said, "Please send me your CV with a photo". I said, "Fuck, no". She said, "How are we going to remember you?" I said, "You're going to remember me because when I leave here I am going to get into my fucking car and drive right through the wall into this office. That's how you're going to remember me".'

I adore him. I can't wait to read about some kamikaze actor driving into the commissary at 20th Century Fox on his instructions.

I have known Matthew Modine for years and adore him, too. He is like a big dog, always charming, still amazing-looking, and so is his wife. Unlike one, they have both aged beautifully.

The lady from the Hollywood Foreign Press is very nice, too. She scores us free jewellery and huge awards at each festival and we stagger back to the hotel with them wondering how on earth we are going to be able to fit them into our luggage with all the dry-cleaning.

As the festivals get smaller the awards seem to get bigger, but it all helps and the film does reasonably well considering that Sky Italia have put little muscle into its promotion. I have lobbied endlessly for more money, more visibility but to no avail and soon it's too late. That's when I catch sight of the CEO Nicola in a boutique on the Via Condotti. I hide in one changing room, while he hides in another. Finally we both realise that we can't wait for the other to leave, so we both appear and vow to have a coffee to discuss the promotion. Of course we never do.

The swirling montage of reviews, trains, planes and flashing cameras moves on to Germany. It is a beautiful May weekend in Munich. There are two premieres in different theatres. Jörg gives a speech thanking the German crew. Speeches in Germany are very formal. The Mayor, the city officials, all with their titles, *herr doktor*, *liebe frau professor*, are thanked in long blank mono-tone phrases, so probably nobody notices that Jörg reads the names of our German crew with difficulty – he has never met them, nor they he – but Jörg is not faint-hearted. He and Philipp have formed a company since the film was made, which in itself is quite surprising. Sworn enemies one day, strange bedfellows the next – it could be a show business mantra.

We all stand in a row, the screen towering behind us, and Jörg mumbles on. The audience watch with polite eager faces – the Germans are very correct, deeply respectful and listen carefully as Jörg and Philipp neatly manage to carve themselves a future – a next step – which eludes the rest of us, by the way, but is the simple rule of thumb for survival in our business. Keep moving. Look busy. Work breeds work. Soon they are producing the new Daniel Radcliffe thriller and have their fingers in a thousand pies while I am back in rep. All hail to them.

Since my fight on the phone I know the future is doomed, but I am grudgingly pleased for Jörg and Philipp. After all they have had to deal with me for the last six years, tricky, deceitful, hot and cold, smart and stupid, but sadly there is an underwater feeling to the whole premiere weekend. Primarily because there has been a major shift in the power structure at our German distributors and we find ourselves – again – part of an ancien régime. In the old days my friend Markus Zimmer was the CEO of Concorde films. We collaborated many times and – for the most part – with a certain success. (*St Trinian's* was our Waterloo. The Germans loathed it.) But on the strength of our former triumphs he bought the film for Germany – for good money, for last year's money, for money that is hard to score these days.

Concorde is owned by Herr Kloiber, who also owns Tele München, and this year he decided to put his son in charge, over Markus. The son, young Herr Kloiber, is good-looking, red-headed, hot-headed, with (red) eyes fixed on Hollywood. Markus – my champion – made a dignified exit and a new regime was installed that was not particularly interested in *The Happy Prince*. Hence they have decided to put the film out at the same time as the World Cup, their premise being that people who don't like the football can go to the cinema.

But this is last year's rule. It no longer applies. Today the football trumps everything and everyone – including old queens – and what it doesn't stop the warm weather does. Concorde threw peanuts into the promotion and the valiant Bavarian fund came up with the rest, but it was already a damp squib as it came under starter's orders. And so my dream of making a wonderful German film went down like a sinking ship as the box office collapsed within a matter of days and the film was buried in a hot May grave.

CHAPTER THIRTY-SIX

A Happy Ending in the Gorbals

I had been secretly dreading the UK release of *The Happy Prince*. You never know which way the wind is going to blow at home and a lady of the night must always prepare for a squall, but in the end London was the most fun part of the whole world circus.

We got some excellent reviews. The audiences were good. Lionsgate did a brilliant job. Justine Picardie from *Harper's Magazine* gave a party at the Café Royal on the night of the premiere. Ruby Wax came. Colin Firth too. And so – very shortly after – did a gigantic heatwave. Day after day of blistering weather reduced the country to a standstill and my nerves to shreds. Nobody goes to the movies when it's hot outside and so we wilted across the country along with everything else. Each day I pictured rows of empty seats in all those sawn-off screening rooms up and down the country, just a somnambulistic usherette sitting at the back and maybe one faithful old fairy eating a sandwich.

But there was a high point, a white summer night at the Glasgow Film Theatre.

I took the train from Euston in the acid trip weather, eyes

glued to the view, the pit in my stomach at the catastrophic turn of events momentarily dissolved by England, Cumberland, Northumberland, Hadrian's Wall, all at their seductive best. The eastern track is the 'high road' to Scotland because the train tears past the coast for a breathtaking stretch. Deep-blue sea, white waves, green hills. And memories.

The first time I took this train was in 1978, more than forty years ago. On that trip I was determined to launch myself on the famous Citizens Theatre where I had heard everyone was a cross-dresser and they all had sex in the showers after the shows. This may seem scant recommendation in today's puritan world but to me it sounded heavenly. I was fully expecting – indeed looking forward to – a bit of rough and tumble on the way up. Or down. With my Glaswegian friend Joe, a child actor I got to know when we were both dressers at the RSC, I arrived for a performance of *Chinchilla*, a play about Diaghilev, by the resident playwright Robert David MacDonald. We were dressed up to the nines, me in my Antony Price spacesuit, Joe decked out as a child star from the forties, in shorts and a pork-pie hat. Heads turned as we entered the theatre and by the interval I had landed myself a job. As an extra, fifteen pounds a week, beginning in ten days. The play was an adaptation of the complete works of Proust, again written by MacDonald. And so began the most successful stretch of my career. There was no sex in the showers but apart from that, Glasgow – city and theatre – lived up to all my fantastical expectations in a way that very little else ever did. The play was called *A Waste of Time* and was the most extraordinary piece of work I have ever been involved in. From then on I worked in Glasgow for Philip on and off until he retired in 2009. I hardly worked for anybody else.

And so at Motherwell my heart began to race as the south side of Glasgow unfolded from the haze, the familiar red stone sidings and hangars flashing past, suddenly close, falling away, purple weeds waving from the tracks, while the train groaned and clanked, suddenly shifting tracks towards the Gorbals, over the Clyde and into Central station, producing an unusual rush in the blistering heat, the smell of diesel and dust igniting that cluster of long-drained brain cells to release their chemical memories, surging through the nerves up to the surface, and I spent the day with tingling skin, sweaty and tearful. The film suddenly seemed like my ultimate expression. I had forgotten how it related to my life in Glasgow so intimately.

Before the screening I walked the few yards from the GFT to see the art school, more or less burnt to the ground for the second time. 'There isn't a God,' said a woman after we had both been standing there for several minutes. 'Otherwise he'd have come down and put it oot.'

The Glaswegian audience is sharp, warm and vocal. They can sniff out a wrong note and have a cruel sense of humour that probably hasn't changed much since the music hall days, but that night at the GFT they were at their most charming. There wasn't an empty seat. Some people there had seen all the plays I was in at the Citizens, which was absolutely thrilling. They laughed at all the jokes. They watched the end poker-faced – no tears in Glasgow – and were generous in their applause. It felt like the wonderful culmination of a long friendship or, as someone in the audience put it, 'the happy ending after a long wank'. You never quite know where the compliment lies.

The next morning, knocked senseless by a terrible hangover, I attempt a photo shoot on the stage at the Citizens Theatre. It feels strangely vacant, unfamiliar, being back in the theatre where my career began, although the French chairs which graced every production I was ever in are still there, one on the stage, a couple in the wings, like old bones sticking out of a graveyard.

There's a crack down the middle of the theatre – a broken heart – that's going to cost £20 million to repair, and the trains no longer grind by on the siding behind the rehearsal room.

All Seats 40p was written across the front of the theatre in large
black letters when I arrived. (Someone tartly observed – Philip
Prowse probably – that mine went for considerably less than that
in those early pre-Aids days.)

Now the facade – such as it is – shrouded in scaffolding awaits
the beginning of its two-year refurbishment and craning up at
it, standing outside on Gorbals Street, I am suddenly disorientated. Don't look up with a hangover. The whole world spins.
The mosque – still magnificently incongruous on the banks of
the Clyde – swings back and forth across the road. But the grim
tower blocks of yesterday have disappeared, replaced by a low
beige town house city basking in the Mediterranean heat.

Nothing remains. Not a whisper of those old streets, hanging
on – even then – from the bygone age, the lone corner pub, the
incongruous tenement preserved from a demolished close. Even
then, in rainy 1979, they were exotic phantoms, bathed in the
orange glow of a Glasgow street lamp late at night. They've all
gone, been paved over, rerouted. Now the traffic hurtles past
in the dusty heat and somebody shouts from a car, 'Gae aff the
road y' lang streak a piss.' Only the indomitable Glaswegian
spirit remains unblunted.

I met Philip in the theatre that long-ago night in 1978 and it
changed the direction of my life. His influence on me over the
years was as constructive as it was destructive. After knowing him
I would never be able to merge successfully into the mainstream.
His withering views sounded strangely shrill coming out of this
nineteen-year-old ventriloquist's dummy. The BBC was run by
tired old leather queens from the Coleherne. Oh really, Rupert?
The National Theatre was a home for the colour-blind and brain-
dead and Merchant Ivory films were second-hand bric-a-brac.

These were the borrowed opinions with which I disguised
the void of my own personality. They cut me off from a whole
world. But on the other hand, genius observed at close quarters

rubs off in one way or another. Philip's eye, his brilliant sense of design, his way of seeing plays and books, his cruel world view, his sudden sympathy, his sense of humour, his view on politics, on paintings – all of which could be one thing one week and the opposite the next – were unlike anyone's I had ever come across before, and with the exception of another director – Tony Richardson – have never encountered since.

Standing there now, I realise it took me a lifetime to become my own person and to release myself from being his female impersonator. Falling out of his orbit and into my own creative atmosphere – if I can call it that – has been a bumpy ride. Philip is a vicious critic. Everything is always wrong from his point of view – he's an only child, after all – and his is the only opinion that counts, but on the other hand I could never have come up with this film without his withering challenges to every one of my ideas, or the inspired ideas of his own, or indeed without having lived through the endless dinners and lunches over the years – first at the Spaghetti House on Sauchiehall Street, or Costanzo's on Bath Street, then as our friendship expanded, to the Ark in Notting Hill and O Sole Mio underneath his flat on Kensington Church Street, where he went every night in the days before he learnt to cook and where the waitress – Maria – declared about every dish, 'Aie eets veeerry nice'.

After thirty-five years I was ready to go out on my own, and I got a blessing of sorts.

'Trouble with you, dear, is you're a magpie without an aesthetic base.'

'Well, that makes me rather a modern person then,' I reply testily.

'Yes. Thoroughly Modern Millie.'

And these are my thoughts as the trip goes into reverse, folding back past Motherwell, Cumberland, Northumberland to Euston in the glorious end of days weather and the haze of memories disappearing over the horizon.

CHAPTER THIRTY-SEVEN

Goodbye to New York

My heart always lurches flying over Manhattan. A bubble of anxiety bursts in my stomach every time the city appears like a bed of nails over the horizon. So much danger in those deep gulleys of glass, so much delusion in the disco ball. One always seems to be driving oneself to the edge in New York and that's probably its black magic allure. Without knowing it one risks everything, and my first visit could have been my last.

It was 1977 and a benign sprite was policing my trip. Hell-bent on drowning myself in the sex pools of the city, I was thwarted at every step. One night I presented myself at that notorious leather club called the Mineshaft. 'No cologne. No Lacoste. No fats. No fems' was written on a sign by the door. I was wearing my new Joseph ballet pumps and a waisted Claude Montana bolero jacket. I was not allowed in.

I didn't return until 1984, this time on a promotional tour for the miniseries *Princess Daisy*, and by then the HIV virus had taken its grip on the city and there was a whispering hysteria in the air. I met an English girl in the street before the press

conference and asked her for news about a mutual friend and
she suddenly looked scared.

'Haven't you heard?' she whispered. 'Gary died. Last month.
I'm sorry. I've got to run.' Before I could say a word she had gone,
melted into the crowd while every cell in my body stood still.

She hadn't said it. She didn't need to.

It should have been the perfect time. I was staying at the
Plaza Hotel. Claudia Cardinale was in the room next door. She
played my stepmother in the series. We made friends during
the shoot, and in New York we went for dinner one night to a
restaurant called Odeon where she held my hand and told me
that Visconti would have loved me. I burst into tears. It was too
late for Visconti. I was going to die.

Only of course I didn't. Over the next five years I was in and
out of Manhattan trying to become a star while the disease
found a name but not a cure. The dying looked like Martians in
the freezing New York winter, tramping the streets, wound up
in scarves and hats, their faces as grey as the dirty snow piled
up at the street corners.

There was no respite. We were all undead, walking in limbo,
terrified of ourselves, of our friends, of everyone. Who knew
when or if the disease would strike? Facing the sick was like
looking into a terrible mirror and one had to fight that primal
instinct to run in the opposite direction, even if it was off the
side of a building because it drove us all mad.

There was no definitive test to take, no reliable warning sign
apart from the famous dry cough which everyone contracted
through sheer terror, the night sweats and then of course the
signature blotches, Kaposi's sarcoma, a little-known cancer, only
named in whispers – more whispers – that appeared like spots of
flicked paint or pebbles rising to the surface of the skin.

Through all this everyone charged on, from the disco to the
hospital, from the dealer to the doctor. The sex clubs closed.

Cholera cells were scraped off the walls of the Mineshaft. Forty-second Street was sold to Mickey Mouse and the rest is history.

Now it's all gone. There is nothing left to remind one of the old times. Even St Vincent's Hospital – the last port of call for the dying, the only place they held your hand without wearing rubber gloves – is now a block of luxury flats. Even the survivors have been bricked over. The West Village is a cake shop. There are no more freaks, or if there are they are lost in the swarms of tourists who gather religiously outside the house in which *Friends* was shot. In short New York is a giant cruise ship and Liberty fell off. Flying over now, that lady looks shrunken, abandoned.

It's hard not to reflect on all this as I stand in the endless immigration line at JFK, and at the seismic shift in my own circumstances since that last glorious evening – just weeks before 9/11 and I was on a speedboat with Harvey Weinstein and Madonna streaking towards Liberty Island and Tina Brown's party for the soon-to-be-defunct *Talk* magazine. What happened! I was the *ami nécessaire* to America's biggest star. I was even a star myself. I was the next best thing! Speeding along, bump bump bump, Madge's hand on my arm, Harvey's on my thigh (kidding), it never crossed my mind that I was on the verge of a new dark age.

Question to self, flying over the Chrysler Building. Why hadn't I realised I could write in those days? It would all have been so much easier – this ten-year torture could have been resolved with a few phone calls in 2001. It remains a great mystery – but God moves in mysterious ways.

In New York everything started out well. An amazing premiere was conjured up by Hamish Bowles from *Vogue*. Anna Wintour was the host, along with Julianne Moore and Colin Firth. The evening took place in an extraordinary cinema with pods instead of seats – for groups of two – where meals were served and the chairs reclined to horizontal in case anyone wanted a quick nap. Anna got a bit antsy when the film didn't start dead on time. She was craning round, looking for assistants. I quickly wrapped up my speech, forgetting in the panic of the moment to thank Hamish Bowles who organised the whole thing. Particularly since I had spent minutes of my speech eulogising Anna in a rather oily way. She (Hamish) forgave me but only after two funerals and a wedding. The after-party was stylish and everyone actually stayed for more than fifteen minutes. Including Candice Bergen (Morgana le Fay to my Lancelot du Lac in *Arthur the Queen*.)

We opened at two cinemas in New York. Sony Classics employed their usual marketing technique – the shoestring – waiting to see if anyone came to see the film before they even considered putting their hands into their pockets. Unfortunately no one did. How could they? One of the cinemas was hidden underground in a grim neighbourhood that was called Trump City until everyone complained. Huge glass towers – ungainly like lollipops – newly constructed and largely unsold squatted over the deserted Cineplex, and in the evening there was just a pool of light under a squashed marquee and the street disappeared into the gloom. No passing trade apart from rodents, and it wasn't really their kind of film.

In LA we lasted five days on Crescent Heights in West Hollywood. After that you had to trek to Pasadena. In short, there was no interest. And so the distributor's enthusiasm flickered and died while I spent a fascinating month on the road – San Francisco, Dallas, Chicago, San Diego, Washington, Seattle, New York. More swirling reviews with trains and planes driving through them, only in this case the reviews were lacklustre. On the other hand the studio moved me around in style. Strange personal greeters like extras from *Rosemary's Baby* were always on hand at the kerb to rush me through security at the airport. They were fascinating sweetheart aliens and knew all the ropes. Characters from the studio met me at each new location. Added to this I was usually accompanied by one of the girls from my publicist's office so it all felt rather grand – like the last tour of a soon-to-be-deposed minor royal before the revolution.

During the screenings I went to dinner or checked out the other films at whichever Cineplex I was appearing – in little sections, not always in the correct order – and I can't recommend this way of seeing a movie enough. The bad ones are really bad and the good ones have their own magic, no matter at what point you join them. My favourite was *Beautiful Boy*. After my own screenings I went on stage to answer questions. The audiences were enthusiastic, generous, and I generally had a lovely time, but still it felt like goodbye. Everything seemed to be full of meaning – the mist over the San Francisco bay, the street in Dallas where Kennedy was assassinated, the restaurant we always went to while shooting *My Best Friend's Wedding* in Chicago.

I passed through all these places like a ghost, looking in windows, in wonder at the passage of time. The red-eye from LA to New York was a flight across my own life – still sloshed, thank God – as the continent slid by again, and I got lost in drunken reflection, watching the sudden rashes of orange light appear out of the void – the cities of the plain; jewels thrown across velvet. How many love affairs, how many plans, how many scrapes had I put on hold flying tipsily over this view, blank and bleary-eyed at the dawn creeping over Arizona, watching the endless straight roads plough through the dirty brown desert, ending – this time – with another wonderful freak trotting me through security to the usual armoured truck purring on the kerb.

I stepped in guiltily, feeling like an impostor. Whatever happened to the lovely old stretch limo with its red plush seats, its low lights, its decanters of whisky and gin, backlit, clinking in time to the potholes in the road?

The tragedy for me – if there was one – was that the LGBTQ world I had pinned my hopes on seemed completely disinterested in my film and me. We didn't even register. Possibly I was the wrong type of queen. Any hope I may have harboured that they would embrace the story of Wilde as a Christ figure for the gay movement, or myself as someone who had at the very least taken the risk, played some sort of role, was squashed early on when I couldn't even get an interview with *Out Magazine* beyond filling in a quiz for LGBTQ moviemakers which included questions like how I felt being a part of the LGBTQ community. Well, not particularly thrilled this week.

On the Sunday before returning to London there was a screening at the Academy of Motion Picture Arts and Sciences. Backstage the rep from Sony whispered, 'We've got a great crowd in there for a Sunday.' I swelled slightly. Something was at last going well. Maybe David's dream of winning four Oscars would come true. This was it. I could see the credits roll through the back of the huge screen. The music swelled and I was ushered into that impressive theatre. Two gigantic Oscars stood guard either side of the screen. I fixed on my friendliest smile and turned to face the crowd.

There was hardly anyone there. It was like a drizzly midweek matinee in the West End, a vast auditorium dotted with people. And Joan Collins wearing a huge cowboy hat with her husband Percy beside her.

'I thought you said it was a good crowd,' I hissed to the Sony rep.

'For a Sunday,' she hissed back, all smiles.

Joan and Percy waved from their seats and I nearly burst into tears because, say whatever you like about Joan, she is a loyal friend. I was extremely touched they bothered to come.

'Joan Collins and Percy are here,' whispered the Sony rep.

'You make them sound like a circus act.'

'I don't understand.'

'You know. Tah-dah. The fabulous Joan Collins and Percy.'

'Oh yeah. I can see her in the circus. Being fired from a cannon.'

Slightly catty but what a wonderful thought, and who knows? Joan is capable of anything. In top hat and tails, pushing Percy around on a trolley before making him jump through hoops of fire was the image that kept me smiling through the Q and A. One could only imagine their touring caravan. Actually being married to Joan was the hoop and Percy has jumped through it with flair and grace, to a standing ovation from all her friends.

Needless to say Joan is having another comeback, this time at the hands of Ryan Murphy, the new king of Hollywood. She is an inspiration but of course I am green with envy. On the other hand I am so relieved we finally made it up after the debacle dinner at The Ivy ten years ago.

'Listen. We're friends, aren't we?' she chirruped.

'We are. Although I feel sorry for anyone sitting behind you in that hat.'

'Darling. There wasn't anyone sitting behind me.'

'And we were in the fifth row,' added Percy for good measure.

And off we went for tea.

And so another stitch is dropped in that rich tapestry called show business. Up and down, in and out. I may have missed dinner, but I made it for tea. Ten years later. You slave through those ten years over an idea and nobody likes it. So what? We're all dealt an unfair hand. Maybe I'm hopelessly out of date, out of synch, out of touch. And maybe I'm not. But actually, now, writing this – hashtag my scars healing nicely – I don't care so much. I wanted to paint a portrait of Oscar Wilde, one that added a new dimension to the debate. I painted him as I felt him to be and of course like everyone who becomes intoxicated with making films I am still drunk on every frame. I adore it, warts and all, and some strange weight has lifted from my shoulders. We throw the dice for immortality in this crapshoot and are quickly forgotten, even the most illustrious of us, but this film will remain, somewhere, lost perhaps, seen only by a Martian cleaning out his mother's spaceship, but still there. My Oscar. And that's that.

Unlike Cinderella, I did not get invited to the Governors Ball in November – which is when you know you're in the running for awards season. Instead, and I suppose typically, I did find myself trapped in a turret room at the Sunset Tower Hotel a couple of months later on the night of the Golden Globes – the awards I had canvassed so unsuccessfully for a nomination – and watched from my window as Richard E. Grant and his wife Joan arrived on the sidewalk for the after-party which was being thrown – as luck would have it – downstairs. Richard was nominated everywhere and he sprang from the limo into the sea of flashlights holding hands with Joan. I wrestled briefly with the idea of throwing myself out of the window and landing – splat – at their feet, ruining their night but saving my film – they'd have to all go and see it then – or would they? Either way I thought better of it. I adore Richard (and also life) so I ordered room service instead and settled down to watch it all on TV, feeling quite relieved in the end to be looking at the view instead of trying to be a part of the picture. Outside the window the Hollywood Hills were near enough to touch. At their feet Sunset Boulevard was a huge electric cable of tail lights and headlights, jammed with celebrities in tanks converging on the tower, disgorging armies bearing their triumphant stars through the paparazzi to the party. Fans bayed like clockwork from behind velvet ropes. It reminded me of my favourite John Schlesinger film *The Day of the Locust*.

I suddenly felt terribly happy, peaceful almost. Sunset coiled around the hills towards the Chateau Marmont twinkling in the distance. Tonight it looked like the castle from *Chitty Chitty Bang Bang*. (In daylight it looked more like a remand home.) I must have inhabited half the rooms in that fairy-tale fleapit at one time or other. I could just make out the huge picture window of Tony Richardson's old house on Kings Road. I could see him sitting there with Christopher Isherwood, Jessica Mitford and Gavin Lambert, playing bridge. All those years ago. Dead stars of course but their lights still shine.

There is no billboard for Oscar Wilde on Sunset as I had dreamt there would be. But it's not the end of the world, I realise, settling down to the marijuana chocolate bar left at reception by a thoughtful friend (thank you, Leslie). The cameras explode like fireworks downstairs as another star streaks into the atmosphere and I get the giggles. Looking out of the window now I feel a surge of affection for these crumbling hills that have been my home on and off over the years. We are dragged in and out with the tide, back and forth to Hollywood, occasionally crashing in on the crest of a wave but mostly beached or swept out too deep so that by the end we are stripped bare in the undertow, recognised only by our dentures in a B-movie, a footnote found drowned in a detective series, finally washed up on Long Beach, trying to make it ashore for pilot season, clinging to a scrapbook of faded reviews. I can feel the pull of the current right now. It's taking me out over Sunset, past Hollywood, Mount Olympus, Seattle Drive, up and over Mulholland, all the places I clung to over the years like a limpet, trying to fit in. This time I'm not going to exhaust myself trying to swim back. This time I will go with the flow and see where the tide takes me. Maybe it comes back round. Maybe not.

CHAPTER THIRTY-EIGHT

Back in the USSR

Three days later, from some reason via Dubai, numb with jet lag, I find myself at the gay and lesbian film festival in Saint Petersburg. Our screening has been cancelled this morning by the Mayor – as usual – it is his party trick. Apparently he always does it. For some reason the theatre is suddenly unavailable – but they show the film anyway in a gym against a sheet pinned to the wall.

Four hundred men and women squeeze into the room, all shapes and sizes, goths and queens, biker girls and geeks. No transsexuals. Too dangerous for them. We can only show the film on a DVD so the image is a bit faded, the screen is wrinkled and the sound is muffled, as if it comes from another room, but despite all this – or maybe because of it – the screening ends up being the most vivid and exciting night of my entire world tour.

I watch from the back of the hall, electrified by the atmosphere of attention from the crowd, their upturned faces grave and ghostly in the light of my film. It feels as if I had travelled back in time. Gay Petersburg reminds me of London or New

York in the old days. They are a disparate group, the ordinary and the freak, the old and the young, the Adonis and the activist, all interacting, rougher, madder, funnier than their counterparts in the puritanical overdeveloped West. You can hear a pin drop at the end of the film. Oscar's life in Paris is not so far removed from the gay experience in Russia today. After the screening the questions are sharp and funny. I feel incredibly proud to be there. It may be getting harder being gay in the West today but it's nothing compared to the cross carried by the Russian queen. The audience tonight have taken a risk just by showing up and the most extraordinary thing is that they really care, they are concerned about Wilde, about me, that I have worked so hard to make the film and have actually bothered to come to them with it. I am thrilled and touched and utterly floored by the affection.

Suddenly everything falls into place – Oscar Wilde, me, the film itself, its chequered reception, the struggle to make it, the fact that I have spent so long in Russia, all those years ago, working with Bondarchuk, the whole thing seems to make sense. THIS is the prize. And it's an unusual one that only I could win. Coming back to Russia and being loved, having some kind of message for this outcast community, and having the opportunity to stand beside them – if only for a moment – means everything.

Standing ovation.

Epilogue

My father is buried in the cemetery at Enford Church. Ten years have gone by since his funeral during a November downpour in 2009.

'When did he pass?' a neighbour asked my mother recently.

'He didn't. He died,' snapped my mother.

For once Mummy and I are in agreement. One is dead. Gone. Croaked. That's that. Thank God.

I now live in his house and own a new dog. He is called Pluto. He is a black Labrador, the great-great-nephew of my last dog Mo. He has arrived with no expense spared from Geneva and is already gigantic. We walk to the church every morning at seven thirty, meeting a variety of neighbours on the way. Fern is a galumphy brown Lab, about the only dog so far who can deal with Pluto's manic energy, and they tear around the graveyard dive-bombing one another. Fern is up for anything and doesn't even mind the dry-humping side of things. Pluto is already sexual even though his little balls – the size of hazelnuts – are still lodged in the stem between his member and the furry purse of his ball sack. No amount of licking them down seems to be working but Pluto already has a very clear idea of sex and Fern is fairly obliging.

Brunswick on the other hand is horrified at P's big snout digging into his permed nether regions. He is a haughty and vindictive sausage dog who lashes out like clockwork but Pluto dances around him like a boxer, springing back, tongue lolling, delighted to be snapped at. Brunswick's owner is charming and rather good-looking, dressed for safari with a luxuriant shock of white hair, and we both get tangled up in our leads, like a couple in a cartoon who are forced by their pets into a kiss.

Claire, the owner of Fern, has warned me about the owner of two whippets, a thin lady who has accused poor Fern of being a bully. I sometimes meet her on the track up to the plain. She is very chic with orange hair, a tailored jacket and a pencil skirt and neatly tied poo bags balanced in each hand like the scales of justice. She is a character from Miss Marple, but then we all are, I suppose. I am the bohemian blob, marooned in the country, found hanged in a ballgown. Did I do it? Murder he wrote. Nobody seems to know where Miss Whippets comes from. I think she's on an observation mission from the Crab Nebula. She's too well dressed to be local.

I am not the only gay in the village. However I do appear to be the only Remainer. It's a lonely role. My mother, who very sensibly has decided to abandon her short-term memory for the loftier vistas of 1961, adores Donald Trump, and thinks Boris is doing jolly well.

And that's village life for you at the end of days, a slightly different vignette than that sketched by my ancestor William Cobbett, who walked through Enford in 1830 and wrote rather drearily about it in a slim tome called *Rural Rides*. I am thinking of borrowing the title for my new country Grindr ID.

Anyway all this is just to say that we walk early to avoid all the dogs and decoys because then Pluto is all mine, easy, friendly, obedient and we can play his favourite game, which involves me chasing him around the churchyard screaming as he desecrates the graves, ripping flowers from their vases, dancing and dodging just out of reach as I try to lunge at him.

On the way home we sit on the bench in the lychgate, Pluto leans up close and I read to him the names of the dead from the two great wars which are engraved on the opposite wall. Wordsells and Dears, Birds and Feys, whole families wiped out for England – three Wordsells in each war. Pluto can't believe it. It's strange to think of all that tragedy, reduced, like a pot of tears on the boil for a century, to a list of barely discernible names engraved on a lychgate. The fatal shot, the haze of gas, the barbed wire crucifixion – all forgotten now, mossed over, embedded in ivy. Most of the families are extinct although old Mrs Fey was still alive in 2015.

Today there is a mist over the water meadow. My dad's gravestone, designed by me – a milestone – sticks out of the fog like an old tooth. I wanted to write on it 'London – 99 miles' with an arrow going one way and 'Paradise – a lot further' next to another going up, but I was not allowed. He is wearing his blue pyjamas and his old red slippers down there and we often wonder – my mother and I – what state of degeneration his earthly remains are in.

During the ten years since his death I have made my film. 'Will you ever get that bloody film off the ground?' he used to ask. And tonight I will finish this book describing those years.

So what next? Never has the future seemed so uncertain, and the village street is a dusky mirage, a bubble floating off into space expanding and bursting into nothing. The church tower still rises above the trees. The bells still ring occasionally. There is the odd service conducted half-heartedly by a lady vicar. (Never have the sacred words seemed so drab.) The track on to the plain is still enchanting, unchanged for hundreds of years, carved into the hill, under a tunnel of hawthorn and quince. Pluto gallops up it, a black silhouette, little ears flapping. Birds, rabbits and weasels escape from the bushes in his wake and tear off across the fields.

Tonight when we get back I shall record an audition on my iPhone. I have constructed a little set, a Turkish cushion, a stone wall, a shadowed light worthy of James Wong Howe courtesy of my dad's old desk lamp. In the scene I must play King Gallarhorn – a part in a gigantic series I am up for. I haven't got a clue what the story is, nor any idea who King Gallarhorn might be. Everything is top secret. I have been sent two pages of dialogue and that's that. The type of approach for which I was vaguely trained – studying the character, knowing the story – is obsolete in today's world. Just the scene – to be learnt by tomorrow. Goodbye all early Alzheimer's sufferers. This could be the moment of truth. My agent tells me the series is going to be as big as *Game of Thrones*. I could suddenly be the new witch on the block.

After about thirty attempts at the scene I give up. The last one is nearly perfect unless you count me saying 'It is dangerous for a soldier like Auron (Our Ron) to study too deeply the art of the enema'. I don't think they'll notice. I take a deep breath and press send. It's like the lottery. I imagine my audition twirling through cyberspace, like the three baddies from the first Superman film, reduced to a kind of record sleeve, up through the iCloud and into the virtual hell of the casting director's inbox. Needless to say, I never hear back.

And there I leave you. A lit window in winter. The patter of rain on a roof. A mad freak crouches in a pool of light. An iPhone towers over him on a tripod. He cranes towards the lens, all cheekbones and hooded eyes (hopefully) in the light of the lamp. A black dog observes, ears cocked. With a heartfelt sigh the animal slumps to the ground and watches from the floor as the freak tries again.

Night falls in Wiltshire and the planet creaks round. The universe expands silently at the speed of light comedy, and somewhere another world ends, bursts into nothing.

Shooting star. Shot.

Picture Credits

Plate Section 1

page 1, top: © David M Benett/Getty Images
page 1, bottom left and right: © Alastair Muir/Shutterstock
page 2, top: © Babinho
page 3, top and bottom: Everett family's private collection
page 4, top left: private collection
page 4, top right: © Richard Young/Shutterstock
page 4, bottom left: © BBC Photo Library
page 4, bottom right: © TCD/Prod.DB/Alamy Stock Photo
page 5, top and bottom: © Rupert Everett
page 7, top: © Columbia/Kobal/Shutterstock
page 8, top left and right: © Celador/20th Century Fox/Kobal/Shutterstock
page 8, middle: © Rupert Everett
page 9, bottom left and right: © Rupert Everett

Plate Section 2

pages 8–9: © John Conroy
page 16, top: © John Devlin
page 16, bottom: © Rupert Everett

All other images in Plate Sections 1 and 2 © Wilhelm Moser

Acknowledgements

Thank you Babinho for putting up with me all these years. And thank you David Colby for all your encouragement and support making *The Happy Prince*. And Willy Moser for taking the pictures for free. Thank you John Conroy for bringing the film home, and Merlin Holland for your generosity and help.

I would like to thank my big sister Connie Fillipello for all the years together. And Robert Fox for his friendship and endless good advice. I would like to thank Oliver Hoare (dead) for the priceless antique rings he lent me for Oscar. Thank you Antonia for guiding me through this book. And everyone at Little, Brown – past and present – for the support. Thank you Ed Victor (dead) for all the fun we had plotting book deals and sequels.